THE WTO CASE LAW OF 2001
THE AMERICAN LAW INSTITUTE
REPORTERS' STUDIES

This book is the first in a new series of annual volumes that will be utilized in the development of an American Law Institute (ALI) project on World Trade Organization Law. The project will undertake yearly analysis of the case law from the adjudicating bodies of the WTO. The Reporters' Studies for 2001 cover a wide range of WTO law ranging from classic trade in goods issues to intellectual property protection. Each of the cases is jointly evaluated by an economist and a lawyer, both well-known experts in the field of trade law or international economics. The Reporters critically review the jurisprudence of WTO adjudicating bodies and attempt to evaluate whether the ruling "makes sense" from an economic as well as a legal point of view, and, if not, whether the problem lies in the interpretation of the law or the law itself. The Studies do not always cover all issues discussed in a case, but they seek to discuss both the procedural and the substantive issues that form the "core" of the dispute.

HENRIK HORN is Professor of International Economics and Deputy Director at the Institute for International Economic Studies, Stockholm University. He has previously worked for the Economic Research and Analysis Division of the World Trade Organization, and has been a judge in the Swedish Market Court (supreme court for competition cases). He is a member of the Editorial Board of the *World Trade Review* and is a research fellow at the Centre for Economic Policy Research (CEPR).

PETROS C. MAVROIDIS is Professor of Law at the University of Neuchâtel and Columbia Law School. He was previously Chair of Competition Law, European University Institute, Florence and a member of both the Legal Affairs Division of the World Trade Organization and the Centre for Economic Policy Research (CEPR). He is Associate Editor of the *Journal of World Trade* and a member of the Editorial Board of the *World Trade Review*, *Columbia Journal of Transnational Law*, and *Columbia Journal of European Law*.

THE WTO CASE LAW OF 2001

The American Law Institute
Reporters' Studies

Edited by

HENRIK HORN AND PETROS C. MAVROIDIS

CAMBRIDGE
UNIVERSITY PRESS

PUBLISHED BY THE PRESS SYNDICATE OF THE UNIVERSITY OF CAMBRIDGE
The Pitt Building, Trumpington Street, Cambridge, United Kingdom

CAMBRIDGE UNIVERSITY PRESS
The Edinburgh Building, Cambridge, CB2 2RU, UK
40 West 20th Street, New York, NY 10011–4211, USA
477 Williamstown Road, Port Melbourne, VIC 3207, Australia
Ruiz de Alarcón 13, 28014 Madrid, Spain
Dock House, The Waterfront, Cape Town 8001, South Africa

http://www.cambridge.org

First published 2003

Printed in the United Kingdom at the University Press, Cambridge

Typeface Minion 10.75/12.75 pt.   *System* LaTeX 2$_\varepsilon$ [TB]

A catalogue record for this book is available from the British Library

ISBN 0 521 83421 X hardback

CONTENTS

FOREWORD

Since 1923, the American Law Institute (ALI) has sought to "restate" American law. This means seeking coherent and progressive doctrine in the confusion of common-law decisions by judges. Note that unlike countries with a unified legal system, the United States has fifty states, each with its own rules as to many areas of public and private law. The ALI, a private organization, is a primary source of legal unification.

The Institute has also worked on reforming other areas of law, for example criminal law and tax law. And in recent years it has sought to be helpful internationally, for example in the project on Transnational Civil Procedure, cosponsored with Unidroit, and in its attempt to assist coordination of transnational bankruptcies in Canada, Mexico, and the United States. Aside, however, from a chapter in our Restatement Third, the Foreign Relations Law of the United States, which antedated the present World Trade Organization regime, the current project represents the Institute's first effort to engage with trade law.

The law of international trade is at an early stage of development. Trade, of course, is old, and so are bilateral and some multilateral attempts to establish rules. But the World Trade Organization (WTO), with its elaborate dispute-resolution system, is only nine years old, and so far there have been fewer than sixty decisions by the Appellate Body. Attempting to describe rules of trade law is like authoring a treatise on contract law in England in the year 1200, when the King's Bench had rendered a similarly modest number of opinions.

Nonetheless, the effort to build legal principles on the framework of the WTO decisions seems worthwhile. If talented economists and lawyers analyze the decisions, those engaged in the process can be drawn into conversation and over time there will be agreement on basic concepts. This will not happen quickly, but the significance for the world economy is great and assisting the effort, even modestly, will be valuable.

This project, whose working title is Principles of Trade Law: The World Trade Organization, is new for the ALI in two ways. First, each portion of the work is being undertaken by both a lawyer and an economist. Second, the two leaders of the project, Henrik Horn of Stockholm University and Petros Mavroidis of the University of Neuchâtel and Columbia Law School, are not Americans. The two Chief Reporters selected three other lawyer/economist teams and the four teams each analyzed a group of 2001 decisions by the adjudicating bodies of the WTO. Those analyses were themselves subjected to critical analysis by the other Reporters at a meeting in October and then by an international group of experts on the law and economics of the world trading system at a two-day invitational conference in February. The resulting set of Reporters' Studies is included in this volume.

As I write, the team of scholars, to which another lawyer and economist have been added, has begun work analyzing the decisions rendered by the WTO in 2002. Our plan is to carry out this "bottom–up" process of analyzing individual trade law decisions for several more years, and only then to attempt to draft general principles based on the analysis of the individual disputes. It should be noted that this preliminary series of Reporters' Studies, of which the present volume represents the first installment, is the work of the participating Reporters themselves rather than of the American Law Institute. We envision these Studies, of tremendous value and importance in their own right, as constituting the essential matrix for developing the broader formulations that we hope eventually to be able to issue under the aegis of the Institute itself.

We are immensely grateful to our Reporters and to those who have criticized the earlier drafts of their work. We are also grateful for the financial support that has made this project possible from Jan Wallander's and Tom Hedelius' Research Foundation, Svenska Handelsbanken, Stockholm, from the Asia-Pacific Economic Cooperation Study Center at Columbia University, and from the Milton and Miriam Handler Foundation.

This is challenging work, but we begin the undertaking confident that our efforts can assist in a small way in the creation of a peaceful and prosperous world.

Lance Liebman
Director
The American Law Institute

A note on the American Law Institute

The American Law Institute was founded in 1923 and is based in Philadelphia. The Institute, through a careful and deliberative process, drafts and then publishes various restatements of the law, model codes, and other proposals for legal reform "to promote the clarification and simplification of the law and its better adaptation to social needs, to secure the better administration of justice, and to encourage and carry on scholarly and scientific legal work." Its membership consists of judges, practicing lawyers, and legal scholars from all areas of the United States as well as some foreign countries, selected on the basis of professional achievement and demonstrated interest in the improvement of the law. The Institute's incorporators included Chief Justice and former President William Howard Taft, future Chief Justice Charles Evans Hughes, and former Secretary of State Elihu Root. Judges Benjamin N. Cardozo and Learned Hand were among its early leaders.

The Institute's restatements, model codes, and legal studies are used as references by the entire legal profession.

The American Law Institute http://www.ali.org

AMERICAN LAW INSTITUTE REPORTERS

KYLE BAGWELL is Professor of Economics, Columbia University.

GENE M. GROSSMAN is Jacob Viner Professor of International Economics, Princeton University.

HENRIK HORN is Professor of International Economics, Institute for International Economic Studies, Stockholm University.

ROBERT HOWSE is Professor of Law, University of Michigan Law School.

MERIT E. JANOW is Professor in the Practice of International Trade, Columbia University.

PETROS C. MAVROIDIS is Professor of Law, Columbia Law School and University of Neuchâtel.

DAMIEN J. NEVEN is Professor of Economics, Graduate Institute for International Studies, University of Geneva.

ROBERT W. STAIGER is Professor of Economics, University of Wisconsin.

ALAN O. SYKES is Frank and Bernice Greenberg Professor of Law, University of Chicago Law School.

JOSEPH H. H. WEILER is Professor of Law and Jean Monnet Chair, New York University School of Law.

Introduction

HENRIK HORN AND PETROS C. MAVROIDIS

1 The project

This is the first annual report of the American Law Institute (ALI) project *Principles of Trade Law: The World Trade Organization.* The project's object of study hardly needs any motivation. The World Trade Organization (WTO) Agreement is one of the most extensive international agreements ever. With 145 Members, ranging from the poorest to the richest countries on the globe, the Agreement covers the vast majority of international commerce in goods and services, and also contains an agreement on the protection of intellectual property.

The WTO contract contains a rarity in international relations – a compulsory third-party adjudication clause – embodying the idea that trade conflicts should be resolved through multilateral adjudication rather than through unilateral actions. As is the case with many contracts, many of the terms in the WTO Agreement[1] are opaque, leaving much discretion to adjudicating bodies to determine the actual content of the obligations. The case law thus provides more than a mechanical execution of clear-cut rules.

The WTO contract and its interpretation by the WTO adjudicating bodies are subject to intensive policy debate, conducted largely by politicians and non-governmental organizations. There is also an ongoing debate among trade law practitioners and legal scholars concerning the appropriate interpretation of the law. Academic economists, on the other hand, with some notable exceptions, very rarely intervene in these discussions.

The aim of this project is to bridge this divide by providing systematic analysis of WTO law based in both Economics and Law. Such an

---

[1] We use "the WTO contract" synonymously with "the WTO Agreement."

interdisciplinary approach is in our view necessitated by the fact that the WTO Agreement has inherently economic objectives. For instance, the Preamble states the Agreement's objectives as:

> . . . raising standards of living, ensuring full employment and a large and steadily growing volume of real income and effective demand, and expanding the production of and trade in goods and services, while allowing for the optimal use of the world's resources in accordance with the objective of sustainable development, seeking both to protect and preserve the environment and to enhance the means for doing so in a manner consistent with their respective needs and concerns at different levels of economic development . . .

Since a thorough analysis of the appropriate design of Trade Law inevitably has to take into account the purpose of the trade agreement, its focus must be on the interaction between the law and the world economy it seeks to regulate. Of course, this is not to deny the possibility that members might also have other objectives in mind when signing the contract.

A fundamental methodological problem facing the project is the lack of a "manual" for how to perform a joint economic and legal analysis of the WTO contract; there is no field, "The Economics of Trade Law," that can be relied upon for the purpose of the project. The relevant specialized fields, such as International Trade Law and International Economics, instead differ widely, both in terms of aims and in terms of method, and lawyers and economists are typically too specialized in their respective fields to be able to undertake a legal-*cum*-economic analysis of the law by themselves. Instead, such an analysis requires the joint efforts of economists and lawyers. The main idea behind this project is to develop such collaboration.

The project will undertake yearly analysis of the case law from the adjudicating bodies of the WTO. The intention is each year to analyze all disputes that in the previous year came to an administrative end, either because they were not appealed, or because they have gone through both the panel and the Appellate Body (AB) stages (even though time constraints may prevent us from covering each and every dispute that falls into this category). Each dispute is to be evaluated jointly by an economist and a lawyer. Their general task is to evaluate whether the ruling "makes sense" from an economic as well as a legal point of view, and if not, whether the problem lies in the legal text, or in the interpretation thereof. The teams of lawyers and economists will not always cover all issues discussed in a case;

they will however seek to discuss both the procedural and the substantive issues that form the "core" of the dispute.

The Reporters' Studies are initially scrutinized in a meeting of all of the Reporters. After revisions resulting from that meeting, the Reporters' Studies are next presented and discussed in a meeting with an external advisory group, comprising both lawyers and economists. The final versions, such as those published in this volume, have been subject to another round of revisions derived from the advisory meeting. Despite these collective efforts, each pair of authors remains solely responsible for the studies it has authored.

The analysis of the WTO case law is meant to serve two purposes. First, given the central role of the Dispute Settlement system in the WTO (and the lack of accountability of its adjudicating bodies seen by some observers), it is of vital importance that the system is constantly and carefully scrutinized. Our yearly independent analysis of the emerging case law will hopefully contribute toward this end.

Second, the yearly scrutiny of the case law is meant to serve as a steppingstone toward an analysis of the core provisions of the contract itself. Depending on the progress that we will make over the years, and our views on the quality of the primary and secondary WTO law, this might eventually take the form of a developed set of Principles, or perhaps even a Restatement, of WTO Law.

Before turning to the content of this volume, we would like to express our gratitude to the American Law Institute (ALI), which welcomed the project under its aegis, and provided it with administrative and financial support. Its Director, Lance Liebman, has been instrumental in taking the project to where it is today. We have also benefited greatly from the support of Michael Traynor, the President of the ALI, as well as from the efficient administrative aid provided by Elena Cappella and Michael Greenwald, Deputy Directors at the ALI, as well as by other ALI staff members. Frank Ravue Ito read the manuscript and provided excellent editorial assistance. We are also extremely grateful for financial support from the Jan Wallander's and Tom Hedelius' Research Foundation, Svenska Handelsbanken, Stockholm as well as from the Asia-Pacific Economic Cooperation Study Center at Columbia University and the Milton and Miriam Handler Foundation.

2 The Reporters' Studies on the WTO Case Law of 2001

The Reporters' Studies have been drafted by the following persons, who have been appointed Reporters for the project by the ALI:

Gene Grossman, Jacob Viner Professor of International Economics, Princeton University, USA.

Henrik Horn, Professor of International Economics, Institute for International Economic Studies, Stockholm University, Sweden.

Robert Howse, Professor of Law, University of Michigan Law School, USA.

Merit Janow, Professor in the Practice of International Trade, Columbia University, USA.

Petros C. Mavroidis, Professor of Law, Columbia Law School, USA, and University of Neuchâtel, Switzerland.

Damien J. Neven, Professor of Economics, Graduate Institute for International Studies, University of Geneva, Switzerland.

Robert W. Staiger, Professor of Economics, University of Wisconsin, Madison, USA.

Joseph H. H. Weiler, Professor of Law and Jean Monnet Chair, New York University School of Law, USA.

This first year of the project focused on the case law of the year 2001. The Reporters' Studies in the volume benefited from extremely helpful discussions with participants in an invitational conference, consisting of practising lawyers and economists, on February 6 and 7, 2003, in Philadelphia:

Professor José E. Alvarez, Columbia University Law School, New York, NY.

Professor George A. Bermann, Columbia University Law School, New York, NY.

The Rt. Hon. The Lord Brittan, Vice Chairman, UBS Warburg, London, England.

Steve Charnovitz, Esquire, Wilmer, Cutler, & Pickering, Washington, DC.

Professor William Davey, University of Illinois College of Law, Champaign, IL.

Claus-Dieter Ehlermann, Esquire, Wilmer, Cutler, & Pickering, Brussels, Belgium.

Susan G. Esserman, Esquire, Steptoe & Johnson, Washington, DC.

Professor Wilfred Ethier, University of Pennsylvania, Department of Economics, Philadelphia, PA.

Dean David W. Leebron, Columbia University Law School, New York, NY.

Professor Mitsuo Matsushita, Seikei University, Department of Law, Tokyo, Japan.

Professor Patrick Messerlin, Institut d'Etudes Politiques, Paris, France.

David Palmeter, Esquire, Sidley Austin Brown & Wood, Washington, DC.

Professor Thomas J. Prusa, Rutgers University, Department of Economics, New Brunswick, NJ.

Professor Donald Regan, University of Michigan Law School, Ann Arbor, MI.

Professor David A. Wirth, Director of International Programs, Boston College Law School, Newton, MA.

The Hon. Diane P. Wood, US Court of Appeals, 7th Circuit, Chicago, IL.

Professor Claire Wright, Thomas Jefferson School of Law, San Diego, CA.

One invitee to the conference, Robert E. Hudec, was unable to attend because of illness. He, nevertheless, provided us with cogent and helpful comments on the materials before his untimely death later in the year. He was a great pioneer in the field of trade law and his death is a major loss to this enterprise.

We briefly summarize the studies in the order of their appearance in the volume:

The *EC – Asbestos* report is presented by Horn and Weiler. The dispute concerned a French health-motivated ban of asbestos-containing construction materials. Canada argued that the French decree was an impermissible discrimination between two otherwise like products (asbestos- and non-asbestos-containing construction material), which operated to the disadvantage of imported products and thus constituted a violation of Article III.4 GATT. The AB dismissed Canada's claim, essentially arguing that the two products were not like due to their different impacts on human health.

The authors do not put into question the outcome, that France had not violated their obligations under the GATT. They disagree, however, with the reasoning underlying the AB's findings, arguing that it lacks logical coherence, and that it adds to the existing uncertainty surrounding what is and what is not a legitimate motive for government intervention. They also find the AB report overly focused on the burden of proof issue, and they provide several examples of situations where the reasoning of the AB in the *EC – Asbestos* case, if replicated elsewhere, might yield unwarranted outcomes. In their study they identify three separate methods of interpreting the non-discrimination provisions in the GATT, and discuss the pros and cons of each.

The *US – Shrimp* (Article 21.5 DSU) report by the AB is discussed by Howse and Neven. This AB report is the final step in the long *US – Shrimp* saga. Very briefly, the United States enacted legislation banning imports of shrimp that were caught in a manner leading to a high incidental taking of sea turtles. At the same time, the United States had negotiated with some, but not all, WTO Members treaties aiming to ensure that the incidental taking of sea turtles would be at acceptable levels. Such treaties, in return, allowed WTO Members that had adhered to them to continue to export shrimp to the United States. A number of countries (Malaysia playing a key role) complained about the US practice.

The AB, reversing the original Panel's findings, upheld the US practice as WTO-consistent but found that the United States had applied it in a discriminatory manner by not offering negotiations to other Members. It also requested the United States to show flexibility in the application of their legislation and to accept methods of fishing shrimp, other than those used by US fishermen, as equivalent to the US method, to the extent that they led to a comparable amount of incidental taking of sea turtles. The AB requested that the United States bring their measures into compliance within the implementation period. To this effect, the United States offered negotiations with a view to signing an agreement with the exporters of shrimps that had not initially been offered such negotiations (that is, when the legislation was first introduced).

Negotiations were unsuccessful and Malaysia complained to the WTO, arguing that the United States had not implemented its obligations in good faith, since no international agreement between them and interested exporters was concluded at the end of the day. The AB dismissed the claim, stating that the United States did not have to guarantee a successful outcome of the negotiations offered. It simply had to ensure (to respect non-discrimination) that it entered into good faith negotiations with those countries that had not been initially offered this possibility.

The AB report also found that the United States, by adopting a flexible approach towards certification of exporters (that is, that exporters do not have to use the same abatement technology used by US fishermen in order to be permitted to export to the US market), complied with the requirement of the chapeau of Article XX GATT to provide flexibility.

Howse and Neven find that, from a strictly legal perspective, the AB's ruling is correct: the United States indeed cannot unilaterally guarantee the success of international negotiations. By offering in good faith this possibility to Malaysia (as they had done vis-à-vis other WTO members before), they complied with their obligations under the WTO. On the other hand, in order to conform to the flexibility requirement, the United States would have to accept imports of shrimp from countries with different but equally efficient (when it comes to incidental taking of sea turtles) abatement technology, which the United States did.

From an economic perspective however, the issue is more complicated. The authors observe that to make imports contingent on the adoption of an abatement standard can be a very effective means of addressing external effects across jurisdictions, at least when efficient abatement technologies are available. In the view of the authors, however, it would have been appropriate for the AB to clarify what is meant by "comparable in effectiveness" when discussing flexibility. Furthermore, the AB should have indicated that comparable effectiveness does not imply that different jurisdictions should reach similar standards, but rather that the marginal effectiveness of resources invested in abatement should be comparable across countries.

Horn and Mavroidis discuss the AB *US – Lamb* report. In this case, New Zealand and Australia complained that imposition of safeguards by the United States on imports of lamb violated various provisions governing safeguards in the WTO. The AB found that the United States indeed had failed to show that the increase of imports was the result of unforeseen developments and that the United States did not properly attribute injury to its various sources. Due to these findings, the AB found the safeguard to be illegal.

The authors do not disagree with the final verdict when it comes to attribution. Indeed, in their view, the US safeguard investigation did not comply with the requirements for attribution as specified in the WTO contract. However, they point out that the AB could have been clearer as to the use of quantitative evidence in this respect. In their view, some form of quantification is typically necessary in order to attribute injury, and to demonstrate the necessity of the measure, in a reasonable manner.

Horn and Mavroidis also see a weakness in the text of the Agreement: imports should be seen as the result of the interaction between more fundamental economic forces, such as foreign supply and demand and domestic supply and demand. An import surge may stem from changes in any of these. To blame imports for injury thus begs the question of who or what is actually responsible for an import surge. The authors also argue that an "unforeseen developments" requirement should be interpreted as an obligation for national authorities entrusted with the administration of safeguards to respect a due diligence standard. This standard should not exonerate them from responsibility for actions that their own government has provoked.

Janow and Staiger comment on the *EC – Bed Linen* jurisprudence. In this case, India complained about the methodology employed by the European Community with respect to anti-dumping duties on imports of cotton bed linen. The latter had based its calculation of the "normal value" for all Indian exporters on sales data for a single company, although the sales at hand were outside the ordinary course of trade (as defined in the WTO anti-dumping agreement). India complained about this EC practice and also about the defendant's practice of "zeroing," whereby dumping margins are calculated on the basis of dumped transactions and all non-dumped transactions are zeroed. The AB found fault with these practices.

Janow and Staiger agree with the finding that "zeroing" can exaggerate the margin of dumping contrary to the letter and the spirit of the WTO Anti-dumping Agreement (Article 2). They further agree with the finding that a weighted average of dumping margins for all Indian exporters based on data from one exporter only can be problematic as well. In their view, however (and in this respect they distance themselves from the formalistic findings of the AB), this is the case because such a procedure is likely to introduce a large element of "noise" into the cost calculation. Finally, the authors point out that from an economic perspective, the foundations of the Anti-dumping Agreement as such are highly problematic.

The *Mexico – Corn Syrup* Article 21.5 DSU compliance Panel decision is examined by Howse and Neven. In this case, Mexico was initially condemned for issuing an anti-dumping order in contravention of various provisions of the Anti-dumping Agreement. Mexico agreed to implement the findings, but, in the view of the United States, this did not occur. The United States requested a compliance panel to evaluate whether Mexico failed to comply with its obligations under the WTO Agreement by improperly analyzing factors of injury laid down in Articles 3.4 and 3.7 of the anti-dumping Agreement. At issue in this dispute was also the appropriate standard of review to be applied by panels when adjudicating disputes under this Agreement (Article 17.6).

The authors conclude that the correct understanding of the standard of review laid down in the Anti-dumping Agreement requires WTO panels to accept the determination of national investigating authorities as such and thus avoid entering into a *de novo* review. In this respect they are in agreement with the final decision by the AB. But they also point to an error by the Panel that was not corrected by the AB, the failure to take into account market segmentation. In the authors' view, isolating the appropriate segment of the market may well enhance the accuracy of an analysis of injury.

Howse and Neven also discuss the *Argentina – Ceramic Tiles* Panel decision. In this case, the European Community complained that Argentina, when imposing anti-dumping duties on imports of ceramic tiles, did not respect its obligations under Articles 6.8 and 6.9 of the Anti-dumping Agreement, which regulate the legitimate recourse to "facts available." The complainant also maintained that Argentina violated its obligations under Article 6.10 of the same Agreement by failing to calculate individual dumping margins for each exporter. Finally, it was argued that Argentina violated Article 2.4 of the Anti-dumping Agreement as well by not taking into account differences in physical characteristics when making price comparisons. The Panel agreed with all claims advanced by the European Community.

The authors do not put into question the Panel's findings on Article 6.8 as such. They would have preferred, however, that the Panel had seen Argentina's recourse to facts available in the wider context of the investigation (this is in their view the appropriate understanding of the standard of review imposed on panels when discussing anti-dumping litigations as laid down in Article 17.6 of the Anti-dumping Agreement). Viewed in this perspective, they find nothing wrong with Argentina's due diligence standard.

The authors disagree with the Panel's understanding of Article 6.9: in their opinion, this Article does not oblige authorities to explain why a final decision will not be based on information supplied by the exporters. The authors further disagree with the Panel's interpretation of Article 6.10. In their view, this provision clearly allows investigating authorities the possibility of not calculating individual margins when the number of exporters appears to be too large, and the provision at the same time offers no specific guidance as to what constitutes a "large number." This element was overlooked because the Panel failed to apply the appropriate standard of review. Finally, the authors find the Panel's conclusions with respect to Article 2.4 sound.

Grossman and Mavroidis comment on the *US – Lead and Bismuth II* dispute. In this case, the European Community complained about the US practice of imposing countervailing duties (CVDs) on exports of steel products of EC companies that had received state aid before they were privatized. The heart of the dispute concerns the extent to which an arm's length privatization of a previously subsidized company suffices to eliminate all subsidies previously paid. The AB concluded that the United States, in their determination to impose CVDs, did not demonstrate why a benefit (in the sense of Article 1 Subsidies and Countervailing Measures [SCM] Agreement) survived the arm's length privatization. By not offering the proof, the United States illegally imposed CVDs on EC exports.

The authors agree with the outcome in this respect: the United States indeed did not demonstrate why subsidies survived privatization. They do disagree, however, with the opinion expressed by the AB that non-recurring subsidies are always extinguished whenever the company that benefited from them is privatized at arm's length. In their view, this is not necessarily always the case. The question that the AB should have asked is whether the original investment would have taken place under market conditions (the private investor test). If the answer is no, then there is at least a possibility that the original subsidy has survived the privatization. To rule otherwise would be tantamount to stating that any time shares of subsidized companies change hands in stock market operations all benefits are ipso facto extinguished.

The *US – Export Restraints* decision is commented upon by Janow and Staiger. The case concerns a long-standing disagreement between the United States and Canada as to the treatment under the GATT/WTO of export restraints by the former. Canada was here attacking the propriety of the legislation itself and not a particular measure. The Panel, by considering both the language of the disputed US statute (the US Statement of Administrative Action) and its practice, concluded that the US measures at hand could not be characterized as mandatory legislation. Following previous case law, the Panel thus concluded that the legislation could not be the subject of a complaint independently of its application. The Panel further ruled that the aforementioned export restraints could not be characterized as subsidies either, since they did not constitute a financial contribution (as required by Article 1.1 SCM).

The authors do not question the soundness of the Panel's approach. In fact, they offer additional reasons why export restraints should not be accepted as tantamount to subsidies: in their view, the specificity requirement is missing. Moreover, if such an expansive interpretation of the term "subsidy" were adopted, then even legal import tariffs could be put into question, since import tariffs implicitly subsidize the consumption of the comparable domestic product. The authors also point to the fact that the SCM Agreement is sometimes hard to reconcile with economic principles, essentially since it does not address in a comprehensive manner the overall welfare implications of subsidies.

Janow and Staiger also discuss the *Canada – Dairy* report. The United States and New Zealand complained that Canada, by using a target prices system in its domestic market and allowing for exports of over-quota milk (which did not benefit from domestic support schemes), was in fact granting an export subsidy prohibited by Articles 3 and 9 of the Agreement on Agriculture. They also held that the import tariff quota imposed by Canada was inconsistent with its obligations under Article II.1b of the GATT. The AB narrowed down the findings of inconsistency by the Panel but still found some aspects of the Canadian measures to constitute export subsidies (by using average cost as a benchmark) and upheld the finding on Article II.1b of the GATT.

The authors voice their concern with aspects of the AB's findings. Although they point to the lack of an economic basis for parts of the SCM Agreement, as in their comment on *US – Export Restraints*, they nevertheless make the point that the existing legal framework still provides WTO adjudicating bodies with sufficient discretion to reach their findings in a legally correct as well as economics-friendly manner. In particular, they stress their dissatisfaction with the benchmark the AB used to establish the existence of a subsidy (average cost). In the authors' view, when sunk investments earn a below market rate of return – which is to be the case in industries receiving government support – the AB's suggested methodology of relying on average total cost becomes problematic.

The last study in this volume is the discussion of the *US – Section 110(5) Copyright Act* dispute by Grossman and Mavroidis. The European Community complained that the United States legislation with respect to enforcement of some copyrights was inconsistent with the TRIPs Agreement. The Panel agreed with the EC allegation. Following the Panel's findings, the parties to the dispute submitted to an arbitrator (under Article 25 DSU) a request to evaluate the extent of injury suffered by EC owners of copyright as a result of inadequate enforcement by the United States. The European Community held the view that the benchmark against which to evaluate the extent of injury should be the case where the United States enforces copyrights in all establishments playing music. The United States, on the other hand, held the view that the benchmark should take into account costs of enforcement. In the US view, it was not obliged to license stores for which costs of enforcement outweighed the combined prospective benefits to the United States and the European Community; in the view of the United States, enforcement costs should be deducted from the amount of money transferred to the European Community. The Arbitrator essentially followed the US approach.

The authors do not dispute the approach of the arbitrator, especially since the legality of the overall US enforcement procedures as such was not put into question in the present dispute: all that was put into question was a relatively minor issue concerning the damage suffered by the European Community as a result of an amendment in US law (the WTO consistency of which is not doubted).

The authors do single out two issues of concern, however: first, they would strongly urge panels to dismiss requests of urgency by the parties to a dispute when urgency may jeopardize the quality of the final report. They voice this concern because the Arbitrator time and again blames the continuous request by the parties for speedy resolution for the insufficient factual basis on which the dispute was adjudicated. Second, in their view, the arbitrator did not properly decide on the time dimension of the EC injury: nothing in the WTO contract as such argues against retroactive remedies, and the arbitrator should have calculated the EC injury as of the point in time when the US illegality was committed.

As can be seen from this brief summary, the studies voice concern about the outcome as well as the reasoning by the adjudicating bodies in several disputes. In order to provide some form of summary statistics on the views expressed in these studies, we have classified the findings of each of them below using two criteria: the extent to which each and every study is in agreement with the adjudicating body's reasoning, and the extent to which it is in agreement with the outcomes of the dispute. This is how we have interpreted the studies:

	Rationale	Outcome
EC – Asbestos	unsatisfactory	correct
US – Shrimp	partly unsatisfactory	partly wrong
US – Lamb	unsatisfactory	partly wrong
EC – Bed linen	partly unsatisfactory	partly wrong
Mexico – Corn Syrup	satisfactory	correct
Argentina – Ceramic Tiles	unsatisfactory	wrong
US – Lead and Bismuth II	unsatisfactory	correct
US – Export Restraints	satisfactory	correct
Canada – Dairy	unsatisfactory	wrong
US – Section 110(5) Copyright Act	partly unsatisfactory	correct

As can be noted, the Reporters disagreed at least partly with the outcome in half of the disputes. However, more significant in our view is the rather general unease with the quality of the adjudicating bodies' analysis: the Reporters found methodological deficiencies in eight of the ten reviewed disputes. Were one to try the difficult task of summarizing this first year's review in one observation, it would probably be that the Reporters expressed overall dissatisfaction with the methodology used by WTO adjudicating bodies in the 2001 WTO case law.

Finally, criticizing is easy, and we should not lose sight of the fact that the task facing the adjudicating bodies is very difficult. The text of the various Agreements is often extremely vague and difficult to interpret in a consistent, reasonable manner. One therefore has to accept an element of trial-and-error in the formation of case law, in particular in the context of the newer Agreements. But while it is understandable that "errors" occur, they need to be highlighted in order to steer the future adjudication in sounder directions. We hope that the Reporters' Studies for this project can contribute to this end.

2

EC – Asbestos
European Communities – Measures Affecting Asbestos and Asbestos-Containing Products*

HENRIK HORN AND JOSEPH H. H. WEILER

1 *EC – Asbestos* as Watershed

Some cases attain "landmark" status because they constitute a jurisprudential paradigm shift. Others attain such status because in them a decisor,
usually a supreme jurisdiction, renders a definitive, "canonical," ruling.
Sometimes it is both reasons. Sometimes, rarely, it is neither. *EC – Asbestos*
is such a rare case. It may well qualify as a landmark. It has, justifiably,
attracted huge attention and, understandably, considerable controversy.
Its reasoning, however, is so decidedly non-definitive that it is not, consequently, possible to say whether it represents a veritable paradigm shift
or is just a badly reasoned case by the Appellate Body (AB), albeit with a
non controversial result.

It is a rare, indeed unique, instance that embedded in the decision
itself a Member of the Appellate Body Division which decided the case
expresses "substantial doubt" as to the core reasoning of the decision.[1]

---

* This study discusses the WTO Dispute Settlement dispute *European Communities –
Measures Affecting Asbestos and Asbestos-Containing Products* (WT/DS135/R, September
18, 2000 and WT/DS135/AB/R, 12 March 2001). We are grateful for helpful discussions
with Petros C. Mavroidis and the other Reporters of the project, and the comments provided
by participants in the ALI meeting in Philadelphia, February 6–7, 2003.

[1] In Recital 154 of the AB decision, the anonymous Separate Opinion opines: "My second
point is that the necessity or appropriateness of adopting a 'fundamentally' economic
interpretation of the 'likeness' of products under Article III.4 GATT 1994 does not appear to
me to be free from substantial doubt. Moreover, in future concrete contexts, the line between
a 'fundamentally' and 'exclusively' economic view of 'like products' under Article III.4
may well prove very difficult, as a practical matter, to identify. It seems to me the better
part of valour to reserve one's opinion on such an important, indeed, philosophical matter,
which may have unforeseeable implications, and to leave that matter for another appeal
and another day, or perhaps other appeals and other days. I so reserve my opinion on this
matter."

And although the AB rejected the reasoning, not the final outcome, of the Panel's decision, the doctrinal implications of the rejection are not clear and continue to be contested.

The importance of *Asbestos* must initially be found in its factual matrix, a French Government Decree of 1966[2] providing, *inter alia*, in its first article as follows:

> I. – For the purpose of protecting workers, . . . the manufacture, processing, sale, import, placing on the domestic market and transfer under any title whatsoever of all varieties of asbestos fibres shall be prohibited, regardless of whether these substances have been incorporated into materials, products or devices.
>
> II. – For the purpose of protecting consumers, . . . the manufacture, import, domestic marketing, exportation, possession for sale, offer, sale and transfer under any title whatsoever of all varieties of asbestos fibres or product containing asbestos fibres shall be prohibited . . .

This is a most typical (arguably the most typical) kind of government measure in the field of consumer and workplace protection taken in Member Countries of rich or poor, North or South, West or East. *EC – Asbestos* thus affects the physiognomy, not the pathology, of government regulation and its entanglement with General Agreement on Tariffs and Trade (GATT) trade rules.

It is also a case that implicates what is arguably the most central of GATT disciplines: National Treatment in the field of Regulation (and, by implication, taxation). There was never a serious doubt as to the material outcome of this case: validation of the legality of the French measure (many suspect that the Canadian government could not have seriously believed the WTO would overturn a ban on asbestos, but that it needed the result as a matter of domestic politics.) Thus, this is not a case about outcomes but about reasoning: the proper way for regulators and adjudicators to think of the application of the most central of GATT disciplines to the most central of government regulatory activity.

It is our belief that the case does not settle this question definitively but is extremely important in putting the methodological question squarely back on the table. It is veritably a watershed case – the full significance of which will emerge in the light of subsequent jurisprudence. Our own methodology will be as follows. The outcome of *EC – Asbestos* is hardly in doubt here. It is, as noted, the framework of methodologies that should

---

[2] *Décret no. 96–1133 relatif à l'interdiction de l'amiante, pris en application du code de travail et du code de la consommation, Journal officiel*, December 26, 1996.

become the central discussion point regarding *EC – Asbestos*, for it will provide a normative yardstick with which both to evaluate the specific decision in this case and to prescribe future evolution. We shall therefore first expound three possible approaches that *EC – Asbestos* exemplifies for interpreting the ambit of the National Treatment provision in GATT as it applies to regulation. Although, following the case, our focus will be on regulation, one cannot fully grasp the issues in the case without extensive reference to the law and case law on taxation. The principal governing norm, Article III.4 GATT is part of a whole (Article III GATT) which situates taxation and regulation side by side under a common *chapeau*. We will then discuss, critically, the main findings by the Panel and the AB in the light of these approaches.

2   Three methodologies for dealing with regulation under GATT 1994

In order to structure the discussion of the adjudicating bodies' rulings in *EC – Asbestos*, we find it useful to distinguish between three possible methods of interpreting GATT 1994, as it applies to health (and other regulatory) measures. These three approaches – or methodologies – do not perhaps correspond exactly to the views put forth by any particular body or individual, but each seems to capture the essence of a distinguishable way of reasoning. It should be emphasized, however, that they are not meant to exhaust the set of possible interpretations. We believe that each of the three represents a reasonably coherent way of approaching the issues in *EC – Asbestos* and, in fact, we see traces of all three in the decision of the Panel and Appellate Body. One reason *EC – Asbestos* has attracted so much attention is precisely because it represents a methodological crossway. We will strive to present the three methodologies in a neutral fashion, even though we do not necessarily find all them equally attractive.

The essential textual matrix of the case in relation to which the three approaches will be examined is as follows:

Article III.1 GATT – the chapeau – applies both to taxation and regulation and provides as follows:

> 1. The contracting parties recognize that internal taxes and other internal charges, and laws, regulations and requirements affecting the internal sale, offering for sale, purchase, transportation, distribution or use of products, and internal quantitative regulations requiring the mixture, processing or use of products in specified amounts or proportions, should not be applied to imported or domestic products so as to afford protection to domestic production.

Article III.4 GATT applying specifically to regulation states:

4. The products of the territory of any contracting party imported into the territory of any other contracting party shall be accorded treatment no less favourable than that accorded to like products of national origin in respect of all laws, regulations and requirements affecting their internal sale, offering for sale, purchase, transportation, distribution or use. The provisions of this paragraph shall not prevent the application of differential internal transportation charges which are based exclusively on the economic operation of the means of transport and not on the nationality of the product.

Article III.2 GATT applying specifically to taxation affirms:

2. The products of the territory of any contracting party imported into the territory of any other contracting party shall not be subject, directly or indirectly, to internal taxes or other internal charges of any kind in excess of those applied, directly or indirectly, to like domestic products. Moreover, no contracting party shall otherwise apply internal taxes or other internal charges to imported or domestic products in a manner contrary to the principles set forth in paragraph 1.

An *ad* to Article III.2 GATT explicates:

A tax conforming to the requirements of the first sentence of paragraph 2 would be considered to be inconsistent with the provisions of the second sentence only in cases where competition was involved between, on the one hand, the taxed product and, on the other hand, a directly competitive or substitutable product which was not similarly taxed.

Finally, Article XX GATT provides as follows:

General Exceptions
Subject to the requirement that such measures are not applied in a manner which would constitute a means of arbitrary or unjustifiable discrimination between countries where the same conditions prevail, or a disguised restriction on international trade, nothing in this Agreement shall be construed to prevent the adoption or enforcement by any contracting party of measures:
(*a*) necessary to protect public morals;
(*b*) necessary to protect human, animal or plant life or health[.]

All three methodologies share a premise as to the reach of GATT in this area: Members retain fiscal and regulatory autonomy under the GATT. But, in the exercise of their fiscal and regulatory autonomy they may not violate the principle of National Treatment as expressed in the legal matrix outlined above.

The interpretation of Article III GATT as it applies to regulation hence hinges principally on the interpretation of three terms:

- *like*
- *so as to afford protection* and
- *treatment not less favorable.*

The three stylized approaches we are to define and discuss differ in their interpretations of these three terms and their relationship to Article XX GATT.

2.1   Methodology I: the "Objective" approach

As will be argued below, this is the methodology used essentially by the Panel in *EC – Asbestos*. We are not trying to summarize the decision of the Panel here, but to present as a matter of theory a methodology which in our view underlies the approach by the Panel. It has also been employed by various panels and the AB in other cases, notably in the area of taxation. The "Objective" approach may be synthesized in the following manner: as mentioned, members retain fiscal and regulatory autonomy. They may impose taxation or adopt regulation as an expression of their specific socio-economic preferences. These may, and usually will, differ from country to country. Violation of National Treatment takes place when their tax or regulatory regimes distort competition between imported and domestic products in favor of the latter. In the words of the AB in *Japan – Taxes on Alcoholic Beverages:*[3]

> Article III obliges Members of the WTO to provide equality of competitive conditions for imported products in relation to domestic products. . . . Article III protects expectations not of any particular trade volume but rather of the equal competitive relationship between imported and domestic products. . . .[4]

The distinguishing feature of the first methodology is to understand the problematic turn of phrase in Article III.1 GATT – *so as* – whereby domestic taxation and regulation

---

[3] WTO WT/DS88, 10, 11/AB/R, Oct 1996.
[4] AB Report, *Japan – Taxes on Alcoholic Beverages*, footnote 58, at 109 and 110.

... should not be applied to imported or domestic products so as to afford
protection to domestic production ...

as indicative of an *objective general prohibition*: taxation and regulation
may not be applied in a way that *results* in protection being afforded
to domestic production. This prohibition applies also to taxation and
regulation which, on its face, is origin-neutral. Critically, the entire phrase
"should not be applied to imported or domestic products so as to afford
protection to domestic production" is understood in this methodology
as applying to the result of the tax or regulatory regime – to its *effect* on
the competitive relationship between domestic and imported products
and not to the intention or purpose of the tax and regulatory regime.

On this approach, a regulatory (or tax) regime which was adopted
with the explicit intention of distorting competition in favor of domestic
production but which, owing, say, to the stupidity of the regulator did
not have that effect, would not be in violation of Article III GATT. The
contrary would be equally true: a regulatory regime adopted on an origin-
neutral basis with no protectionist purpose at all, but which, nonetheless,
happened to ". . . afford protection to domestic production" would fall
under the prohibition imposed by Article III GATT.

Under this method even if the State adopted the regulatory or tax
measure with non-protective reasons in mind, indeed, with other com-
mendable reasons such as protection of consumers or the environment,
etcetera, a regulatory or tax measure that had the effect of affording protection to domestic production by distorting the competitive relationship
of an import in favor of domestic production could be retained only if
justified in accordance with Article XX GATT.

Articles III.2 GATT and III.4 GATT on this reading set out the precise legal conditions which would trigger a legal violation of the general
principle enunciated in the *chapeau* in the case of taxation and regulation
respectively. Specifically, in relation to regulation,

> The products of the territory of any contracting party imported into the
> territory of any other contracting party shall be accorded treatment no
> less favourable than that accorded to like products of national origin in
> respect of all laws, regulations and requirements affecting their internal
> sale, offering for sale, purchase, transportation, distribution or use.

Two issues in particular require elucidation: which products are covered by the non-discrimination discipline? What conduct amounts to a
violation of that discipline?

The first condition relates to the products – domestic and imported – to which the discipline applies. Article III.4 GATT speaks of "like" products. Article III.2.i GATT also refers to "like" products and Article III.2.ii GATT glossed by the *ad* note includes as a second category "directly competitive or substitutable products."[5] Consequently, "likeness" in Article III.2 GATT

---

[5] Tantalizingly, the *ad* to Article III speaks of direct competition *or* substitutability. Could there be a situation where substitutable products would not be in competition with each other? A high degree of functional substitutability between two products should naturally contribute to a competitive relationship in the market. But, the competitive relationship is determined by the interaction of the demand and the supply side. Therefore, if firms are constrained in their capacity to increase production, there is not a very competitive relationship in the market, despite the fact that products are highly substitutable on the demand side. On the other hand, it seems less likely that a competitive situation would arise in a situation where products are rather poor substitutes.

We would also like to make a comment on the common argument that likeness should not be determined "in the market place." It is argued that consumers may gradually change their consumption patterns habits through learning if imported products were to become substantially cheaper. For instance, after some time, kiwis are recognized by most consumers as a valid substitution to many other "juicy fruits" and find themselves in a competitive relationship with such fruit. But that might not be the case at the moment of introduction into the market. This argument has been invoked in case law in, for instance, *Korea – Alcoholic Beverages*, where the AB speaks of "latent demand" alluding to the situation where the very tax or regulatory regime under consideration would have shaped consumer preferences in a way that as an empirical matter two products which could (as evidenced in, say, some other market) be considered as objectively substitutable, do not appear to engender robust competition and thus would not be considered under the objective test as like. In some respects a similar phenomenon exists in relation to any new product, though functional similarity is much easier to communicate to potential consumers than taste.

This argument has an important grain of truth, but is at the same time a bit misleading. One has to distinguish between the notion that market competitiveness is what should ultimately determine likeness under Methodology I, and the practical question of *how* to determine this competitiveness. Heuristically, we may here distinguish between three types of situations with regard to the role of potential competition. In the first, the magnitude of the alleged discrimination is small, in the sense that the measure would not change prices, etc., in the market outside the range in which they normally vary. In this case, no fundamental problem stemming from potential competition seems to be involved. In the second type of situation the measure does shift prices, significantly outside the range where they normally vary. Here there is a problem, since we would have to "extrapolate" outside the range for which we have observations, and the further outside this range we go, the more uncertainty there is concerning the trustworthiness of the assessment. But, as far as we can see, there is no presumption that the errors we would make would be biased toward underestimating the degree of competitive relationship. A third type of situation would be one where some form of learning process is indeed involved. For instance, consumers may learn gradually about the characteristics of an imported product from their consumption of the product. Information obtained from a period of very high import prices, and low consumption, may then be of limited value to predict the consequences of a substantial reduction in the price of imported products, where consumers have learnt about the foreign product. In this third situation we can hardly rely on market data to determine

has been construed narrowly. The AB is emphatic in *EC − Asbestos* that the "like" products in Article III.4 GATT may not be the same as the "like" products in Article III.2 GATT and must be interpreted far more broadly. In fact, in order for Article III.4 GATT to successfully give expression to the general principle enunciated in the chapeau, "like" products in Article III.4 GATT must be understood as covering products which are competitive and/or substitutable even if in terms of their characteristics they may not be quite so like as products under the first sentence of Article III.2 GATT. Whilst there surely will be, according to the AB, some products whose degree of substitutability is so insignificant as to exclude them from the discipline of Article III.4 GATT, under the first approach, any appreciable degree of competition would bring the products within the purview of Article III.4 GATT.

Under Methodology I, "likeness" for the purposes of Article III.4 GATT is thus to be determined in the market place: it is only when products are in an appreciable (i.e. not *de-minimis*) competitive relationship that a less favorable treatment of an imported product can have the effect of protecting a domestic product. We will not deal here with the means for determining the existence of a competitive relationship in the market.

Once established that two products are in such a competitive relationship and are, thus, "like" products and subject to the discipline of Article III.4 GATT, the second legal condition relates to the conduct or content of the measure that will amount to a violation, by forbidding *less favorable treatment* of like imported products. Put differently, Article III.4 GATT gives specific expression (to use a term employed by the AB) to the general principle enunciated in III.1 GATT that regulation may not be applied *so as to afford protection* to domestic production by instructing that imported products ". . . shall be accorded treatment no less favourable . . . ."

It is important at this juncture to explore further the comparison of the "which" and "what" between Article III.2 GATT and III.4 GATT, since the construction of Article III.2 GATT could arguably provide some support for Methodology I.

the competitive relationship, since there is a presumption that data stemming from a period before learning would be biased toward undervaluing the degree of competitive rivalry. As a result, one may have to rely on evidence that does not directly stem from observations of the market in question. Note however, that the problem here is "only" one of empirically estimating the competitive relationship in the market. In particular, we have not questioned the basic premise that the competitive relationship − "the marketplace" − determines the degree of likeness. Hence, this is not an argument against the conceptual basis of the likeness definition, but about the possibility to use for instance standard econometrics to assess the competitive relationship.

As noted above, Article III.2 GATT provides two replies to the which question: the discipline of national treatment applies to "like products" *simpliciter* as well as products which are in "direct competition or are substitutable" even if not "like" in a narrow sense. According to the AB, "like products" in the sense of Article III.2 GATT has to be interpreted narrowly. The term would thus denote products which are very substitutable, in a high degree of competition and sharing physical and other characteristics. Products included under the second sentence of Article III.2 GATT may not share as many physical and other characteristics and the degree of substitutability and/or competition may not be quite as high.

What difference does it make? A critical one. Under the Methodology I, in the case of Article III.2 GATT "like" products, the trigger for violation is *any* taxation on the imported product in excess of that imposed on the like domestic product. Any taxation in excess would represent that: even the smallest difference would constitute a violation. Any taxation in excess would constitute a violation: whatever its intention and purpose.

In relation to the other broader category of products in Article III.2 GATT, this is arguably not the case. When products are "merely" in competition with each other but not amounting to "like" products, Article III.2 GATT contemplates the possibility of the imposition of a tax on the imported products in excess of the domestic one which does not constitute a violation. Instead, in relation to that category, the trigger will only be taxation which is inconsistent with the principles of Article III.1 GATT – notably ". . . so as to afford protection to domestic production."

What is the logic of the text which tells us that when products are "like" – meaning very, very similar to each other – any excess tax, even the smallest, would affect the competitive relationship and hence constitute a violation, but when products are not so similar though in competition with each other or being substitutable, a small difference in tax even in excess may not affect the competitive relationship and hence not constitute a violation?

Arguably, it would not make sense to avoid a subjective-intention test for "like products" but to introduce, through the words "so as to afford protection", such a test for products which are not "like" but are in competition with each other. Instead, it is more plausible on this reading to argue that the distinction turns on a different reasoning. It may have been thought that when products are not so similar and are only partially substitutable, a small difference in taxation would not affect consumer demand more than marginally and hence not affect the competitive relationship between products in any significant way. Only a difference in tax which was sufficiently big to noticeably "afford protection" would be caught.

What is important is that this distinction may seem to give some support to the hermeneutics of the objective methodology – since one possible way of reading it is to say that, in relation to the broader category, only a difference in taxation which has the effect (e.g. by being big enough) to afford protection between products which are only partially in competition, will trigger a violation. This reading would it could be argued, constitutes another reason not to read purpose or intent into the phrase ". . . so as to afford protection" but to see it as indicating an objective state reflecting a tax or regulation which distorts competition whether intended or otherwise.

To conclude, under the Objective Methodology of Article III:

- Likeness measures the degree to which products are in actual or potential competition in the market place.
- The yardstick for determining whether "less favorable treatment" has been rendered does not take into account any rationale for differential treatment, such as differences in health impact, but only captures the effect of the measure.
- Such less favorable treatment to imported products is a necessary and sufficient requirement for the measure to be such so as to afford protection.

2.2   Methodology II: the "Effect and Purpose" approach[6]

The second approach to interpreting Article III GATT shares one important feature with Interpretation I: products must be in competition with each other for Article III.4 GATT to apply at all. And the measure in question, at least *ipso facto*, would have to give some advantage to the domestic product and so afford protection to domestic production. But these would be only necessary conditions, not sufficient ones for a finding of an Article III GATT violation. Methodology II maintains that any advantage given by origin-neutral regulation (or taxation) to domestic production must have been applied *with that purpose* to be illegal.

On this reading, the mutual promise among all members ex Article III GATT was not to refrain from any taxation or regulation which would

---

[6] We avoid "aims and effect" because that has attained a certain canonical meaning in doctrine from which we prefer to be unencumbered. Of course our Methodology II shares much with aims and effect.

merely have the effect of giving protection to domestic production, but to refrain from imposing such regulation or taxation with that purpose.

A hard version of Interpretation II would insist on detecting such purpose, almost as a "*mens rea*" test in the regulatory process. A weaker, arguably more workable and defensible, version, adopted by the United States in *Japan – Alcoholic Beverages II* would be more holistic:[7] the failure of the importing country to provide at the adjudicatory stage a plausible explanation to the measure producing the disparate impact, would create a presumption of bad purpose. We would refer to this as constructive purpose.

Applied to *EC – Asbestos*, this approach would result in a finding of no violation of Article III GATT since on the hard version it would be hard to impute bad purpose to the French measure. On the soft version, France could plausibly (and realistically) explain that its origin-neutral measure was not applied so as to afford protection to domestic production but so as to afford protection to consumers and workers. The case would not on this reading ever reach Article XX GATT.

It should be noted that under Methodology I, a State seeking to justify a measure that was on the face of it in violation of Article III GATT, would be subjected in almost all situations to the Least Restrictive Measure test – it would not be allowed to keep the measure in place, as written, if it could be shown that the objective sanctioned by Article XX GATT could be reasonably achieved in a manner which was less burdensome to trade. Under the Effect and Purpose methodology this examination is folded into the Article III GATT analysis. The non-choice by the State of readily available less restrictive measures would need to be justified unless the presumption of bad purpose were triggered.

To summarize, according to Methodology II:

- Likeness measures the degree to which products are in actual or potential competition in the market place.
- The yardstick for determining whether "less favorable treatment" has been rendered does not take into account any rationale for differential treatment, such as differences in health impact, but only captures the effect of the measure.
- For a measure to be caught by the "so as to afford protection requirement," it is necessary that it *intentionally* provides such less favorable treatment (or that the State cannot give an adequate rational explanation for such treatment whereby intention will be implied).

---

[7] Submission of the United States of August 23, 1996 in the Appeal to *Japan – Taxes on Alcoholic Beverages II* (AB 1996–2).

The difference compared to Methodology I is hence the requirement of not only protective effect, but also such intent – actual or constructed. If the Purpose and Effect approach were to be applied in *EC – Asbestos*, the measure would most likely be accepted, since it would be found to lack protective intent.

2.3   Methodology III: the "Alternative Comparators" approach

Methodology II introduced one source of difference to Methodology I: the subjective requirement of purpose as a condition for illegality. Methodology III is a variation, but an important one, on Methodology II. Purpose is an important component also in Methodology III. But Methodology III takes a further step away from Methodology I, since it operates on a different trajectory of reasoning with regard to the determination of likeness.

Every determination of likeness for the purpose of determining the existence of discrimination embodies, explicitly or implicitly, a comparator. It also involves the exclusion of certain factors as illegitimate comparators. In the case of, say, sex or race discrimination, we take as the comparator the essential humanity of the subjects. In the light of that comparator men and women, or whites and blacks, or Jews and Gentiles, are held to be "like" and the norm of "like" treatment is triggered. Differently put, we exclude as comparator color of skin, or gender, or race and religion: as a matter of policy those are determined to be irrelevant comparators. If color of skin were a legitimate comparator, then for the purposes of that comparator whites and blacks would be "unlike" and could (and even should) be treated differently since treating the "unlike" in a like manner is equally discriminatory to treating the "like" in an unlike manner.

Under both Methodologies I and II, the implicit comparator is market functionality of the product. It is the comparator reflective of the vocabulary of substitutability, competition, consumer preference. Products are considered "like" and hence subject to the discipline of National Treatment because they meet similar needs of the consumer and consequently compete with each other in the eyes of the consumer on the market. Methodology I and II share the same conception of likeness deriving from the same market place comparator.

Methodologies I and II differ in the way they treat the plea of the State that the less favorable treatment accorded the imported product was in pursuance of a legitimate purpose. Under Methodology I such a plea of legitimate purpose will exculpate the overall illegality of the State measure if found to fall within the parameters of Article XX GATT. The State will have been found to discriminate since two "like" products were treated in an unlike manner and thus Article III GATT was violated, but the discrimination will be considered justified in pursuance of an overriding other policy sanctioned under Article XX GATT.

Under Methodology II there is no finding of discrimination and thus of violation of Article III GATT since even though like products have been treated in an unlike manner, violation of Article III GATT is construed as considered to take place only when the less favorable treatment is imposed with the purpose – actual or constructed – of protecting domestic production.

Under Methodology III, the very comparator is put into question. The relevance of the functional comparator does not disappear altogether: the complaint establishing a *prima facie* violation and the requirement of the State to defend itself will be triggered on the basis of alleged discriminatory treatment of products in competition with each other. This is the unifying thread among all three methodologies. The functional market comparator is the default position. The response of the State would however be different in that it would challenge the very use of that comparator.

An illustration will serve to bring out the nuanced difference between the methodologies. In a famous tax case, Italy had a high tax on refined engine oil and a low tax on recycled engine oil. It did so for ecological reasons – to provide an economic incentive to recycle oil thus enhancing conservation and responsible disposal of used oil. From a market-functional perspective refined oil and recycled oil meet the very same needs of the consumer and are in competition with each other. Indeed, in their properties they are so similar, they are indistinguishable. The user can not, from its properties, tell the difference between refined and recycled oil. Taxing imported refined oil at a high rate and domestic recycled oil at a low rate would certainly amount to treating a functionally like imported product in a less favorable way.

Using Methodology I – Article III will have been held to have been violated, but the State may justify its measure under Article XX.g GATT. Under Methodology II, since the purpose of the tax was not to protect domestic production (even if this was its effect) but to protect the environment, no violation of Article III GATT will have taken place. Under Methodology III the two products are not considered like, because the implicit comparator of the measure is not market functionality but an alternative comparator – ecological efficiency: ecologically efficient products (such as recycled oil) are taxed at a low rate and ecologically inefficient products (refined oil) are taxed at a high rate. Under this methodology, by employing an alternative comparator, refined oil and recycled oil simply do not come under the discipline of National Treatment and Article III GATT – any more than diamonds and oranges would.

Note that under Methodology III it is not the set of values of the adjudicator which determine the outcome. It is the choice of comparator by the regulating state. In this respect the role of the adjudicator under Methodology III is not radically different to his or her role under Methodology II: the adjudicator has to decide whether the State has made a convincing argument concerning the choice of comparator underlying the regulatory or tax distinction. Under Methodology II the adjudicator has to pronounce on the claimed purpose. Note too that under Methodology III once the comparator is defined, the test of less favorable treatment and so as to afford protection do not differ from Methodology I – they are market-based and look at effects of the measure on the competitive relationship between the like products (defined, however, according to the relevant comparator). Thus, crucially, even if the adjudicator accepts the claim of an alternative comparator, she can still find discrimination if, *by reference to the categories created by the alternative comparator (e.g. ecologically efficient and ecologically inefficient products)*, imported products are treated less favorably than domestic products.

Applied to asbestos, the comparator implicit in the French Decree is health risk or more specifically carcinogenic potential. The Decree, on this reading, differentiates (in origin-neutral fashion) between carcinogenic and cancer-risk-free products. By reference to the comparator of "carcinogenicity" the two products are simply unlike products and not caught by the discipline of national treatment and non-discrimination.

To summarize, the complaint is based on a claim that a "like" imported product, defined in market terms is treated less favorably than its domestic counterpart. If that is credibly alleged a *prima facie* violation is established and the regulating state is required to defend its action.

Under Methodology III:

- Likeness is defined by reference to the implicit or explicit comparator underlying the measure.
- A product is understood to be treated less favorably in the traditional way – with reference to the effect of the measure on the competitive relationship between the like products (defined, however, by the appropriate comparator).
- Protection is afforded when a like imported product (defined by the appropriate comparator) is treated less favorably.

2.4 Reflections on the three methodologies: what's in the choice?

We do not here take position but are more concerned to explain the choices made by the adjudicating bodies of the GATT and WTO. The *EC – Asbestos* Panel certainly reflected a preference for Methodology I. By contrast, there is a conflict in the jurisprudence of the Appellate Body and it is possible to read as validating, in different cases, all three strands. *EC – Bananas III* was a clear affirmation of Methodology I. *Chile – Taxes on Alcoholic Beverages* has distinct language affirming some variant of Methodology II. *Japan – Alcoholic Beverages II* is the most tantalizing. It avoided the chance for a "full affirmation of purpose" as advocated in the United States Appeal. It rejected purpose for the interpretation of Article III.2 GATT first sentence but used language that could be read as consistent with purpose analysis for the second sentence of Article III.2 GATT.[8]

Although Methodology III has not featured, as such, in either literature or jurisprudence, there is a strand of reasoning in *Japan – Alcoholic Beverages II* which is not only consistent with it, but seems to employ it. The Appellate Body does, after all, accept that taxation by reference to the alcoholic content of a spirit, broken down even to very small differences, is a legitimate practice. Without stating so conceptually, they are allowing the State, in response to the allegation of *prima facie* violation based on the contention that products in competition with each other are treated differently (i.e. default comparator) to explain their tax regime by reference to an alternative comparator, namely alcoholic content. Had the tax steps followed in some coherent sense the logic of the alternative comparator – alcoholic content – Japan would not have been found to be in violation of Article III GATT even though the effect of the tax would be to affect competition between like products – highly suitable from the consumers' point of view.[9]

Instead of trying to argue which approach, hermeneutically or from a policy perspective, remains the "right" or "correct" approach, we would rather assess some of the arguments advocated for the different approaches.

One hermeneutic argument should be dispelled quickly enough, that to employ Methodology II (or III) would render Article XX GATT

---

[8] This raises a delicate issue: since "like products" in Article III.4 GATT is considered to cover more than "like products" in Article III.2 GATT, would this possible distinction drawn by the AB in *Japan Alcoholic Beverages II* indicate a similar bifurcated approach to Article III.4 GATT depending on the degree of likeness of the domestic and imported products?

[9] We are assuming that a difference of, say, one degree of alcoholic content is irrelevant to consumer preference.

redundant. Article XX GATT would retain its place in relation to other Articles of the GATT such as Article XI GATT as well as to those situations where there actually was purposeful discrimination under Article III GATT in the cases where, for example, the State employs non-origin-neutral regulations.

It is also often stated that one big difference between Methodology I and Methodology II concerns burden of proof. Formally, this would seem to be the case. Under Methodology I, once it is established that a violation of Article III GATT has taken place by reason of an imported product receiving less favorable treatment than a "like" domestic product (likeness objectively determined), the burden of justification falls on the defending State. It is usually thought that under Methodology II the burden on the complaining State would be much greater since not only would the complaining State have to prove likeness and less favorable treatment, but also bad purpose. Forensically we think this argument is often overstated. If one examines the American Appellate brief in *Japan – Alcoholic Beverages II* as a benchmark for the actual operationability of Methodology II, it would seem that in practice once less favorable treatment of the imported like product were established, there would be a presumption of protectionist purpose unless, very much in Article XX GATT fashion, the defending State did not justify its practice by reference to a legitimate purpose.

The differences between the two methodologies seem to rest elsewhere – both practically and conceptually. One alleged practical consequence would be the range of policies available to the State. Under Methodology I, this range would be limited to the policies of Article XX GATT. Under Methodology II (and Methodology III) other policies could be employed. In particular it may be thought that, given the great difficulty of amending the Agreements, it would be unwise to force States to lock themselves into a list of policies which may remain static for decades. In our view, from a practical point of view, this difference should not be overstated. Article XX GATT is broad and sufficiently open-textured to cater for most exigencies and the WTO decision-makers have shown themselves ready to adopt such dynamic hermeneutics in interpreting the provisions of Article XX. To the extent that Panels and the AB have resisted Methodology II (and III), it is not because they feared that actual policies unsanctioned by Article XX GATT would have to be validated under this methodology.

Two other considerations may have played a role in explaining the reluctance to move away from Methodology I. The first is the perception by panels and the AB of their own legitimacy. The obsessive rhetorical (though not substantive) reliance of the AB on the plain and ordinary meaning of words is an indication of legitimacy anxiety by a new body in a new adjudicatory situation. The panels and the AB may simply feel more comfortable in legitimating State action which treats imported products less favorably when anchored in the explicit text of Article XX GATT than in the more abstract legitimation process ex Article III GATT.

We are not arguing that they are right in that perception: after all, the application of Methodology I by the Panel in *EC – Asbestos* which led to the characterization of the French health measure as a violation of the principal GATT discipline of National Treatment requiring justification under Article XX GATT may have been even more "delegitimating" than application of Methodologies II or III. But this might be so only because the justification alleged by the State in this case was in a category which so squarely fell within the policies approved by Article XX GATT and the policy was so clearly perceived as applied in good faith and for good reasons. Change the facts just a little and the wish of panels and the AB to rest within the security of Article XX GATT may be more comprehensible.

They may also feel that to link the justification to Article XX GATT enhances (and is, thus, preferable) the *multilateral* dimension of the WTO whereas to employ the other Methodologies enhances the autonomy, sovereignty and "unilateral" dimension of the Agreement. One should not understate the significance of this factor. In a very large number of these cases the defendant belongs to the economically powerful, notably the US, the EC, Canada, etc. The more "objective" elements of Methodology I may appear to shackle these States more firmly as well as to "protect" the Panel and AB from the need to evaluate and contest their subjective assertions of purpose.

The strongest argument for the other Methodologies are not, in our view, of a crude pragmatic nature – i.e. leading to tangible different results but in the realms of concept and symbol. First there is something that comes under the concept of "naming and shaming." It is wrong, it can be argued, to deal with the case of a State which adopts an origin neutral measure for a totally legitimate purpose, but which has the coincidental effect of giving an advantage to domestic production, as a violation of a non-discrimination provision requiring justification. Even if the result is the same, there is value in having cases dealt with in a correct normative context and in not diluting the notion of discrimination with activities which should not be so branded.

There is, it is also argued, a "truth"-based argument which goes beyond the lexical hermeneutics of the text of Article III GATT, namely that there can be no discussion of discrimination which does not imply, in some way and at some level, examination of purpose and an agreed comparator.

We may agree that there should be no discrimination between men and women, which means that we exclude gender as a relevant comparator for different treatment. But, assume that we want to write our laws in a way which would, say, take account of the fact that women, not men, fall pregnant. We might, in view of this fact, want to have special provisions in our labor code concerning leave, grounds of dismissal and the like which would, of course, treat men and women differently. One way would be to say that such laws were discriminatory but were exculpated by an overriding justification. Another way, perhaps with more conceptual coherence, would be to argue that for the purposes of childbirth men and women are not "like" and therefore treating them differently is not a matter of discrimination at all. The question is not which is the advisable policy (e.g. special laws to protect pregnant women against dismissal), but the understanding that what we are doing in relation to these issues is to discuss the legitimacy of alternative comparators, and/or the legitimacy of the purpose of the legislation which presumes a difference or results in a difference.

At an even deeper level, the difference between Methodologies I and II/III can go to the very symbolism of political identity. Methodology I – even if very solicitous to diverse socioeconomic choices in the construction of Article XX – establishes a normative hierarchy whereby the default norm is liberalized trade, and, for competing norms to prevail, they have to be justified. This is not a question of technical burden of proof. It is a question of constitutional identity, the way a society wants to understand its internal hierarchy of values. Methodologies II and III reverse that default. The default value is autonomy of political and moral identity which requires justification only if purposefully abused.

In our view the Agreements in general and Article III GATT specifically can be read in a way which would sustain either of these understandings. This, however, might lead us to yet another contingent reason why some prefer Methodology I. For the decisor, Methodology I does not involve a value judgment at the level of comparator – it takes as the only relevant comparator the competitive relationship in the market. This is akin to the adjudicatory comfort argument mentioned above when it comes to violation.

But there is yet another consideration. At the end of the day, the GATT norms are addressed principally to regulators. Very often they are addressed to the very same regulators which just yesteryear were responsible for articulating, implementing, and justifying protectionist regimes. It may be thought wise in such a circumstance, as a contingent matter, to aim for an "objective" regime determining both likeness (competitive relationship in the market place) and violation (less favorable treatment leading to a protective effect) precisely for the "naming and shaming" effect. This would serve as a means of habituating national regulators to take the regime of non-discrimination seriously; to have their hand slapped, so to speak, every time a regulation is made, or defended, which would treat competing imported products differently. One can envision, on this reading, that with time, with the internalization of the norms of equal treatment, a different approach may be adopted.

3   EC – *Asbestos* in the light of the three methodologies

We will now turn to a discussion of the Panel and AB reports in *EC – Asbestos*, from the perspective of the three approaches identified above.

3.1   *The Panel report*

Generally speaking, the Panel in *EC – Asbestos* employed Methodology I. It found first that the products were "like" on a market-based test. Consequently the French measure violated Article III GATT since it had the effect of providing less favorable treatment to imported products and thus was such as to afford protection to the domestic producers. It then found that the measure was justified under Article XX.b GATT.

According to Methodology I, there would be an entire range of products, notably in the building and do-it-yourself sectors where different technologies would be used to give certain materials an insulating capacity, asbestos being one of such technologies. Accordingly, most of these products, from a functional point of view, would be appreciably substitutable and at least in partial competition with each other and, hence, caught within the definition of likeness ex Article III.4 GATT. The violative trigger would be easily pulled here since the effect of the State measure in question is not simply to burden the competing import but to exclude it entirely from the market place. The violation of Article III.4 GATT would thus be relatively easily established and the State would have to justify the maintenance of such measures ex Article XX.b GATT − not a difficult task given the serious risk factor of asbestos.

3.2   The AB report

The AB report devotes considerable attention to the determination of whether asbestos products are "like" other products not affected by the French *Decret*. We believe that the essential points made by the AB are the following (the number in parenthesis refers to the respective recital):[10]

1. A determination of "likeness" under Article III.4 GATT is, fundamentally, a determination about the nature and extent of a competitive relationship between and among products. (99)
2. The four criteria listed in the *Border Tax Adjustment* (BTA) dispute can be used to assess likeness, but do not constitute a closed list. (102)
3. The Panel did not correctly employ these criteria, since having adopted the BTA procedure, the Panel should have considered *all* four criteria separately. (109) Instead the Panel:
   (i)   confused the discussion of physical characteristics and end-uses; (111)
   (ii) failed to take into account the physical differences between asbestos products and other products; (114)
   (iii) did not provide a complete picture on differences in end-uses; (119)
   (iv) did not appropriately consider differences in consumers' tastes and habits; (120–21) and
   (v)   did not fully analyze the implication of different tariff classification. (124)
4. Health risk should in general be included in the determination of likeness. But in the case of asbestos products, this could be addressed when assessing physical properties and consumer perceptions. (113)
5. Panels must examine fully the physical properties of products, and in particular those that are likely to influence the competitive relationship in the marketplace. (114)
6. The carcinogenicity of asbestos products is a main factor making it physically different from substitute materials, and has to be taken into account when examining likeness. (114)

---

[10] We concentrate on the relationship between cement-based products containing chrysotile asbestos fibres and those containing PCG fibres.

7. Under Article III.4 GATT, evidence relating to health risks may be relevant in assessing the *competitive relationship in the marketplace* between allegedly "like" products. The same evidence should be used under Article XX.b GATT to assess whether there is sufficient basis for adopting or enforcing a WTO-inconsistent measure on the grounds of human health. (115)

8. The end-use and consumer habits and tastes criteria involve certain of the key elements relating to the competitive relationship between products. Evidence of this type is of particular importance under Article III GATT 1994, precisely because that provision is concerned with competitive relationships in the marketplace. If there is – or could be – *no* competitive relationship between products, it is not possible legally for a member through internal taxation or regulation, to protect domestic production. (117)

9. Had the Panel performed the analysis of consumers' tastes and habits, it would have found that consumers did not view products as like. The reason is that consumers are in this case manufacturers, and "[a] manufacturer cannot, for instance, ignore the preferences of the ultimate consumer of its products. If the risks posed by a particular product are sufficiently great, the ultimate consumer may simply cease to buy that product." (122)

10. Employing the BTA approach, the AB finds that the products are physically different. A heavy burden is consequently placed on Canada to show a competitive relationship, in order to overcome a non-likeness finding. (136) Failing to provide such evidence, products are found to be not like, and the AB thus reverses the Panel's finding that the products are like. (141)

3.2.1   Which interpretation did the AB employ?

By rejecting a finding of violation of Article III GATT, the AB in *Asbestos* seemed to be moving away from a robust version of Methodology I. In Recital 100 we even find the following statement:

> [E]ven if two products are "like," that does not mean that a measure is inconsistent with Article III:4. A complaining Member must still establish that the measure accords to the group of "like" *imported* products "less favourable treatment" than it accords to the group of "like" *domestic* products. The term "less favourable treatment" expresses the general principle, in Article III:1, that internal regulations "should not be applied . . . so as to afford protection to domestic production." If there is "less favourable

treatment" of the group of "like" imported products, there is, conversely, "protection" of the group of "like" domestic products. However, a Member may draw distinctions between products which have been found to be "like," without, for this reason alone, according to the group of "like" *imported* products "less favourable treatment" than that accorded to the group of "like" *domestic* products.

This statement could indeed be a platform from which to embrace an intent test along the lines of Methodologies II or even III. Here comes the tantalizing phrase whereby a member *may draw distinctions between products which have been found to be like* without that resulting in less favorable treatment and hence violative of Article III GATT. What could the AB possibly have in mind? If, after all, from a market point of view the imported products are "like" the domestic products and are given less favorable treatment, how could that not amount to protection?

Let us go back in mind to the recycled-oil case: recycled oil and refined oil are, from a market point of view, like products. But, to use the language in Recital 100, drawing a distinction based on ecological efficiency between these two products which have been found to be like from a functional/market sense and taxing them or regulating them according to this distinction, would not, for this reason alone, accord the imported product less favorable treatment than that accorded the domestic product. This is not the rhetoric and reasoning of Methodology I, nor is it the rhetoric and reasoning of Methodology II (since under Methodology II there is a finding of less favorable treatment). Could it be that there is no less favorable treatment because in accordance with the distinction drawn by the State these are simply not like products? This would be the rhetoric and reasoning of Methodology III.

The language of "distinctions" is also consistent with our earlier reading of *Japan – Alcoholic Beverages II*. The fact that products are within a generic group – e.g. spirits – within which there is competition, does not mean that the State cannot draw distinctions on which tax differentiation may take place. In making these distinctions the State may employ alternative comparators. We already saw how products within the spirits group could be differentiated according to alcoholic content and taxed accordingly. One could easily imagine other scenarios: automobiles may constitute the general group of "like" products, but in constructing the tax regime the State may employ the alternative comparator of engine displacement or level of emission and tax accordingly. Reading the enigmatic Recital 100 in the light of the holding of the AB in *EC – Japan Alcoholic Beverages II* would suggest that so long as there was a measure of coherence between the tax rate and the steps suggested by the alternative comparator employed in making these "distinctions," there would not be a violation of Article III GATT.

However we may read Recital 100, in the rest of the report of the AB there is little else to indicate an endorsement of Methodologies II or III. The reason the AB reached a different result to that of the Panel was not because of a different methodology but because, within the parameters of Methodology I, it came to the conclusion that the two products were not like products. It arrived at this conclusion by looking at the health consideration not as a factor in determining the purpose of the measure, or the basis of the comparator, but as a means to determine, factually, whether there was a competitive relationship between the two products. Here is a typical quote:

> Under Article III:4, evidence relating to health risks may be relevant in assessing the *competitive relationship in the marketplace* between allegedly "like" products. (emphasis in the original)

Weighing heavily in the AB's finding of unlikeness was the fact that asbestos was a well-known carcinogenic, the presence of which would surely affect the competitive relationship in the marketplace.

The core of the AB's reasoning with regard to likeness seems to be as follows:

1. The test for likeness is in the marketplace, since absent likeness there can be no protection. (99, 117)
2. The market view of likeness is not directly observable, so we instead have to rely on various indicators providing partial information about the relationship. The BTA list contains some possible indicators, all of which are informative of the relationship. (102)
3. It is well known that the products involved in the dispute are very different in their health impact, due to their different physical properties. (114, 136)
4. The end-use criterion is difficult to evaluate since it is not clear to what extent there is overlap in the use between asbestos-containing products and substitute products. (138)
5. The consumers' habits and tastes criterion is also hard to employ, since no evidence is presented by Canada on this point. (139) However, the fact that the differences between products in riskiness are well known, combined with the economic incentives of buyers to take into account

final consumers' aversion to dangerous products (122), suggest that products would indeed be found to be unlike from the buyers' point of view, if this analysis were to be performed.

6. With strong evidence on differences in risk, and with little or no evidence on end-uses and consumers' tastes and habits, one is led to conclude that products are not like in the marketplace.

In this circuitous and forced reading, this appears to be an endorsement of Methodology I even in the circumstances of *EC – Asbestos*. The AB extricated the WTO from the embarrassment of characterizing the legitimate policy of France as a violation of its core discipline of National Treatment. But, paradoxically, it reached that result by using the methodology which is most likely to produce again and again the conclusion of the Panel.

3.3   Concluding remarks

The outcome of *EC – Asbestos* is not at issue. Clearly the French measure to ban asbestos is justified under the Agreements. Methodologically, however, both legally and economically the case is not without serious problems.

Technically, and this is our first point, the case turned on burden of proof – Canada failed the burden necessary to establish likeness. That is an unsatisfactory basis for the decision. Should the result of the case have been different if Canada had simply provided evidence that *some* consumers would still buy the products, risk notwithstanding, and would maybe even comforted by the fact that in the age of Government regulation the absence of a prohibition gives some indication that "the Government" does not consider the product truly beyond a reasonable consumer choice?

An important link in the reasoning above, showing how the AB likeness criterion might be viewed as only concerning market relations, was that buyers in this market would take risk differences into account. This was based on a simplistic belief in the working of the market, according to which the buyers (who are not end-users) had to do this since they would otherwise lose customers.

We do not want to suggest that this knowledge on the preferences of the ultimate consumers would not be an important factor limiting the usage of asbestos products. But there are a number of arguments to suggest the potential for the exposure to asbestos to be higher than socially desirable. For instance, because of costly information one should not expect all final consumers to be fully informed about all hazards. There are likely to be severe negative externalities associated with asbestos products, since final users of asbestos products may not care about the negative health impact of their use of asbestos-containing products for third parties. For instance, asbestos in the brakes of an auto may not cause much of a health hazard to the owner, but it contributes to the spreading of asbestos in the air.

Market failures are also likely to arise from fixed costs in litigation. For instance, the health damage from exposure to asbestos from a particular building might be limited, if it is a building in which most people spend a very limited time. But being exposed to asbestos in many such buildings may have severe negative consequences. But since each individual only suffers minor damage from any particular building, it might not pay to litigate. Or, the possibility of being sheltered by bankruptcy may adversely affect buyer behavior. For all these reasons one should expect that products containing asbestos are over-consumed relative to what would be socially efficient if the market were left unregulated. This is indeed precisely why government intervention is needed. It is the fact that buyers tend to treat the products as closer substitutes than they are from the government's point of view that motivates the regulation.

Was not the very fact that the products are considered substitutable and in competition with each other and that, at least to some degree, the risky product would be used, among the reasons which prompted the French government to institute the ban? If so, was it not a bit too emphatic to claim that there was no evidence of a competitive relationship in the marketplace? Moreover, in Recital 121 the AB criticizes the Panel for concluding that products are like without examining evidence on consumer habits and tastes, and with weak evidence on end-uses (119) which

> ... involve certain of the key elements relating to the competitive relation-
> ship between products ... (117)

On the basis of the same material, the AB is able to conclude that products are *not* like. This determination comes as a result of the presumption for likeness created by physical differences, and Canada's unwillingness/inability to provide evidence on consumers' tastes and habits. While the latter obviously weakens Canada's case, it is hard to see how this can be taken as evidence of lack of likeness, rather than of the fact that the issue is unresolved. Once again we confront the systemic weakness of the Dispute Settlement Understanding which does not allow the AB to remand a case back to the Panel for a new factual determination. But we doubt very much if the AB is truly serious about this point and whether it has not simply decided that in some essentialist sense, independently of the market, carcinogenic and non-carcinogenic products cannot be "like."

Third, the logic of the AB reasoning may lead to the following very puzzling result: when a product has a well-known risk factor and the State regulates on that basis, there is no violation of Article III GATT. But imagine another product which is equally dangerous and where the State takes an identical regulation to protect consumers, the only difference being that in the second case the nature of the risk is less well known by the public. Should this fact alone determine that in the second case there was a violation of Article III GATT?

Fourth, would the AB's reasoning allow France simply to tax the imported product more highly without violating Article III.2 GATT since the products have been determined not to be like products? Imagine such an occurrence resulting in a marketplace in which carcinogenic asbestos-containing products were sold alongside non-carcinogenic asbestos-free products at the same price. This could be the result of competitive market conditions, where the imported product yields a smaller profit because of the need to absorb the higher tax in order to remain price competitive. In such a case there would be no health impact of the measure, which would only serve as a revenue-generating tax on imports.[11] And yet, under the reasoning of EC – Asbestos it would be permitted.

Finally, although the AB reaches a result that differs from the Panel's, it is in the same methodological ballpark. One cannot escape the feeling that although the surface language of the AB is concerned with the alleged preferences of consumers and the competitive relationship in the marketplace of the two products, the deep structure of its discourse is very different: the belief of the AB that it simply cannot be that under the WTO a State cannot accord different treatment to carcinogenic and non-carcinogenic products without being branded as violating the principle of National Treatment and having to justify itself ex Article XX GATT.

Caught up by some of the considerations discussed in our analysis of the three methods, the AB could not bring itself to say that the products are not "like" because the State may legitimately employ in its tax and regulatory regimes non-market comparators (such as health risk or ecological

---

[11] Since the definition of likeness under III.4 seems to overlap with the combined definition of likeness of III.2.

efficiency) or instead, that although the products were like products, the measure of the State itself according less favorable treatment to one over the other was not a violation of Article III GATT, since it was not applied with the purpose of affording protection to domestic production, but with the purpose of affording protection to would-be users of the product. It thus reverted to an attempt to push these other concepts into the straightjacket of market competition. The result is a decision that, while correct in terms of outcome, has added to the uncertainty concerning the method by which to determine the legality of domestic regulations under the WTO contract.

3

US – Shrimp
United States – Import Prohibition of Certain Shrimp and Shrimp Products: Recourse to Article 21.5 of the DSU by Malaysia*

ROBERT HOWSE AND DAMIEN J. NEVEN

1 Introduction

This study discusses the ruling of the Appellate Body (AB) in the recourse to Article 21.5 of the DSU by Malaysia in the context of the US import prohibition of certain shrimp and shrimp products from a legal and economic perspective. The first part of the chapter (section 2) discusses the background of the case, and, in particular, presents the main issues at stake in the Panel and AB decisions in the original case as well as their main findings. Section 3 discusses the key elements of the compliance panel and its subsequent appeal and identifies a few issues that are discussed in further detail. In section 4, in the context of a simple model, we first consider the consequences of making imports contingent on the adoption of environmental measures in exporting countries. We find that the attractiveness of such measures depends heavily on the characteristics of abatement technology and the range of policies available in the exporting countries. Finally, section 5 briefly discusses the trade-off between flexibility in the imposition of environmental standards and the enforcement of dispute settlements' rulings.

2 Factual background[1] and summary of legal issues and findings

2.1 Protection of sea turtles by the United States

Several species of sea turtles are endangered. In the 1980s, in an effort to protect these species, the United States enacted measures to reduce the

---

* This study was prepared in the context of the American Law Institute project on the Principles of World Trade Law.
[1] The material in this section draws heavily on Howse (2002).

number of sea turtles killed by US trawlers. The most important measure was a requirement that every US trawler fishing waters inhabited by sea turtles be equipped with a Turtle Excluder Device. In 1989, the United States attempted to impose the Turtle Excluder Device requirement on shrimp trawlers elsewhere in the world.

Section 609 of the law on the "Protection of sea turtles in shrimp trawl fishing operations" contained several elements. First, it required the US State Department to (1) commence negotiations as soon as possible for concluding bilateral and multilateral agreements to protect sea turtles and to (2) promote other international environmental agreements to better protect sea turtles. Second, it required the State Department to report to Congress within a year on the practices of other countries affecting the mortality of sea turtles. Third, it prohibited the importation of any shrimp harvested using commercial fishing technologies that might harm sea turtles, unless the exporting country is certified by the US administration as having a regulatory program to prevent incidental turtle deaths comparable to that of the United States, or is certified as having a fishing environment that does not pose risks to sea turtles from shrimping. Until 1995, the State Department had only applied the requirements of this section to the Caribbean area and did so on the basis of a program to require trawlers to be equipped with Turtle Excluder Devices. In 1995, environmental NGOs challenged the decision of the State Department to limit the application of section 609 to the Caribbean area before the US Court of International Trade.

The Court of International Trade held that there was no statutory basis for limiting the law to the Caribbean region. In a subsequent court action, the State Department asked the court to extend the deadline for application of the embargo to other countries beyond 1996, arguing that this deadline would provide inadequate opportunity for other countries to adopt the measures necessary to be certified. The Court of International Trade denied this request. This led the State Department to promulgate a series of guidelines for enforcement of the statute, which permitted entry into the US of shrimp that were declared to be caught with Turtle Excluder Device technology, even if the country concerned could not be certified as having a regulatory program comparable to that of the US. These guidelines were in turn challenged by NGOs in further proceedings at the Court.

The Court held that Congress had intended that the main operative provision of section 609, which banned shrimps caught with commercial fishing technology harmful to endangered species of sea turtles, in fact applied to all shrimps not originating from certified countries, regardless of whether the imported shrimps themselves were caught by boats equipped with Turtle Excluder Device technology.

On the day of the Court of International Trade judgment, India, Malaysia, Pakistan, and Thailand took the matter to dispute settlement at the WTO. The United States chose not to dispute explicitly the complainants' argument that the shrimp embargo was a violation of Article XI GATT, which bans non-tariff prohibitions or restrictions on imports. The United States based its defense of the measure strictly on the claim that they were justified under Article XX.b or g GATT. Article XX GATT provides exceptions (to Article XI GATT) for measures that are "necessary" to protect human and animal health (XX.b) and measures enacted "in relation to" the conservation of natural resources (XX.g).

2.2   The original Panel and Appellate Body rulings

While much of the legal arguments of the parties, as well as their factual claims, addressed whether the embargo could be justified under Article XX.b or g GATT, the Panel chose to pin its legal analysis exclusively on a consideration of whether the embargo satisfied the chapeau, i.e. the general provisions of Article XX GATT. It stipulated that measures should not be applied "in a manner which would constitute a means of arbitrary or unjustifiable discrimination between countries where the same conditions prevail, or a disguised restriction of international trade."

The Panel ruled that unilateral measures conditioning market access to the adoption of certain policies by exporting countries were not consistent with the chapeau. According to the Panel, if such unilateral measures were accepted, the WTO agreement could "no longer serve as a multilateral framework for trade among Members as security and predictability of trade relations under those Agreements would be threatened. This follows because if one WTO Member were allowed such measures, then other Members would also have the right to adopt similar measures on the same subject but with differing, or even conflicting, policy requirements. Indeed, as each of these requirements would necessitate the adoption of a policy applicable not only to export production, but also to domestic production, it would be impossible for a country to adopt one of these policies without the risk of breaching other Members' conflicting policy requirements for the same product and being refused access to these other markets."

The United States appealed this ruling. The AB reversed the findings of the Panel on two important issues. Importantly, the AB also went forward to apply the law, as correctly understood, to the facts of the case.

2.2.1   Negative findings

First, the AB found that the Panel had made an error of law in assuming that unilateral measures that condition market access on the policies of exporting countries were, as a matter of principle, not justifiable under Article XX GATT. In particular, paragraph 121 reads:[2]

> In the present case, the Panel found that the United States measures at stake fell within the class of excluded measures because section 609 conditions access to the domestic shrimp market of the United States on the adoption by exporting countries of certain conservation policies prescribed by the United States. It appears to us, however, that conditioning market access to a Member's domestic market on whether exporting Members comply with, or adopt, a policy or policies unilaterally prescribed by the importing Member may, to some degree, be a common aspect of measures falling with the scope of one or another of the exceptions (a) to (j) of Article XX. It is not necessary to assume that requiring from exporting countries compliance with, or adoption of, certain policies (although covered in principle by one or another of the exceptions) prescribed by the importing country, renders a measure *a priori* incapable of justification under Article XX. Such an interpretation renders most, if not all, of the specific exceptions of Article XX inutile, a result abhorrent to the principles of interpretation we are bound to apply.

This finding represents a radical shift in approach from the Tuna/ Dolphin cases. To the extent that the AB did not have to rely on this finding to reverse the Panel decision, some interpreted this paragraph as *dicta*, of uncertain legal significance in future cases.

Second, the AB found that the Panel should have applied a sequential approach in dealing with Article XX GATT, such that it should have first considered whether the measure could be justified under one of the heads of Article XX GATT and then only if there was such provisional justification, to consider whether the party maintaining the measure was

---

[2] WTO Appellate Body Report on *US – Import prohibition of Certain Shrimp and Shrimp Products*, WT/DS58/AB/R, October 12, 1998.

in compliance with the chapeau. The AB stressed that the chapeau is concerned only with the application of measures, not whether the measures themselves are justified under Article XX GATT. According to the AB (paragraph 15),

> In the present case, the Panel did not expressly examine the ordinary meaning of the words of Article XX. The panel disregarded the fact that the introductory clauses of Article XX speak of the "manner" in which measures sought to be justified are applied. What the panel did, in purporting to examine the consistency of the measure with the chapeau of Article XX, was to focus repeatedly on the design of the measure itself. The general design of a measure, as distinguished, from its application, is, however, to be examined in the course of determining whether that measure falls within one or another of the paragraph of Article XX following the chapeau.

2.2.2   The positive findings

The AB went on to complete the sequential analysis. The first stage involved the question whether the measure was covered by any of the specific heads of Article XX GATT. The AB considered that turtles could be seen as an exhaustible resource within the meaning of Article XX.g GATT and further analyzed whether the measure was "in relation" with its conservation. In doing so, the AB applied a "rational connection" or reasonableness standard and easily found that the measure met this standard.

There is some evidence however that, beyond rational connection, the AB was using some conception of proportionality. Thus, the AB not only held that there was a direct connection between the main features of the US scheme and the conservation of sea turtles, but also found that "section 609, cum implementing guidelines, is not disproportionately wide in its scope and reach in relation to the policy objective of protection and conservation of sea turtle species." What the AB appears to mean here by proportionality in scope and reach, is whether all the trade-restricting features of the scheme have some reasonable connection to turtle conservation. It does not appear to be balancing in any way the environmental benefits against the costs to trade entailed in the measure. Thus, the AB does not engage in the analysis of the trade-off between the benefits of the measure in terms of environmental protection and its costs in terms of trade restrictions.

With respect to the second stage (whether the implementation of the measure met the conditions of the chapeau), the AB found that the failure of the State Department to negotiate seriously with the complainants constituted "unjustifiable discrimination." This was a failure in implementation since section 609 itself contained a requirement to negotiate with all relevant countries. In addition, the AB found that the implementation involved unjustifiable discrimination because (i) the Panel were applying a rigid, extraterritorial extension of US law to other countries and because (ii) the Panel wholly disregarded the conditions prevailing in other countries.

To be certified and hence gain access to the US markets, all countries were required to have a Turtle Excluder Device program essentially identical to that of the US, regardless of the conditions prevailing in those countries. This was certainly discriminatory in comparison to the agreement embodied in the Inter-American Convention for the protection and conservation of sea turtles, which allowed the specific circumstances of the exporting countries to be taken into account in determining the means they adopted to satisfy the US conservation objectives. It was unjustified because, as the AB suggests, other measures more acceptable to the exporting country might have achieved the legitimate conservation objective of the US. Section 609 itself allowed for the possibility of certification in the case of a turtle conservation program *comparable* to that of the US.

The AB also noted that since the US guidelines did not allow for shipment by shipment certification, shrimp caught with a Turtle Excluder Device could be barred because they happened to have been caught in waters that were not certified. The AB saw this as evidence that section 609 was applied more as an extraterritorial extension of US law than a global conservation measure. The AB also found the existence of arbitrary discrimination in the manner in which section 609 was applied, citing lack of transparency in the certification process.

3   The Compliance Panel and Appellate Body ruling

Following the AB ruling, the US modified the guidelines implementing section 609. The revised guidelines dropped the requirement that exporting countries should use Turtle Excluder Devices and allowed for certification if the exporting countries could show that they were enforcing a regulatory program without devices that was comparable in effectiveness to those using devices. The revised guidelines also allowed for certification if fishing conditions in the exporting country did not pose a threat of incidental capture of sea turtles. Finally, the revised guidelines allowed for shipment by shipment certification, and greater transparency and due process.

3.1   The Panel decision

Of the complainants in the original action, Malaysia alone filed a complaint under 21.5, alleging that the changes that the United States made in the manner of implementation of section 609 did not satisfy the conditions of the chapeau as articulated by the AB. The Panel found that, in all relevant respects, the United States had met its obligations under the chapeau and that its measure was now in conformity with the requirements of the GATT treaty. The core of the Panel's decision related to its interpretation of the kind of "flexibility" that the AB was requiring in order for the United States to meet the requirements of the chapeau; this core aspect was the basis of Malaysia's further appeal of the 21.5 Panel ruling to the AB. Thus, we will discuss it below in our analysis of the AB 21.5 ruling. However, there are several curious or troubling features of the 21.5 Panel ruling that were not the subject of appeal or cross-appeal, and did not attract direct comment by the AB. These we briefly elaborate on in what follows.

3.1.1   Jurisdiction of the 21.5 Panel; the threshold question

It has been repeatedly held by the AB that a panel *may* only consider claims based on articles of the Covered Agreements that are listed in the request for a panel. The *minimum* level of specificity at which these must be listed is the article itself; however, a *greater* degree of specificity may be required where necessary for the defending party to be fully apprised of the case against it.

In Malaysia's request for a 21.5 Panel, Malaysia did not cite *any* articles of the covered agreements with which it was claiming the new US measures were inconsistent (Recourse by Malaysia to Article 21.5 DSU, WT/DS58/17). In Article 5.10 of its report, the 21.5 Panel stated that it took no position on whether pursuant to the interpretation of DSU 6.2 in AB reports, Malaysia had failed to state the provisions of the covered agreements on which it was relying in its claim with adequate specificity. This was an error of law.

The request for a panel is a crucial element in the establishment of the panel's jurisdiction (*European Communities–Bananas III*, Report of the Appellate Body, adopted September 25, 1997, WT/DS27/AB/R, paragraph. 141), and the Panel erred in assuming that it possessed jurisdiction without determining the adequacy of the request for the panel in light of DSU 6.2. The Panel's justification for so proceeding was that the United States did not claim that the request for the Panel was inadequately specific. However, the *minimum* requirement that the articles of the DSU upon which a member is relying be stated in its request for a panel is not one that can be waived by the defending party. This is a matter of due process in dispute settlement generally and goes to the panel's jurisdiction.

A request for a panel alerts *all* WTO members to the substance of the complaining Member's claim and may affect their decision as to whether to seek third-party rights in a given proceeding. As the AB re-emphasized in the *Korea – Dairy* case, a panel has a duty to consider carefully the request for the panel, and to make a decision on its adequacy as against the standard set out in Article 6.2 of the DSU (*Korea – Dairy*, paragraph 122). To be sure, by listing an article of a covered agreement in its request for a panel, and claiming this article to have been violated, a complaining Party may be able to make a claim concerning *other* provisions of the covered agreements, where these other, *unlisted*, provisions are incorporated by reference, as it were, through the *listed* articles. However, Malaysia's request for a Panel does not contain a list of *any* articles of *any* covered agreement with which Malaysia claims the new US measures are inconsistent.

Unless otherwise so specified, or unless such an interpretation would be manifestly absurd or unreasonable, provisions of the DSU that apply to a panel apply, *mutatis mutandis*, with respect to a 21.5 panel: the term "panel" is an expression with a special meaning within the DSU, and, applying Article 31.4 of the Vienna Convention, this special meaning as defined in numerous provisions of the DSU should be given to its usage within 21.5 except where the treaty text itself modifies that meaning in the case of 21.5 panels (for example, time limitations). Article 21.5 panels have consistently assumed that provisions of the DSU and rules of panel procedure apply to 21.5 proceedings – a recent example is *Brazil – Export Financing Programme for Aircraft*, Second Recourse to Article 21.5 of the DSU, where the Panel examined Brazil's claim concerning confidentiality of documents against the provisions of the DSU applicable generally to *panels* (paragraphs 3.1–3.15).

3.1.2   Country-by-country vs. shipment-by-shipment inspection

In completing the analysis in the original AB decision in this case, the AB identified several differences in the manner in which the US scheme was applied to different shrimp-exporting countries, which amounted "*cumulatively*" to unjustifiable discrimination within the meaning of the chapeau. *One* of the features in question that *contributed* to the existence of "unjustifiable discrimination "was" country-by-country application of the legislation." Thus, even where a particular shipment of shrimp was fished in a manner consistent with the conservation objectives of the United States, it would not be permitted to enter the United States unless the country of origin was certified to have a regulatory program for turtle conservation essentially identical to that of the United States.

In its report the 21.5 Panel correctly found that the United States' change to shipment-by-shipment certification was one respect in which its new measure could be considered not to contribute to the existence of "unjustifiable discrimination." However, the 21.5 Panel went further and held that "[t]his condition is addressed separately from the broader category concerning lack of flexibility and insufficient consideration of the conditions prevailing in the exporting countries because, in our opinion, it required a specific solution, while the other findings left more discretion to the United States" (paragraph 5.106).

This treatment of country-by-country vs. shipment-by-shipment certification is unwarranted by anything in the AB report. The AB considered the country-by-country aspect of the scheme, in one of a series of continuous paragraphs in the section of its report under the heading "Unjustifiable Discrimination," in which it dealt with all the other aspects bearing on "unjustified discrimination" as well; the section as a whole ends in a *single* finding of unjustifiable discrimination in the ultimate paragraph, based upon the *cumulation* of the various aspects identified throughout the section.

The paragraph in which country-by-country certification is discussed (165) begins with the word "Furthermore," and is followed by a paragraph that begins with the expression "Another aspect . . ." This makes it clear that country-by-country certification is being dealt with by the AB as one of a series of aspects of the application of the scheme that, *cumulatively*, result in "unjustifiable discrimination" within the meaning of the chapeau. Contrary to the implication of the Panel, the AB did not suggest that country-by-country certification required a "specific solution." Its recommendation, in paragraph 188 of its report, is the standard recommendation that the US bring itself into conformity with the provisions of the covered Agreement in question, and there is no suggestion of a "specific solution," nor any distinction drawn between, on the one hand, elements of discretion in the means taken by the US to implement the

AB report and, on the other, actions that the AB believes *must* be taken by the US in order to bring itself into conformity.

3.1.3   Article XX GATT as an emergency clause

In paragraph 5.88 of its report, the 21.5 Panel makes the following statement:

> Finally the Panel would like to clarify that, in a context such as this one where a multilateral agreement is clearly to be preferred and where measures such as that taken by the United States in this case may only be accepted under Article XX if they were allowed under an international agreement or if they were taken further to the completion of serious good faith efforts to reach a multilateral agreement, the possibility to impose a unilateral measure to protect sea turtles under 609 is more to be seen, for purposes of Article XX, as the possibility to adopt a *provisional* measure allowed for emergency reasons than as a definitive "right" to take a permanent measure. The extent to which serious good faith efforts continue to be made may be assessed at any time. For instance, steps which constituted good faith efforts at the beginning of a negotiation may fail to meet that test at a later stage.

Here, perhaps, the Panel merely wished to point out that, inasmuch as it imposes conditions on the exercise of rights under Article XX GATT that relate to the *application* of measures, any ruling of a 21.5 panel concerning consistency with the chapeau is of a contingent or provisional character. A ruling that US officials are *currently* applying section 609 in a manner consistent with the chapeau could hardly immunize *future* acts of US officials from review under 21.5. In this sense, all the rights in Article XX GATT are indeed provisional, as the *continuing* justifiability of the measure under this article depends on the *ongoing application* of the measure being consistent with the chapeau.

However, in making this point, the 21.5 Panel went too far, in suggesting that, as a matter of law, the US in order to maintain its measure as justified under Article XX GATT, must never cease to make further serious good faith efforts to negotiate a multilateral agreement. Whether any particular shortfall or curtailment of negotiating efforts at a future point in time might constitute "unjustifiable discrimination" within the meaning of the chapeau, would have to be assessed by a 21.5 panel at that point in time, in light of all the facts. For example, if the United States were to curtail or suspend negotiating efforts after the failure of prolonged, costly, and intense negotiations to produce an agreement, such a decision would far from necessarily amount to unjustifiable discrimination between countries where similar conditions prevail. Moreover, certain wording in this state-ment by the panel ("may *only* be accepted under Article XX..." [emphasis added]) suggests that the 21.5 Panel may have misunderstood the AB as reading a condition into the chapeau of Article XX GATT that is not based on the treaty text, rather than simply interpreting and applying the words "discrimination" and "unjustifiable" in the *particular* facts of *this* dispute.

The chapeau of Article XX GATT does not contain a positive duty to negotiate, regardless of the unilateral character of the measures in ques-tion; however, the elements of unilateralism discussed by the Appellate Body, might well lead to *discriminatory* behavior in respect of negotia-tions crossing the threshold of *unjustifiable* discrimination. But this is a matter of applying, on a case-by-case basis, the *text* of the chapeau to the full factual record and legal context. Here, it should be noted that the duty of cooperation pointed out by the AB in its discussion of the law of sustainable development in its original decision in this dispute is a duty on *all* States affecting and affected by the global common problem at issue (paragraph 168, citing Article 5 of the Convention on Biodiversity): any assessment of the future negotiating behavior of the United States would also require a concomitant consideration of the related behavior of other States implicated in the same environmental situation.

3.2 The AB ruling

Malaysia appealed on two grounds. First, Malaysia claimed that the Panel did not properly fulfill its mandate. According to Malaysia, the Panel considered the consistency of the compliance measure implemented by the US with the recommendations of the AB in the original decision but should have considered whether the compliance measures were consistent with GATT's agreement.

Second, Malaysia disagreed with the Panel's conclusion that the re-formed guidelines are consistent with the chapeau of Article XX GATT, namely that they no longer constitute an arbitrary or unjustifiable dis-crimination between countries where the same conditions prevail.

3.2.1 Scope of the review

With respect to the first claim, the AB confirmed that the mandate of the Panel is to consider the compliance measure in its "totality" and indeed to consider the consistency of the compliance measures with respect to GATT's agreement but that the task of the Panel is limited by the claims made by the parties. The AB thus concluded that it would be inappropriate to consider issues that have not been raised.

One issue however arose with respect to the interpretation of what is meant by the "totality" of a compliance measure and in particular whether the Panel should have considered again those aspects of the compliance measures that were found to be GATT-consistent by the original Panel. The AB did not rule this out (paragraph 91) suggesting that, since section 609 of the law was part of the new measure, it was not immune from scrutiny. However, the AB also reiterated the distinction between the measure adopted by the US (namely section 609) and the implementation of the measure through guidelines.

The AB emphasized that only the implementation of Section 609 had been considered unlawful by the original decision (i.e. did not benefit from the exception of Article XX GATT) and not section 609 itself. The AB found that the *application* of the original measure that denied the original measure the benefit of Article XX GATT were unrelated to the original measure itself. Accordingly, the AB concluded that the panel did not have to consider again the consistency of section 609 with GATT's agreement. The AB agreed with the Panel's finding that the "revised guidelines do not modify the interpretation given to section 609" and that there is "no evidence" that the revised guidelines have modified in any way the meaning of section 609 vis-à-vis the requirements of paragraph (g), as interpreted by the AB.

3.2.2   Requirements of the chapeau

Malaysia claims that the revised guidelines still violate the chapeau of Article XX GATT on, essentially, two grounds. First, Malaysia claims that the US should have not only negotiated but also concluded an international agreement on the protection of sea turtles before imposing an import prohibition. Malaysia points out that if the requirement is only to negotiate, as long as the negotiation is not concluded, defendants could end up imposing unilateral measures which would constitute "unjustifiable" discrimination.

The AB ruled that a requirement to conclude an international agreement would be unreasonable – essentially because it would grant a veto right to every single party to the negotiation on whether a country fulfills its WTO obligations (paragraph. 123):[3]

---

[3] Report of the AB, US – Shrimp; Recourse to Article 21.5 of the DSU by Malaysia, WT/DS58/AB/RW (October 22, 2001).

Requiring that a multilateral agreement be concluded by the United States
in order to avoid arbitrary or unjustifiable discrimination in applying the
measure would mean that any country party to the negotiations with the
United States, whether a WTO Member or not, would in effect have a veto
right over whether the United States could fulfill its WTO obligations. Such
a requirement would not be reasonable.

Second, Malaysia challenged the panel's interpretation of the chapeau's
flexibility requirement. As indicated above, the original AB decision found
that the US could not require other countries to adopt its own regime
of protection of sea turtles. According to the AB, this would constitute
arbitrary discrimination.

The Compliance Panel found (relying on the original AB decision) that
a requirement that foreign programs should be comparable in effectiveness would be compatible with the chapeau of Article XX GATT and hence
would not constitute arbitrary discrimination. Malaysia disagreed and
noted that the US will retain the power to decide which programs can be
considered as comparable in effectiveness. According to Malaysia, award-
ing a veto right to the US with respect to alternative programs implies
that the US measure results in arbitrary or unjustifiable discrimination.

Malaysia further argued that the AB's ruling in the original case that
"conditioning access to a Member's domestic market on whether exporting Members comply with, or adopt, a policy or policies unilaterally prescribed by the importing Member may, to some degree, be a common
aspect of measures falling within the scope of one or another of the exceptions (a) to (j) of Article XX," was mere *dicta*.

The AB emphasized that the principle expressed by this statement was
not mere *dicta*, but rather a principle that was "central" to its ruling. The
AB further amplified the distinction between the imposition of identical
measures and the imposition of measures that are comparable in effectiveness. The AB emphasized that the latter gives sufficient latitude to
the exporting countries to adjust to the specific conditions that they face
(paragraph 144).

> In our view, there is an important difference between conditioning market
> access on the adoption of essentially the same program, and conditioning
> market access on the adoption of a program *comparable in effectiveness*.
> Authorizing an importing Member to condition market access on exporting
> Members putting in place regulatory programs comparable in effectiveness
> to that of the importing Member gives sufficient latitude to the exporting
> Member with respect to the program it may adopt to achieve the level of

effectiveness required. It allows the exporting Member to adopt a regulatory program that is suitable to the specific conditions prevailing in its territory. As we see it, the Panel correctly reasoned and concluded that conditioning market access on the adoption of a program comparable in effectiveness, allows for sufficient flexibility in the application of the measure, so as to avoid "arbitrary or unjustifiable discrimination." We, therefore, agree with the conclusion of the Panel on "comparable effectiveness."

3.3   Issues raised by AB ruling

The AB 21.5 ruling raises at least two important issues. First, the AB compliance ruling, has confirmed, *definitively*, that imports can be made contingent on environmental standards that are determined unilaterally by the importing nation. The importance of this final determination should not be underestimated. It effectively reverses the initial Panel ruling but also stands in stark contrast with the general approach adopted by panels in other cases where environmental measures were at stake. For instance, in both Tuna/Dolphin cases, the Panel had ruled that an embargo on tuna which was not fished in a dolphin friendly manner, could not be justified under Article XX.[4]

It is thus not surprising that this new doctrine has been subject to controversy. For instance, Bhagwati (2001) commenting on the original AB decision (which was confirmed by the AB compliance ruling on this point) suggested that the AB had indulged in illegitimate judicial activism. He offered the judgment that the AB had been unduly concerned about "the political pressures brought by the rich-country environmental NGOs and essentially made law that affected the developing countries adversely." He saw this as an instance where the AB should have deferred more to the political process.[5]

Section 4 of the chapter will consider the issue further and explore in the context of a simple model the consequences of allowing market access to be made contingent on the adoption of environmental standards and consider whether such concerns for "green protectionism" are well founded.

---

[4] These panel reports were however never adopted.

[5] Howse (2002) discusses Bhagwati's criticisms and shows that it is unwarranted from the perspective of the jurisprudence.

The second issue raised by the AB ruling concerns the design of compliance measures. The trade-off between the flexibility of the compliance measures and the incentives to comply are briefly discussed in section 5.

4   Imports contingent on environmental measures

The *US – Shrimp* case can be described as a situation where the production of one commodity (shrimps) imposes a negative externality on the citizens of one country (say, the US). The external effect arises because US citizens attach some value to the preservation of sea turtles and to the extent that the production of shrimps reduces the likelihood that turtles will survive, they suffer from a negative externality when shrimps are produced. As long as production takes place in the country concerned, the external effect can be internalized, for instance by the imposition of appropriate externality (Pigouvian) taxes. However, when production takes place in another country (say, Malaysia), for which citizens of the first country (the US) cannot design and implement regulation, external effects will not be internalized by the producing country.

Depending on the instruments available, both countries concerned may however implement policies that will effectively reduce the incidence of the external effects. Making trade contingent on the adoption of particular abatement policy or at least the adoption of particular standards towards the external effect, as explicitly allowed by the *US – Shrimp* ruling, is one of the possible instruments. Others may include the negotiation of international agreements between the countries concerned on the internalization of the external effects. These agreements may or may not involve a link with trade flows.

In what follows, we will focus on instruments involving trade. We will explore the welfare consequence of allowing for the *US – Shrimp* solution, i.e. making import contingent on the adoption of standards toward the external effect in the exporting country, in the context of a simple model. We will evaluate this instrument in different regulatory environments in the exporting country, considering for instance the effect that additional instruments like Pigouvian taxes will have on the final allocation. We will compare the *US – Shrimp* solution with a number of alternatives like free trade, the first best allocation, and unconstrained trade policies for both importing and exporting countries.

4.1   A simple model

We use a simple model, which is a variant of the framework proposed by Ludema and Wooton (1994).[6] There are two countries; the importing country (H) and the exporting country (F). All consumption takes place in H while production takes place in both countries. Let x be the quantity of the good that is traded. Assume that inverse demand for imports is linear:

$$p = a - bx$$

The good is produced under perfect competition and the foreign inverse supply curve is also linear, where q is the foreign price:

$$q = f + gx$$

The domestic import price is given by the foreign price supplemented by any specific import tariff (r) or export tax (t).

Assume that production in the exporting country generates a non-pecuniary externality on the importing country, which reduces utility at a rate z per unit of output.[7] Welfare in the importing country is then given by the sum of consumer surplus, domestic producer surplus, and tariff revenues less the externality:

$$u(x, r, z) = \frac{bx^2}{2} + (r - z)x$$

having normalized autarky welfare to zero.

Similarly welfare in the exporting country, which is the sum of producer surplus and tax revenues, can be written as:

$$v(x, s, z) = \frac{gx^2}{2} + tx$$

We further assume that abatement technology is available. In the absence of any abatement, the utility cost of the externality is equal to $z = \bar{z}$ per unit of output. Abatement can however reduce the externality cost at

---

[6] Ludema and Wooton (1994) consider a two-stage game in which the exporting country can commit to an externality tax in the first stage and in which both countries set their commercial policy (respectively a tariff and an export tax) in the second stage. They also consider a game where the importing country sets a standard and the exporting country sets an externality tax. The results that they obtain for this game are fully discussed below.

[7] In other words, the externality is defined in terms of utility units and the externality is a constant fraction of output.

levels $z < \bar{z}$, and the abatement cost per unit of output is given by $C(z)$, with $C'(z) < 0$, $C''(z) > 0$. That is, a firm which produces x units of output and reaches an externality level of z will have to spend $C(z)x$ on abatement.

This framework thus assumes consumption of the good and external effects in the exporting country and the generation of external effects from production in the importing country. In a complete model, consumption in the exporting country would thus impose a negative externality on the importing country and production in the importing country might also impose a negative externality on the exporting country. Our framework effectively sets the utility cost of the external effect to zero in the foreign country. Given this, the other ingredients will be unimportant as long as optimal domestic policies are implemented.

In particular, if production in the importing country generates an external effect at home, it can be addressed by an appropriate Pigouvian tax. And consumption in the exporting country can be insulated from the effect of a production tax by an appropriate subsidy. In other words, the simple framework considered here focuses on the external effect across countries and the ability to affect the terms of trade as the only sources of distortion. From this perspective, it is best positioned to isolate the interaction between trade and (non-pecuniary) external effects across countries and trace out the consequences of the *US − Shrimp* solution.

Note that the external effect modeled here cannot be fully characterized as an instance of "global common" or "global public good." A problem of "global commons" would involve the adequate provision of a commodity that brings indirect costs to both countries. For instance, if both the US and Malaysia attached some value to the preservation of sea turtles, the US would set its preservation policy without considering the effect on Malaysia and vice versa. By having assumed that Malaysia does not attach any value to the preservation of sea turtles, our model is admittedly one that would have to be adapted in order to answer adequately how trade can affect the solution to global commons.[8] Rather, it focuses on narrower

---

[8] One can only speculate about the effect of a Shrimp/Turtle solution on a true problem of global commons. The external effect of consumption in the exporting country on itself could be internalized by appropriate taxes imposed by the government of the importing country. As in the current framework, the external effect of production in the exporting country on the importing country could be met by making imports contingent on the adoption of appropriate policies in the exporting country. The external effect that production and consumption in the importing country would impose on the exporting country could be met by making *exports* contingent on the adoption of appropriate policies in the importing country.

circumstances, where the external effect only flows from one country to the other. This may be a better description of a situation where there is a spillover across jurisdiction, such that, for instance, shrimping in Malaysia affects the annual migration of sea turtles toward (say) the US which in turn destabilizes the ecological system there.

4.2 Commercial policy without abatement

As a background, we first describe the outcome of free trade, the first best, and the imposition of a unilateral tariff, in the absence of any abatement technology. All formal derivations will be relegated to the appendix. In the text, we will present the main insights and illustrate them through an example. Our example assumes that $a = b = g = 1, f = 0$ and $\bar{z} = \frac{1}{4}$. These values are chosen in such a way that the importing country is indifferent between free trade and autarky.

Let us first note that the first best (which maximizes overall welfare) requires the imposition of a Pigouvian (externality) tax at the rate $t = \bar{z}$. The imposition of a unilateral import tariff will result from the traditional motive, namely to affect the terms of trade and the effect that tariff has on the external effect through the reduction in imports. Hence, the unilateral tariff will exceed the level that that would obtain in the absence of an externality.

In this framework, an externality tax in the foreign country is equivalent to a production tax and in turn is equivalent to an export tax. Hence, if the foreign country can impose a Pigouvian tax and the domestic country can impose an import tariff, the outcome will be equivalent to unconstrained trade, where both countries freely set their commercial policy (respectively an import tariff and an export tax). Given the nature of underlying incentives (which conforms to Prisoner's dilemma), the Nash equilibrium of the game where the domestic country sets an import tariff and the foreign country sets an export (Pigouvian) tax will thus involve higher overall protection than the unilateral tariff. In this instance, the Pigouvian tax reduces the external effect but is purely driven by the terms of trade motive.

Some preliminary observations can be made. First, given the presence of an external effect, it is not a surprise that free trade does not maximize welfare and involve trade in excess of the first best. Second, the imposition of a unilateral tariff might actually yield a better outcome in terms of overall welfare than free trade. This arises because the unilateral tariff reduces the flow of the external effect. Some of the benefit that the importing

Table 3.1 *Output and welfare without abatement technology*

	X	Welfare H	Welfare F	Total welfare
FT	0.500	0.000	0.125	0.125
FB	0.375			0.141
UT	0.250	0.094	0.031	0.125
UT + PT	0.188	0.053	0.053	0.105

FT = free trade, FB = first best, UT = unilateral import tariff
UT + PT = unilateral import tariff and Pigouvian tax abroad.

country obtains from the imposition of the tariff does not come at the expense of the exporting country. In the context of our example, free trade actually leads to the same level of welfare as the imposition of a unilateral tariff (see table 3.1). It is easy to check however that relative to this benchmark both a more elastic supply curve and a less elastic demand curve would lead to higher welfare with a unilateral tariff than under free trade.

Third, the simultaneous imposition of a unilateral tariff and a Pigouvian tax in the exporting country, which involve more protection than the unilateral imposition of a tariff, might also lead to higher welfare than free trade. As one would expect, this arises when the external effect is particularly strong. Specifically, a sufficient condition for free trade to dominate is that the external effect is sufficiently weak that trade is equivalent to autarky for the importing country (as in our benchmark case). If free trade is worse than autarky (i.e. when the utility cost of the externality is larger than in the benchmark case), then the simultaneous imposition of a unilateral tariff and a Pigouvian tax will yield higher welfare than free trade.

Fourth, the Nash equilibrium will be highly asymmetric with a higher import tariff than a Pigouvian tax. This arises because the importing country has a higher incentive to impose a tax (the terms of trade and the external effect). The welfare of the exporting country could still increase relative to free trade, if the foreign supply is sufficiently elastic (a higher supply elasticity raises the equilibrium Pigouvian tax and shifts surplus towards the foreign country).

Finally, it is worth considering the possibility that imports could be made contingent on the adoption of a Pigouvian tax (say e) in the exporting country. In particular, we assume that the level of tax is determined by the importing country, but that the revenue from the tax accrues to the exporting country. Note that such an arrangement has some desirable incentive properties – to the extent that the importing country has no incentive to set the tax in order to shift the terms of trade but solely in order to correct the external effect (while taking into consideration the consequences of reduced output in its own jurisdiction). Even if the actual Shrimp/Turtle case refers to the adoption of an abatement technology, nothing in the wording of the AB decision would seem to rule out other environmental policies like a Pigouvian tax.

To return to the original AB ruling, in considering whether the US scheme itself (as opposed to its manner of application) was consistent with Article XX GATT, the AB examined whether, within the meaning of Article XX.g GATT, the scheme was "related to the conservation of exhaustible natural resources" and noted that such a rational connection existed. The AB observed as well, as we discuss at the beginning of this study, that the scheme was not "disproportionately wide in scope and reach" relative to the policy objective. Thus, there is room for the adjudicator to consider the extent to which the policy instrument chosen, as opposed to other possible policy instruments, represents an appropriate fit with the objective, or whether it overreaches, causing superfluous harmful effects.

In the context of our model, it appears that the importing country will choose a corner solution; it will either choose not to impose a Pigouvian tax as a condition for imports, when the external effect is weak, or to impose a prohibitive tax, when the external effect is sufficiently strong. This arises because the imposition of a Pigouvian tax abroad deteriorates the terms of trade without reducing the external effect per unit of output. The discrete nature of the solution may be due to our assumptions that demand is linear (so that surplus is quadratic) and the assumption that the external effect is a constant fraction of output.

If the external effect per unit of output increased with the output level, an intermediate solution may be found such that imports can be made contingent on a positive but non-prohibitive Pigouvian tax. In this instance, both the importing and the exporting countries would benefit relative to autarky. More importantly, the exporting country might also benefit relative to free trade (import prices increase and the government obtains the revenues from the Pigouvian tax).

To sum up, these preliminary results first illustrate that the imposition of a environmental policy abroad (through externality taxes) affects the terms of trade. In the simple model considered here, it is even equivalent to an export tax.[9] Exporting countries will have an incentive to set these externality taxes at a level which has nothing to do with the externality at stake but which will simply improve their terms of trade.

Second, these results confirm that allowing for unconstrained commercial policies may actually do better than free trade. Third, it also appears that making imports contingent on the adoption of externality taxes in the foreign country could actually improve the welfare of exporting countries. Making trade contingent on environmental protection does not necessarily hurt developing countries *even if* they do not value the resources being protected.

4.3   Contingent imports with abatement technology

As discussed above, the *US – Shrimp* ruling allows for imports to be made contingent on the adoption of an abatement technology or at least the adoption of a particular standard with respect to the external effect. This is modelled in our framework as a policy where the domestic country chooses a level of external effect z and in which the exporting country can meet this level of external effect through the adoption of the only abatement technology available. As before, we will consider the adoption of such a policy both when the exporting country is allowed to impose a Pigouvian tax and when is it barred from doing so.

Consider first the imposition of a standard, which can only be met by the adoption of the available abatement technology, without a Pigouvian tax abroad. In general, the imposition of a standard involves a trade-off as it will increase the cost of the foreign firms, which translates into lower output and higher import prices, but it also reduces the external effect per unit of output. Relative to a unilateral tariff, the imposition of a standard will also involve less distortion as the domestic country does not gain from the increase in the cost of foreign firms which results from the adoption of abatement technology.

In the context of our model, the government of the importing country will find it profitable to suppress the external effect altogether, i.e. to impose maximum abatement when the abatement technology is

---

[9]   The precise equivalence is however an artefact that results from the absence of consumption in the exporting country.

Table 3.2 *Output and welfare with abatement technology*

	X	Welfare H	Welfare F	Total welfare
FT	0.500	0.000	0.125	0.125
FB	0.375			0.141
UT	0.250	0.094	0.031	0.125
ST	0.438	0.096	0.096	0.191
$(k = 0.5, z = 0)$				
ST	0.375	0.070	0.070	0.141
$(k = 1, z = 0)$				
ST				
$(k = 2, z = 0)$	0.250	0.031	0.031	0.063
ST	0.250	0.010	0.031	0.042
$(k = 3, z = 0.083)$				

ST: Shrimp-Turtle solution
FT = free trade, FB = first best, UT = unilateral import tariff

relatively efficient. In this instance, the *US – Shrimp* solution can actually improve welfare relative to free trade. It might also do better than the first best that can be achieved in the absence of abatement technology. It may also be attractive for the domestic government relative to the imposition of unilateral import tariff (despite the fact that the latter would bring revenues). The fact that the *US – Shrimp* solution is so attractive in this instance should not come as a surprise: it effectively provides an incentive to the government of the exporting country to use a very efficient technology that it has no incentive to use otherwise. Of course, the *US – Shrimp* solution always reduces welfare in the exporting country. This is illustrated in table 3.2, which for the sake of illustration assumes a linear abatement technology of the form $C(z) = k(\overline{z} - z)$, with $k = 0.5$.

Table 3.2 also illustrates the outcome of a *US – Shrimp* policy in the case where the resource cost of reducing the externality (per unit of output) is equal to its utility cost, i.e when $k = 1$. In this instance, the government of the importing country still imposes a policy of complete abatement and, unsurprisingly, the *US – Shrimp* solution then replicates the first best that can be achieved without abatement.

For less efficient abatement technology, the government of the importing country will still impose complete abatement. As long as the resource cost of abatement is reasonably close to the cost of the external effect

($k < 1.1725$, in our benchmark case), the *US – Shrimp* solution will still do better than free trade. This arises because even though the *US – Shrimp* solution reduces output and trade, it also suppresses the external effect.

The importing country's government will actually find it profitable to impose a complete abatement even for very inefficient technologies, up to a resource cost of abatement which is twice as high as the utility cost (i.e. up to $k = 2$) in the context of our benchmark. The importing country's government will thus impose very high standards and obtain little benefit from them overall but impose a strong burden on the exporting country. For even less efficient technologies, the importing country's government will choose incomplete abatement standards. Its optimal policy does not involve further reductions in output – so that the welfare of the foreign country does not fall any further. This is illustrated at the bottom of table 3.2, which presents the *US – Shrimp* solution for $k = 2$ and $k = 3$.

Let us now allow the exporting country's government to impose a Pigouvian tax. In this context, the firms will have the choice between adopting the abatement technology or paying the Pigouvian tax. We assume that they will choose the combination which minimizes cost. As shown by Ludeman and Wooton (1994), for any level of Pigouvian tax chosen by the exporting country, the importing country's government will have an incentive to set a standard which is binding, i.e. which requires an abatement level in excess of the abatement that would be induced by the tax. Since higher taxes induce higher abatement by exporting firms, the best reply of the importing country's government will involve an even higher standard (a lower z) than what would be implied by the tax.

The reaction of the importing country's government is thus downward sloping (in the (e,z) space). Considering the incentive of the exporting country's government, for any level of abatement chosen by the importing country, it will have an incentive to set an externality tax which at most induces the abatement which is imposed by the importing country. If it chooses a tax which exactly induces the abatement imposed by the importing country, since higher abatement standards (a lower z) are induced by higher externality taxes, its reaction will be downward sloping. If it chooses to set a tax below the level which would induce the abatement standard imposed by the importing country, it will impose the optimal export tax. As shown by Ludema and Wooton (1994), this tax is also declining with the level of abatement chosen by the importing country, so that the reaction function of the foreign government is also downward sloping. The reaction function of both governments (in the (e,z) space) are thus downward sloping.

Hence, allowing the exporting country's government to introduce Pigouvian taxes will lead, if anything, to even higher abatement standards and lower output than the ST solution considered above. In the context of our benchmark model, the importing country's government found it profitable to impose full abatement for a wide range of abatement technology, in the absence of a Pigouvian tax abroad. For relatively ineffective abatement technologies, the outcome will be unaffected. There will be full abatement and, as a consequence, the externality tax will be not yield any revenue.[10]

5   Conclusion

From a legal perspective, the AB's most significant holding in the 21.5 ruling, that a multilateral agreement does not have to be concluded (even imminent) for Article XX.g GATT to be invoked, follows logically from the text and structure of XX.g, as well as the AB's original holding that nothing in Article XX GATT excludes from its ambit measures that are aimed at conditioning imports on the policies of another WTO Member (original AB ruling, para. 121). On its face, Article XX.g GATT creates rights that can be exercised by a WTO Member acting without the consent of other States. It is thus different from some other kinds of limitation or exception provisions in the GATT, which do imply that the actions in question must take place within some kind of collective framework; for example, Article XX1.c GATT creates an exception that can only be invoked where Members are taking action "in pursuance of... obligations under the United Nations Charter for the maintenance of international peace and security."

Nor is the conception of a unilateral invocation of Article XX.g GATT rights at odds with general notions of sovereignty in international law. Environmentally based trade action, like that of the US in this case, has often been attacked as "extra-territorial." However, no control over foreign territory is being asserted; the US is merely deciding not to allow imports to enter *its* territory unless they meet certain conditions. It is not prescribing any environmental standards that would be binding on the territory of any *other* state (see Howse and Regan, 2000). The International Court of Justice has held that economic pressure on another state

---

[10] Our benchmark model is however ill-suited to consider this case. With linear abatement technology, the choice of whether to abate or pay the tax is discrete – so that there is either full abatement or no abatement at all.

to change its policy, including in the form of an embargo, is not a per se violation of any rule of customary international law.[11]

It is true, in a general (non-legal) sense that the United States is in effect imposing on the exporting State some of the costs of the externality arising from sea turtles being endangered. *But, some of these costs have been created in the first place by the economic activity of the exporting State.* Why should the exporting State's "right" to create such externalities and impose them on the community of States be a more legitimate or superior attribute of sovereignty, than the sovereign "right" to take actions, otherwise legal under international law, to shift back some of those costs onto the exporting state? If one were to analyze the problem in this manner, and take into account the commitment to sustainable development in the Preamble of the WTO Agreement, the hierarchy would, if anything, be exactly the reverse.

From an economic perspective, it appears first that the *US – Shrimp* solution, which makes imports contingent on the adoption of an abatement standard can be a very effective way of addressing external effects across jurisdictions, at least when efficient abatement technology is available. In this instance, it provides exporters with appropriate incentive to adopt an efficient technology that they would not adopt otherwise and the *US – Shrimp* solution will typically yield a more efficient allocation than free trade.

However, when abatement technology is poor, the *US – Shrimp* solution will be very inefficient. In this instance, the importing country will impose strict abatement standards that hardly improve on its own welfare but greatly reduce welfare abroad and the Shrimp/Turtle solution will do much worse than free trade. Second, it appears that when abatement technology is inefficient, making trade contingent on the adoption of externality taxes in the foreign country would yield a superior outcome.

Third, the implementation of the *US – Shrimp* solution always reduces welfare in the exporting country, relative to free trade. By contrast, making trade contingent on the adoption of Pigouvian taxes (at a rate determined by the importing country) can increase the welfare in both importing and exporting countries, relative to free trade.

Fourth, it appears that the effectiveness of the *US – Shrimp* solution is affected by the range of policies available in the exporting country, and in particular whether the exporting country can charge Pigouvian taxes as a response to the imposition of abatement standards.

[11] *Military and Paramilitary Activities (Nicaragua v. United States)* 1986 I. C. J. 14, 125–26.

These observations provide at least two insights with respect to the *US – Shrimp* ruling. First, in future cases, in considering the fit between a Member's measure and its environmental objective, the adjudicator should take into account the relative efficiency of the various policy instruments that a Member may choose to impose on another Member as a condition of access for its imports. In designing the conditions for imports, the adjudicator may also want to consider the range of policies available to the exporting country.

Second, it appears that the AB's acceptance that the US allowance for policies comparable in effectiveness to the Turtle Excluder Devices standard provided adequate flexibility could have inefficient consequences (although not necessarily). Indeed, if there are large differences in the cost of abatement across jurisdictions, it will be efficient to induce an allocation of abatement effort such that the marginal cost of abatement is uniform (assuming that the marginal benefit is constant). This will lead to the imposition of different environmental standards across jurisdictions. Hence, it would have been appropriate for the AB to clarify what is meant by "comparable in effectiveness" and indicate that comparable effectiveness does not imply that different jurisdictions should reach similar standards[12] but rather that the marginal effectiveness of resources invested in abatement should be comparable across countries.

The framework that we have used has focused on the external effect and the ability to affect the terms of trade as sole sources of distortion. The analysis reveals that when other distortions do not matter, and, in particular, when conditions of supply are competitive, the *US – Shrimp* solution has desirable features. Arguably, however, this framework does not do justice to the concern being voiced about green protectionism.

In our framework, the domestic government has no incentive to raise the cost of foreign firms. Such an incentive may arise in the presence of imperfect competition to the extent that an increase in the cost of foreign firms will then shift profits to domestic firms.[13] The domestic government may then be tempted to exploit situations where domestic abatement costs are low relative to abatement costs abroad. If the *US – Shrimp* ruling is interpreted as allowing for the achievement of similar

---

[12] The fact that the AB refers to policies that are comparable in effectiveness to TED suggests that the AB may have been thinking in terms of policies that yield comparable results – at least if one assumes that Turtle Excluder Device technology is equally effective across jurisdictions.

[13] As usual, a bias in favor of producer surplus induced by a particular political economy environment would yield the same result.

standards, it will offer the scope for such "green protectionism." However, if the *US – Shrimp* ruling is interpreted as imposing the investment of abatement resources with comparable marginal effectiveness, the scope for protectionism will be greatly reduced. This further underlines the need to clarify what is meant by "comparable in effectiveness."

This discussion also implies that an effective implementation of the *US – Shrimp* solution requires some knowledge of abatement costs across jurisdictions. Whether the AB is well placed to evaluate these facts is an open question. It also raises the prospect that exporting countries may want to adopt policies, prior to the imposition of the *US – Shrimp* solution, to induce the importing country to infer that its cost of abatement is higher than the actual cost that would be incurred. Countries with low abatement costs could for instance generate large external effects so as to "pool" themselves with countries with high abatement costs.[14]

Our discussion of the *US – Shrimp* solution has also not considered many alternatives, and in particular it has not taken into account whether international negotiations on environmental policies could be expected to achieve a more efficient outcome.[15] It is beyond the scope of this report to comment on this issue in depth. Let us only note that international agreements on environmental policies face considerable problems of compliance[16] (see for instance, the survey by the OECD, from 1999).

The solution allowed in *US – Shrimp*, by contrast, may be less prone to compliance problems: if the exporting country has an incentive to shirk and not implement the policy, the importing country maintains clear incentive to monitor its implementation and a credible threat to prevent imports in case of non-compliance.

---

[14] Chang (1997) discusses such a mechanism in the context of international agreements. Given the problems of pooling that he identifies, he advocates the use of *US – Shrimp* type instruments (what he refers to as sticks – rather than the carrots that are assimilated with international agreements). Our discussion suggests however that a proper implementation of a *US – Shrimp* solution would also require addressing information asymmetries. In both instances, it would be necessary to separate high abatement countries from low abatement ones. The problems of asymmetric information that he identifies are pervasive.

[15] As discussed by Howse (2002), the *US – Shrimp* solution could also be seen as a threat that could help ensure compliance in international agreements. One may not however want to presume that the *US – Shrimp* solution will be *always* inferior to the outcome of an international agreement.

[16] The extent to which international agreements can effectively address external effects is sometimes questioned (irrespective of implementation issues). It may be useful to note in this respect that even in the US, which achieves a remarkable degree of coordination between constituent states, external effects across states are poorly internalized (see for instance, Revesz, 2000).

Finally, our framework has not considered the complexities that would arise in the case of several importing nations, which could make their imports contingent on different abatement standards.[17] To the extent that the implementation of standards is subject to scale economies, it would seem that the standards imposed by large importers would have a better chance of prevailing.

As noted above, the AB in the original case ruled that the blanket imposition of Turtle Excluder Devices would violate the chapeau. The AB has also ruled that conditioning access on the implementation of policies that are comparable in effectiveness would be compatible with the flexibility requirements of the chapeau.

The ruling of the AB was clearly motivated by the desire to accommodate local circumstances. However, a situation might arise where a Member requires only that the exporting country adopt a scheme comparable in effectiveness in achieving a given level of environmental protection, without specifying a particular *instrument or technology* that will be deemed to satisfy this standard. Of course, this was not the case in the *US – Shrimp* dispute, because it was *always* possible under section 609 for an exporting country to comply by adopting Turtle Excluder Devices, if it so chose.

But where there is no clear benchmark, flexibility may in turn raise *additional* concerns about protectionist abuse, which would need to be addressed under the chapeau. Assume, for instance, that one importing country is motivated by the desire to protect its domestic industry and uses environmental protection merely as an instrument for raising import barriers. This country will have an incentive to accept only those programs that are excessively costly to the exporting country and its industry.

Such behavior could of course trigger further complaints in WTO dispute settlement about the application of the scheme in question. However, in the current framework of dispute settlement, the importing country would be allowed to implement its strict certification until a final ruling by the AB and it would never be asked to pay compensation for the period preceding the ruling if its certification is considered to be unlawful. The importing country could then seemingly comply but make only cosmetic changes to its certification and obtain the benefit of protection until the final compliance ruling. In principle, nothing would actually prevent the

---

[17] As indicated above, these complexities were emphasized by the panel ruling in the original case.

importing country from endless rounds of cosmetic changes and from never actually complying (see Anderson, 2002).[18]

Of course, the scope for such opportunistic behavior will be greater if the equivalence between abatement programs is formulated in general principles rather than precise rules. General principles will allow for a more precise tailoring of abatement programs to local conditions. But precise rules, whose implementation is easy to verify, will be more difficult to abuse.

Overall, it appears that it may be appropriate for the AB to insist that flexibility be accompanied by transparent guidelines or rules that limit the discretion of authorities in making case-by-case decisions as to which programs are effective in meeting the environmental objectives. In fact, this is consistent with the emphasis on due process and transparency in the portion of the original AB ruling that addresses "arbitrary discrimination" under the chapeau. In this respect, in order the ensure that the application of a scheme is consistent with the chapeau, the scheme itself, or at least rule-making pursuant to it, may have to contain certain kinds of features.

This raises an important point about the relationship of the chapeau to the measure itself. While, as the AB correctly has held in *US – Shrimp*, the chapeau conditions concern *application* of a measure, there may be certain cases where the design of the measure itself may be highly relevant to whether its application will violate the chapeau or not. The adjudicator may then need in certain instances to concern itself with aspects of the measure *itself* in applying the chapeau, something that was of course not the case on the *US – Shrimp* facts. But this is consistent with the view of state responsibility in the S. 301 panel – there may be features of a scheme that do not as such compel a violation of WTO rules, but which create a *serious threat* that the rules will be violated when the scheme is applied.

References

Anderson, K. (2002), Peculiarities of retaliation in WTO dispute settlement, *World Trade Review*, 1(2), July.

Bhagwati, J. (2001).

Chang, H. (1997), Carrots, sticks and international externalities, *International Review of Law and Economics*, 17, 309–324.

---

[18] If such opportunistic behavior is allowed to prevail, the incentive to use the dispute settlement mechanism and the incentive to reach a multilateral agreement in the first place may be seriously impaired.

Howse, R. (2002), The Appellate body rulings in the Shrimp/turtle case: a new legal baseline for the trade and environment debate, *Columbia Journal of Environmental Law*, 27(2), 491–521.

Howse, R. and D Regan (2000). The Product/Process Distinction – An Illusory Basis for Disciplining "Unilateralism" in Trade Policy, *European Journal of International Law*, 11(1), 249–283.

Ludema, R. and I. Wooton (1994), Cross-border externalities and trade liberalization: the strategic control of pollution, *The Canadian Journal of Economics*, 27(4), 950–966.

OECD (1999), *Trade measures in multilateral environmental agreements*, OECD, Paris.

Revesz, R. (2000), Federalism and regulation: extrapolating from the analysis of environmental regulation in the United States, *Journal of International Economic Law*, 219–233.

Appendix

1. The free trade solution, the intersection between export supply and import demand is given by:

$$x = \frac{a - f}{b + g}$$

2. The first-best solution maximizes the sum of importing and exporting countries' welfare, with respect to an externality tax and the constraint that demand is equal to supply, i.e.

$$\max_{t} \frac{bx^2}{2} + (t - \bar{z})x + \frac{gx^2}{2},$$
$$s.t. \ x = \frac{a - f - t}{b + g}$$

The first-order condition for this problem implies:

$$t^* = \bar{z} \quad \text{and}$$
$$x = \frac{(a - f - \bar{z})}{(b + g)}$$

3. The optimal unilateral import tariff solves:

$$\max_{r} \frac{bx^2}{2} + (r - \bar{z})x,$$
$$s.t. \ x = \frac{a - f - r}{b + g}$$

Solving the f.o.c yields:

$$r^* = \bar{z}\left(\frac{b+g}{b+2g}\right) + \frac{(a-f)g}{b+2g}$$

$$x = \frac{(a-f-\bar{z})}{b+2g}$$

4. The externality tax on which trade can be made contingent solves:

$$\max_{e} \frac{bx^2}{2} - (\bar{z})x,$$

$$s.t. \; x = \frac{a-f-e\bar{z}}{b+g}$$

The problem is convex and the objective function is equal to zero for $e = \frac{(a-f)}{\bar{z}}$. Hence if $(bx - \bar{z}) > 0$, for $e = 0$, the maximum is reached for $e = 0$. If $(bx - \bar{z}) < 0$, for $e = 0$, the maximum is reached for $e = \frac{(a-f)}{\bar{z}}$. In this case, the externality tax is prohibitive. It is set at a level which prevents trade.

5. The Nash equilibrium of the game in which the importing country sets an import tariff and the exporting country sets an externality tax simultaneously solves:

$$\max_{r} \frac{bx^2}{2} + (r - \bar{z})x \quad \text{and} \quad \max_{e} \frac{gx^2}{2} + e\bar{z}x,$$

$$s.t. \; x = \frac{a-f-(r+e\bar{z})}{b+g}$$

The solution to this problem is given in equation (8) of Ludema and Wooton (1994) and replacing $e\bar{z} = s$.

6. The *US – Shrimp* solution solves the following problem:

$$\max_{z} \frac{bx^2}{2} + zx,$$

$$s.t. \; x = \frac{a-f-C(z)}{b+g}$$

Assuming that $C(x) = k(\bar{z} - z)$, the f.o.c for the problem yields:

$$z^* = \max\left[0, \frac{(a-f-k\bar{z})(kb-(b+g))}{(2k(b+g)-k^2 b)}\right]$$

For $(kb - (b+g)) > 0$ and $(2k(b+g) - k^2 b) > 0$, we have $z^* > 0$.

4

US – Lamb
United States – Safeguard Measures on Imports of Fresh, Chilled or Frozen Lamb Meat from New Zealand and Australia: What Should be Required of a Safeguard Investigation?*

HENRIK HORN AND PETROS C. MAVROIDIS

1 Background

The United States (US) imposed, in July 1999, a safeguard on lamb meat, in the form of tariff rate import quotas, which were to be applied for a period of three years. The measure was based on findings by the US International Trade Commission that increased imports of lamb meat were a substantial cause of threat of serious injury to the US industry producing the like product. Following complaints by New Zealand and Australia that the measure was inconsistent with Articles I, II and XIX of GATT 1994, and several provisions of the Agreement on Safeguards, the World Trade Organization (WTO) Dispute Settlement Body established, in November 1999, a panel to review the consistency of the US measure with the mentioned WTO rules.

The Panel found that:[1]

---

* This study reviews the WTO Appellate Body Decision *United States – Safeguard Measures on Imports of Fresh, Chilled or Frozen Lamb Meat from New Zealand and Australia* (WT/DS177/AB/R, WT/DS178/AB/R, May 1, 2001). It is prepared for the American Law Institute project "Principles of Trade Law: the World Trade Organization." We are grateful to, in particular, Bill Davey, Wilfred J. Ethier, and Joseph Weiler for helpful discussions. We have also benefited from discussions with Eyal Benvenisti, David Strömberg, and Jonas Vlachos as well as with the participants in ALI meetings in Philadelphia on October 24–25, 2002, and February 6–7, 2003.

[1] *United States – Safeguard Measures on Imports of Fresh, Chilled or Frozen Lamb Meat from New Zealand and Australia*, WT/DS177/R, WT/DS178/R, December 21, 2000.

(i) the US had failed to demonstrate that the import surge was the result of *unforeseen developments* as required by Article 1 SGA, which incorporates by reference Article XIX GATT;

(ii) the US had made too broad a definition of *domestic industry* inconsistent with Article 2.1 and Article 4.1c of the Agreement on Safeguards;

(iii) the Complainants failed to establish the deficiency of the methodology employed by the US International Trade Commission to establish *threat of serious injury* (and hence rejected their claims in this respect);

(iv) the US International Trade Commission investigation based its finding on non-representative data, inconsistent with the requirements of the Agreement on Safeguards; and

(v) the US International Trade Commission investigation did not establish, as required by Article 4.2 SGA, a *causal link* between increased imports and the threat of serious injury, nor that this threat could *not be attributed to other factors.*

The Panel thus found that the US had acted inconsistently with Article XIX.1.a GATT and with several provisions in the Agreement on Safeguards.

All three parties to the dispute appealed the Panel Report. In its report,[2] the Appellate Body (AB):

(i) upheld the Panel's finding that the US International Trade Commission had failed to demonstrate unforeseen developments;

(ii) agreed with the Panel that the US International Trade Commission had used too wide a definition of domestic industry and had relied on non-representative data;

(iii) in contrast to the Panel, found the method employed by the US International Trade Commission to assess the threat of serious injury to be deficient; and

(iv) reversed the Panel's interpretation of the causality requirement, but for reasons other than those advanced by the Panel upheld the finding that the US International Trade Commission did not fulfill this requirement, nor the non-attribution requirement.

---

[2] *United States − Safeguard Measures on Imports of Fresh, Chilled or Frozen Lamb Meat from New Zealand and Australia* (WT/DS177/AB/R, WT/DS178/AB/R, May 1, 2001).

The purpose of this study is to provide an economic and legal analysis of this dispute, subsequently referred to as *US – Lamb*. In order to set the stage for the discussion to come, we will start in the next section by sketching a theory of an economic rationale for safeguard provisions in trade agreements. Section 3 provides the context of the legal dispositions that we discuss in the rest of the paper. Section 4 then very briefly lays out the legal provisions of particular relevance to this dispute, which are further analyzed in more detail in section 5 ("unforeseen developments"), Section 6 ("... causal link between increased imports ... and serious injury or threat thereof ..."), and in section 7 ("... of the effects of obligations incurred under this Agreement ..."). Section 8 provides some concluding remarks.

2   The role of safeguards in trade agreements

Safeguards are temporary trade barriers, and, as such, hurt trading partners. A natural question is, therefore, whether they could nevertheless be defended from an efficiency point of view, that is, whether the existence of such an instrument in a trade agreement increases the "size of the cake" that its members share. We will argue that safeguards may indeed play such a role, but that their practical implementation is beset with the risk of abuse.[3]

2.1   The case for safeguards

The economic environment is constantly changing: new products and production technologies are discovered, consumer tastes change, governments come and go, there are wars, investments are made, new firms see the light of day. For a trade agreement to be fully efficient, it would need to adapt to these changes. This adaptation could be fully achieved *only* under very special circumstances. If the parties could perfectly foresee the path of events, then they could sign a contract at the outset that would specify how the contract terms would change along this path. In the absence of such information, the parties may renegotiate the contract any time a change occurs. Alternatively, the parties could write a "fully state

---

[3] See Sykes (1990, 1991) for analysis of the role of safeguards in trade agreements, in particular as viewed from the perspective of public choice theory. See also Deardorff's (1987) treatment of the role of tariff and non-tariff safeguards when social preferences are represented by a Corden "conservative social welfare function."

contingent" contract, which would detail commitments for each possible outcome of the underlying economic environment.[4]

Under either of these circumstances, it would be possible to specify a trade contract that *ex post* ensures the desirable levels of trade. If desirable, this contract could also allow for a gradual adjustment to the changed environment. Hence, in neither case would there be a role for any provision that allowed for an *ex post* change in tariff bindings.

Tariff bindings in actual trade agreements are typically not conditioned on external events, however. There is therefore a need for instruments that allow for *ex post* adjustment of effective levels of bindings – that is, for *escape clauses* – and the GATT includes several provisions to this effect. Article XII enables the adoption of protective measures in response to economy-wide monetary disturbances, but most contingent protection instruments are enacted as remedies to problems in specific industries. Article XXVIII permits renegotiation with other contracting parties of particular bindings, and might thus allow for more long-run, but also presumably more time-consuming, solutions to problems of *ex post* inefficient tariff bindings.

What is, then, the role of Article XIX GATT safeguards in this arsenal of escape clauses? Safeguards may be unilaterally imposed, and might for this reason represent a quicker response to changes in the economic environment in particular industries (depending on the administrative requirements imposed on safeguard investigations) than for instance an Article XXVIII renegotiation.[5] But Article XIX GATT safeguards are not the only measures that can be unilaterally imposed – both anti-dumping duties and countervailing duties can be imposed without negotiation with the exporting country. However, Article XIX GATT safeguards differ from the latter measures in that they are meant to *temporarily slow the pace of adjustment* to changes in the external economic environment, whereas anti-dumping measures and countervailing duties can be in place for as long as the dumping or subsidization continues.[6]

---

[4] The difference between the two scenarios is that in the former, the contract would specify the commitments of the Members at each date. These would then vary over time in response to changes in the external environment. In the latter case, since the realization of these external events would be unknown at the contracting date, the contract would specify for each date commitments for each possible realization. This would thus be a significantly larger contract, but would in principle achieve the same thing as the first contract.

[5] We implicitly assume that there are costs associated with contracting, so that the parties do not negotiate a new contract each time the environment changes.

[6] Suppose that the European Community imposes a four-year safeguard measure on steel. At the end of this period, the EC has two options: either they extend the measure for

The question thus arises of whether such an instrument can be defended from an economic point of view, in the sense of whether it might enhance the efficiency of the trade agreement, that is, increase the size of the "pie" the parties to the contract share through the agreement.

As we will argue below, in order for there to be a need for an instrument seeking to slow the adjustment speed, it does not suffice that tariff bindings be rigid. But a combination of rigid bindings and *"adjustment costs" that depend on the pace of adjustment* may indeed provide a role for safeguards.

2.1.1   Safeguards as means to reduce adjustment costs

The economic notion of "adjustment costs" is amorphous.[7] The interpretation we have in mind refers to the cost accruing due to the *transition* from one equilibrium to another (and does thus not involve a comparison of the final outcome with the initial situation). To define more precisely such costs we need to agree on the criterion according to which costs are evaluated. We here start by considering adjustment costs from the point of view of social welfare maximization. But we will discuss other objectives as well.

Consider an import-competing domestic industry – lamb-meat production, say – that has suffered a severe negative shock – foreign capacity has permanently expanded, and prices have fallen significantly as a result. As matters stand, the industry has to shed 12,000 people. Suppose first that they could all *immediately* find employment in the beef-meat industry, but at lower wages. This lowering of the wage would obviously be costly to workers, but would not be considered as an adjustment cost, since it would simply reflect differences between two equilibria, with no transitional period in between: the lowering of the wage is not a cost incurred during the transition from one employment situation to another.

Let it now take each worker six months to find new employment, no matter what the circumstances, and during this period the worker has to

up to four years (Article 7.2 SGA), or alternatively they do not extend the measure. In the first case, assuming the EC decided to extend the original safeguard for four years, it has to wait for another eight years before imposing a safeguard measure on steel anew. In the second case, they have to wait for four years. No similar rule applies in the case of anti-dumping, where after the sunset of a measure five years after its imposition (11.3 Anti-dumping Agreement), the importing country can effectively extend the anti-dumping measure.

[7] Trade theory often pays lip service to the existence of adjustment costs, but relatively little work has been done on their sources and consequences. For analysis of some basic aspects of adjustment costs, see Mussa (1981) and Neary (1981), and other contributions in the volume edited by Jagdish Bhagwati (Bhagwati, 1981).

remain unproductive. This would be a social adjustment cost: during the transition period the economy is temporarily producing at less than its long-run full capacity. But this cost does not depend on the speed of adjustment, since each worker by assumption has to be unemployed for six months, no matter what. This period of reduced output is essentially an unavoidable investment in a more efficient production pattern. It would hence not provide a rationale for a safeguard that would gradually move workers into the beef industry, since such a measure would not affect the total magnitude of adjustment costs, but would just cause a costly delay to the necessary adjustment.

As a third possibility, assume that each quarter 6,000 vacancies are opened in the beef-meat industry. A finely tuned safeguard that gradually reduced the work force in the lamb-meat industry could then ensure that 6,000 workers were reallocated during the first quarter, and another 6,000 the next, without anyone having to be temporarily unemployed. On the other hand, if all 12,000 had to leave the lamb meat industry immediately, 6,000 of them would be unemployed for a quarter.[8] The *speed* at which the adjustment takes place thus affects the aggregate adjustment costs, and there is a case for a safeguard. This provides efficiency-enhancing rationale for safeguards: *to temporarily reduce the pace of adjustment in order to reduce adjustment costs.*

There are several things to note:

1. The example presumes that the alternative to the safeguard is that all 12,000 workers immediately leave the industry. But why do not 6,000 workers remain in the lamb industry during the first quarter and offer to work at sufficiently low wages for the industry to want to retain them? If wages were reduced this way, there would be no unnecessary loss of output during the transition, and hence no case for a safeguard (or at least a weaker case). The reason must be some form of inflexibility in the wage, arising from, for instance, labor union resistance to wage cuts, or minimum wage legislation.

   More generally, in order for government intervention to have an efficiency-enhancing role to play, the privately perceived incentives to cope with adjustment must be incorrect from a social point of view (or from a government point of view). If the private sector puts the same emphasis on these costs as the government, and has access to

---

[8] To make the case even stronger, suppose that workers lose productive skills during their period of unemployment, or lose self-confidence and thus search less intensively for new jobs, or suffer mentally from the unemployment.

the same (possibly imperfect) information about the future evolution of the economy, and the economy is not distorted in other respects, it does not suffice that there are adjustment costs that depend on the pace of adjustment, for a role for safeguards to exist. For instance, in the example above, the implicitly assumed wage rigidity implied that the cost of labor perceived by the lamb meat industry exceeded the true social cost of this labor, which should reflect the opportunity cost of workers.

2. The example presumes that the shock to international prices is permanent, and the economy will therefore eventually have to change to the new circumstances. If the shock were temporary, a safeguard could under certain circumstances serve a slightly different role, by preventing adjustment costs from arising from resources first moving out and then back into the industry. Again, for such a role to arise it must be that the owners of these resources do not have the right incentives, as perceived from a social point of view, to avoid these adjustment costs by letting resources remain in the industry during the temporary slump.

3. The argument above helps identify circumstances under which a safeguard might improve matters relative to a situation where nothing is done. It has not been argued, however, that an import restriction would be the *best* way of coping with the problem. To start with, if the source of the wage rigidity cannot be removed, it might still be preferable to use employment subsidies, or production subsidies, since these do not distort consumer prices to the same extent.[9]

4. The examples above presume for simplicity's sake that the government has full information about relevant aspects of the future. In practice, there is of course often considerable uncertainty about whether negative shocks are transitory or permanent, and this uncertainty may influence the appropriate length and magnitude of a safeguard measure. But this uncertainty does not in itself add any reason for a government intervention in the form of a safeguard, as long as the government is not better informed than the private sector.

5. In the examples above, the adjustment costs stemmed from the reallocation of labor. But one can establish similar parallelisms with the reallocation of other factors of production, such as machinery, for instance.

---

[9] Of course, if the concern is not efficiency but equity, temporary income support might be better.

6. Very little is known empirically about the magnitude of social-adjustment costs. Economists traditionally dismiss these as being small and swamped by the gains from trade liberalization, even though it is acknowledged that they typically fall upon a few individuals, while the benefits from trade liberalization are spread over many more. Even less is known empirically about the extent to which adjustment costs depend on the speed of trade liberalization. But, for what it is worth, our intuition suggests that the speed of adjustment can indeed often importantly affect aggregate adjustment costs.

7. The reasoning above showed how social-adjustment costs might provide a rationale for social welfare-maximizing governments to include a safeguard provision in a trade agreement. But such costs should also be of concern to governments that are more sensitive to the influence of special interest groups. The weight that such a government puts on these costs may depend on who is carrying them, but the fact that the economy's productive capacity is reduced from a rapid rate of adjustment should reasonably be of concern to a broad range of government types.[10]

8. We have neglected any impact that the safeguard may have on the incentives to eventually move out of the industry, by implicitly assuming away any form of strategic interaction between the private sector and the government at a later stage. In practice, firms and workers often remain in the protected industry with the rational expectation that the government will continue to adjust them also in the future. More generally, there are severe potential problems of abuse associated with safeguards, an issue to which we will return below.

2.1.2   Safeguards and the incentive to liberalize

The reasoning has so far identified two desirable properties of safeguards, which both contribute to enhancing the efficiency of a trade contract: in their capacity of providing escape from inflexible contract terms, they

---

[10] Are adjustment costs in the sense of reduced aggregate output *necessary* for governments to rationally include a safeguard provision in a trade agreement? Here we have to speculate, since we are not aware of any literature to lean against. But just as an accident involving a large number of casualties seems to attract more media and political attention than several smaller accidents combined, there also seem to exist "political adjustment costs" that depend on the speed of adjustment. For instance, large layoffs may be more costly politically than the same number of layoffs when spread over a period of time, even if the total amount of unemployment remains the same in both cases, due to more negative media coverage. If so, there would be a role for a safeguard mechanism, even without adjustment costs in the sense discussed above.

may even, in the absence of adjustment costs that depend on the speed of adjustment, increase the efficiency of the contract after external shocks. But they also have a separate role to play: to temporarily reduce the rate of adjustment in order to reduce the total amount of adjustment costs.

But there may be a related, additional source of efficiency gains from safeguards, a source that is often emphasized in the policy debate: safeguards may induce countries to liberalize further. Consequently, the combined effect of the induced liberalization as well as the possibility of increasing tariffs *ex post*, may result in a fall in the average level of protection.[11]

Another version of this argument, more based on a public choice approach where governments are driven at least partly by motives other than social welfare maximization, is discussed by Sykes (1991). The argument here is that after trade negotiations governments may face strong pressure for protection in certain industries. A safeguard mechanism makes it possible to give in to such pressures, and thus to avoid political setbacks if participating in liberalization. As a result, governments are more prone to liberalize *ex ante*. While this is not a unique feature of safeguards (it is shared by other escape clause mechanisms), the potential of safeguards to avoid adjustment costs might serve as an additional motive for governments to liberalize.

2.2 Potential drawbacks of safeguards

We have so far painted a rather rosy picture of safeguards (and escape clauses more generally). Some of the problems (and virtues) associated with such schemes are illuminated by viewing them as *insurance* mechanisms, a useful but inexact analogy.[12] An essential character of both trade agreements and insurance contracts is that one side in the contractual relationship may be subject to an adverse shock after the signing of the agreement. In an insurance contract there is a net transfer of resources

---

[11] Important as this effect may seem, we are not aware of any serious empirical evidence of its existence.

[12] Such a perspective on safeguards is natural also from a theoretical point of view, since malfunctioning private insurance markets may serve as a basis for welfare-enhancing unilateral trade policy interventions, as demonstrated by Newbery and Stiglitz (1981), for instance. Of relevance to the issues discussed here is also the "tariffs as insurance" literature; see for instance Eaton and Grossman (1985), and Dixit (1987, 1989a, b).

from the insurance company to the insured party. Similarly, Article XIX GATT permits a Member that is exposed to a sufficiently severe negative shock to increase a trade barrier. Formally, the Member had to provide "substantially equivalent" compensation to its trading partners, but it seems likely that trading partners will not achieve full compensation: they would have to go through a possibly lengthy and costly dispute procedure to obtain the compensation, which would serve to reduce their incentives to insist on full compensation.

The similarity between safeguards and insurance schemes does not stop here, however. Just like regular insurance contracts seek to limit the possibility of abuse through complex restrictions on their applicability, many of the features of Article XIX GATT and the Agreement on Safeguards can be seen as attempts to limit such problems. For instance, a basic problem in the case of regular insurance contracts is the conflict between risk-sharing and moral hazard: on the one hand, it is desirable to reduce the risk that a risk-averse party is exposed to by letting a less risk-averse party carry more of the risk. The fact that this is efficiency-enhancing (yields gains from trade), is evidenced by the insured party's willingness to pay an insurance premium to be relieved of the risk. On the other hand, the insurance may adversely affect the insured party's incentives to avoid risk – it may cause a *moral hazard* problem.

It is easy to identify potential moral hazard problems in the context of safeguards: in particular, countries could be tempted to refrain from undertaking measures that would prepare the economy for shocks that might occur in a liberalized trade environment in the expectation of being able to rely on safeguards should a problem arise. A number of the requirements in Article XIX GATT and in the Agreement on Safeguards are naturally seen as means to limit such incentives. For instance, a safeguard can only be invoked in the case where the injury *inter alia* stems from increased *imports*. A "first-best" risk-sharing contract (the optimal contract in a situation without moral hazard problems, etc.) would not restrict the insurance to injury from increased imports. But if any domestic negative shock could to a significant extent be passed on to trading partners, the incentive for countries to pursue reasonable policies would be diminished. On the other hand, when disturbances emanate from abroad, it is less likely that they are the result of negligence or beggar-thy-neighbor behavior by the importing country. Furthermore, in order to verify that increased imports are really the source of injury, Members are required to establish a *causal link* between the two, just like regular insurance contracts require the insured party to verify any claims. Another defense against moral hazard is the requirement that the safeguard solves a problem that could not have been prevented through diligent behavior – the import surge must be *unforeseen*.

Another generic problem facing the design of an insurance contract arises when the outcome is not perfectly observable. For instance, theft is often by its very nature hard to verify, and an insurance company largely has to trust that reported theft has actually occurred (even though it is also aided by laws against fraudulent insurance claims). When certain outcomes are not observable to the party providing the insurance, the contract needs to be designed so as to guarantee that the insured party has incentives not to over-report, or such that it is only based on circumstances that are verifiable by the insurer. A very similar problem may arise in the context of safeguards in trade agreements, where there is a need to prevent Members from claiming injury that has not occurred. In response, a country wanting to impose safeguards has to provide evidence that its industry is suffering *serious injury*, or imminent threat of such. Both the distribution of the burden of proof, as well as the fact that the injury must be serious, tend to ease the observability problem.

2.3   Conclusion

There are at least two potentially efficiency-enhancing features of escape clauses in general: they allow for *ex post* correction of contract terms in response to changes in external events, and they may thereby also provide incentives for further *ex ante* liberalization. A distinguishing feature of Article XIX GATT safeguards is that they are temporary measures that can be invoked *ex post* in response to external shocks. They are more quickly administered than Article XXVIII renegotiations, and they are not conditioned on a finding of dumping by foreign firms, or subsidization by foreign governments.

We have argued that there is an economic rationale for such an instrument, that is, that safeguards might enhance the efficiency of trade agreements, not only for welfare-maximizing governments, but also for governments motivated at least partly by other considerations. We can consequently meaningfully discuss a suitable implementation of this provision from an economic point of view. Had the provision instead been found to be totally undesirable from an economic perspective, it would have been difficult to discuss an economically meaningful implementation of the GATT safeguard provisions.

3 The legal setting

Article XIX.1.a GATT on "Emergency Action on Imports of Particular Products" states:

> If, as a result of unforeseen developments and of the effect of the obligations incurred by a Member under this Agreement, including tariff concessions, any product is being imported into the territory of that Member in such increased quantities and under such conditions as to cause or threaten serious injury to domestic producers in that territory of like or directly competitive products, the Member shall be free, in respect of such product, and to the extent and for such time as may be necessary to prevent or remedy such injury, to suspend the obligation in whole or in part or to withdraw or modify the concession.

The Agreement on Safeguards provides more details on the determination of injury, on the application of safeguards, on the causal link between imports and injury, and on a series of procedural issues. But there are some discrepancies between the Agreement on Safeguards and Article XIX GATT, and the relationship between Article XIX GATT and the Agreement on Safeguards is hence crucial for the interpretation of the safeguards mechanism. The AB addressed this issue in a couple of disputes preceding *US – Lamb*, concluding that safeguard measures have to be consistent with *both* Article XIX GATT and the Agreement on Safeguards,[13] to be WTO-consistent, a position taken by the AB also in *US – Lamb*. We will accept this premise without further discussion.

US – Lamb concerns a safeguard measure against threat of serious injury. Article XIX GATT specifies a number of conditions for such a measure to be legal. These include that:

   (i) an *unforeseen*
  (ii) *import surge* has
 (iii) *due to obligations incurred under* the Agreement
  (iv) *caused*
   (v) an *unstable* situation that will, absent other changes, *lead to*
  (vi) *serious injury* to
 (vii) a *domestic industry*
(viii) producing a *like or directly competitive* product,
  (ix) and the safeguard is *necessary* to prevent such injury
   (x) from occurring in the *future*.

[13] The Appellate Body report on *Argentina – Safeguard Measures on Imports of Footwear* (WT/DS121/AB/R of December 14, 1999) reflects this approach. See §§83, 84, 93, and 94.

Much of the discussion in the Panel and AB reports in *US – Lamb* concerns the extent to which these conditions were fulfilled in the case at hand. In what follows, we will discuss the treatment by the AB, in particular, of several of the conditions listed above.

The Preamble of the Agreement on Safeguards contains the following passage:

> Recognizing the importance of *structural adjustment* and the need to enhance rather than limit competition in international markets . . .
>
> (emphasis added)

The Preamble is of limited legal value. Article 2 SGA, which lays out the conditions for a lawful imposition of safeguards, does not include a reference to structural adjustments. Consequently, although WTO Members do not have the binding legal obligation to undertake structural adjustment whenever they have recourse to a safeguard, the Agreement expresses a wish that this be the case.

4   ". . . unforeseen developments . . ."

Article XIX.1.a GATT stipulates that the safeguard measure must be taken in response to "unforeseen developments." There was dispute as to whether the unforeseen requirement had survived into the WTO era, since this requirement is not explicitly mentioned in the WTO Safeguards Agreement, contrary to Article XIX GATT. In its report on *Argentina – Footwear (EC)*, the AB held the view that, by virtue of the explicit link to Article XIX GATT in Article 1 SGA, WTO Members cannot lawfully impose safeguards unless they satisfy the unforeseen requirement as well.[14] *US – Lamb* is the first dispute where a WTO Member's allegation that an event was unforeseen has been rejected by the AB. A purely descriptive

---

[14] WT/DS121/AB/R of December 14, 1999. The legal correctness of this approach is dubious. It seems that the AB confused two different issues: Article 1 SGA is entitled "General Provision" and refers to Article XIX GATT explicitly only to describe which measures should be understood to be safeguard measures. Article 2 SGA, which is entitled "Conditions," by contrast mentions the legal requirements that have to be fulfilled for a safeguard measure to conform to the SGA. Article 2 does not mention at all the unforeseen developments requirement. The AB imported into Article 2 SGA a requirement which does not exist. Article 1 SGA, as its title and accompanying text indicates, was not intended to discuss the conditions for lawful imposition of safeguards. It was meant to describe what form a safeguard measure can take. Unfortunately, in the present case, the AB followed this case law, which seems to lack legal merit.

statement, which does not explain the reasons why developments were unforeseen, does not suffice in the view of the AB.[15]

4.1   Implications of the notion of "unforeseen"

4.1.1   Unforeseen means "unlikely" and not "unforeseeable"

Leaning against the AB report in *Korea − Dairy*, the panel argued that "unforeseen" should not be interpreted as "unforeseeable." Unforeseeable events are by necessity unforeseen, but unforeseen events

> . . . may nevertheless be foreseeable or predictable in the theoretical sense of capable of being anticipated from a general scientific perspective . . .
>
> (7.22)

We concur with this interpretation. As we understand this statement, it distinguishes between what is unlikely and what can not be conceptualized. For instance, taking imports as an exogenous factor, what matters to domestic producers is the supply of imports, the volumes and/or prices at which imports are supplied. If the import volume a certain year is 100, it might appear very *unlikely* that it will next year be 200, and an occurrence of such a high volume might be "unforeseen" in the sense of "surprising." However, it is a different matter to say that an import volume of 200 is *unforeseeable* in the sense that producers could not conceptualize such a volume. The latter would clearly be an unreasonable criterion. It can also be noted that the interpretation of "unforeseen" as "unforeseeable" in this sense does not sit well with the argument that the safeguard mechanism makes Members more willing to liberalize.

An important question in practice is of course *how* unlikely a development should be to allow for a safeguard. Neither Article XIX GATT, nor the Agreement on Safeguards, gives any guidance on this. It is also not possible in practice to lay down rules in terms of probabilities. But given the incentive problems associated with this type of instrument, we would argue that the reasonably perceived probability for a negative shock to the domestic industry must have been very low, for a safeguard to be allowed, if serious injury were to materialize.

---

[15] It appears as if in GATT 1994 "unforeseen" is only used once in the Agreement on Import Licensing Procedures, and once in the Understanding on Dispute Settlement. Neither case seems to provide any light on its intended interpretation.

4.1.2   Unforeseen implies "not being the deliberate cause of"

The interpretation of unforeseen as unexpected has another desirable consequence: it implies that safeguards cannot be employed in situations where the problems are caused by willful mismanagement or neglect by the government, to the extent that the serious injury should reasonably be expected from this type of behavior. Unforeseen thus also seems to imply "not being the deliberate cause of."

This implication of "unforeseen" has in turn important ramifications for the notion of "increased imports" as a necessary condition for a safeguard. An import surge can be caused by the country seeking to impose safeguards simply by an internal measure that reduces domestic supply, or increases domestic demand. From an economic point of view, it is natural to argue that the government should understand this consequence of the internal measure, and that there would be no ground for a safeguard in such a case.

How detailed an understanding of the economy should the government then be required to have? After all, the economic system is extremely complex – this complexity is indeed what economists make a living on – and a policy intervention somewhere in the economy might have consequences very "far" away in the system that are practically impossible to predict. The link between the policy measure and these developments can in a certain sense be said to be "unforeseeable." The question is then whether the inability of the government to understand how a certain action affects the economy is a sufficient ground to classify the resulting developments as "unforeseen."

In our view, one cannot demand of governments to be able to foresee all economic consequences of their actions. It also seems reasonable that serious injury that is caused by the importing government's interventions for clearly different purposes should not necessarily be disqualified as a ground for safeguards. But governments should obviously be expected to have a "reasonable" understanding of the working of the economy. It is not possible to specify exactly what can and what cannot be foreseen in this sense – this has to be left to the discretion of the adjudicating bodies in each separate case. But the government should be able to demonstrate that it could not reasonably have expected the import surge to result from its policy intervention, in order to legally impose a safeguard. That is, there should be a "due diligence" standard to be respected by national administrations. At any rate, safeguard measures imposed by a government after it has knowingly provoked an import surge should be considered as inconsistent with the Agreement on Safeguards.

One might take the argument even further, however, and include the behavior of the private sector. For instance, governments do not normally know the details of specific industries, but have to rely on the industry to warn them of future problems. What if an industry does not spend enough efforts on forecasting future developments due to mismanagement? Or, what if the industry allows for wage hikes that it cannot afford without protection? Maybe the industry has strategically put itself in the adverse situation in the rational expectation that it would be bailed out through safeguards if a problem were to arise. More generally, should serious injury caused by "reckless" behavior by the private sector be a legitimate ground for a safeguard? If so, will not this induce moral-hazard-like problems, whereby protectionist-minded governments tacitly encourage this type of behavior on the part of the industry?[16]

This discussion of the appropriate restriction on the applicability of safeguards has been pursued from a strictly economic perspective. It suggests that safeguards should not be permitted in response to private-sector reckless behavior, since this would invite moral-hazard problems. But from a legal perspective, for a WTO Member to be liable, there must be an active behavior attributable to the Member. It would therefore be difficult to make the legality of the measure dependent on the behavior of the private sector, unless, following the ruling in *Japan − Trade in Semiconductors* dispute,[17] the government has actively induced the private sector behavior. There thus here seems to be conflict between the principles of economics and of law.

---

[16] The problems that arise in this context are similar to those discussed in macroeconomics concerning the use of government policies to counter cyclical variations in economic activity. Much of the discussion there has focused on the possibility that the private sector learns to see through the government's incentives to intervene. For instance, the expectation by the private sector that the government will accommodate rising unemployment through inflationary monetary policy, may induce the private sector to show less restraint to wage increases, thus causing unemployment that will trigger expansionary monetary policy. The government's control of the money supply − this is the counterpart of its access to a "safeguard mechanism" − thus creates a situation where it is forced to increase money supply, the end result being higher inflation but the same level of, say, unemployment. One of the main reasons why the control of money supply increasingly is delegated to independent central banks is precisely to avoid these problems. One should think that there should be a lesson to learn from this also for safeguard mechanisms in trade agreements.

[17] *Japan − Trade in Semiconductors*, (GATT Doc. BISD 35S/116 of May 4, 1988).

4.2   When should the event have been unforeseen?

Yet another issue in this context is the *time* at which the import surge should have been unforeseen.[18] Neither Article XIX GATT, nor the Agreement on Safeguards, gives any guidance on this issue. There seem to be at least two natural possibilities here. One is to interpret the contract date as the time at which the external event must have been foreseen. Clearly, if the parties could foresee the future change at the time of signing the trade agreement, a safeguard could hardly be motivated.

The opposite situation, where the change is not foreseen at this date, is more problematic. A trade agreement such as the Uruguay Round may regulate trade for a number of years. Clearly, the longer the period between agreements, the more likely that unforeseen developments will occur. Therefore, *some* events occurring after the signing of the agreement could qualify as unforeseen developments. Then, could *any* event occurring after the signing of the contract serve as a basis for a safeguard? We would argue no.

To illustrate, consider the example discussed above with the declining lamb-meat industry. In this example, had the government known one quarter (or longer) *before* that an import surge was forthcoming, it could have induced 6,000 workers to leave the industry during this quarter, and let the rest leave the first quarter after, thus making the safeguard unnecessary. The legality of a safeguard in this case would thus depend on whether a due diligence standard would require the government to have foreseen the shock to come the quarter before. More generally, for the safeguard to be legal it should hence be required that the cause of the serious injury *could not reasonably be foreseen at a time when action was necessary in order to avoid it.*

4.3   How to establish what was unforeseen

As argued above, the essential feature of an unforeseen development must be that the government reasonably attributed a low probability to it occurring, and that it then nevertheless materialized. It is not a trivial exercise to empirically determine such probabilities. Of course, it does not suffice to establish the occurrence of a sharp increase in imports, since it may

---

[18] This question is not to be confused with the issue of whether the occurrence of previously unexpected events has to be established publicly as part of the investigation before the safeguards are invoked.

have been well understood at the time of signing the agreement that such developments would take place, perhaps even as a result of the agreement.

The existence of the safeguard regime itself adds further complexity to the practical determination of whether events were reasonably unexpected or not. For instance, a tempting possibility would be to use stock prices, the idea being that the stock market could be a suitable indicator of what can be reasonably expected. If stock prices did not deteriorate until the import surge actually set in, the surge might be argued to be unexpected. The problem with this approach, however, is that the scenario where the lack of reaction in stock prices motivates safeguards, might not be distinguishable from the one where the stock market actually foresees the import surge, but in the expectation of safeguards does not alter its valuation of firms in the industry to any noticeable degree.

Consequently, it seems clear that it might be very difficult for a country wanting to impose safeguards to verify in a more scientific fashion that an import surge was unexpected given a due diligence standard. We nevertheless believe that Members seeking to impose safeguards should be requested to provide some statistical verification of the claim that an unlikely situation has arisen, given the information at hand. Such an exercise can on few occasions decisively determine whether the unforeseen criterion has been established, but might serve to add some rigor to an otherwise very "soft" test. The importing country would then need to explain why it cannot statistically support its claim, if this is the case. At the end of the day, however, it seems difficult to avoid having to rely on a discretionary judgment concerning whether the developments were unforeseen or not.

4.4   An awkward feature of safeguard investigations

There is a somewhat awkward aspect of the safeguard mechanism with regard to the "unforeseen developments" criterion. The essence of such an investigation is that a government agency evaluates whether past mistakes by itself, or possibly some other agency, in forecasting industry developments, were indeed acceptable despite a due diligence standard. Only when the agency behaved correctly when making the forecast mistake can a safeguard be permitted. This somewhat odd arrangement makes it all the more important that the adjudicating bodies in the WTO maintain clear standards for what is acceptable and not as a basis for a safeguard.

4.5   Were "unforeseen developments" established in US – Lamb?

The US argued in US – Lamb that there is no legal obligation for the USITC to include in the published report an examination of whether the developments were unforeseen, since this can be done if a dispute arises. The AB did not accept this reasoning, and ruled that a demonstration of unforeseen developments must be made prior to the application of the safeguard.

The US also claimed that the change in the product mix of imports as well as an increase in the cut size of imported lamb factually constituted unforeseen developments, and that these developments were documented in its report. The Complainants did not contest the existence of these changes, but maintained that they were largely the consequence of the removal of subsidies under the Wool Act, and that these consequences could and should have been foreseen.

In the Panel's view, the US only provided descriptive statements of the import surge, and did not establish as a matter of fact that they were really unforeseen:

> . . . it is our view that these USITC statements concerning the change in product mix or the increase in cut size, on their face, are simple descriptive statements, and cannot be construed as a conclusion as to the existence of "unforeseen developments" in the sense of GATT Article XIX:1.

> (7.43)

The AB basically upheld this view, stating that

> . . . we see no indication in the USITC report that the USITC addressed the issue of "unforeseen developments" at all . . .

> (73)

. . . even though the AB also said that it did not agree with every aspect of the panel's reasoning. It is not clear to us, however, what exactly they did not agree with.

We share the adjudicating bodies' view that the US did not convincingly demonstrate that the developments motivating the safeguard were unforeseen, and we believe that such a demonstration should be an integral part of the safeguard investigation. As far as we can see, there is nothing that would prevent the use of some form of econometric/statistical analysis in a case like US – Lamb. As mentioned above, such analysis might not be decisive, but should serve to provide much better ground for a judgment; we will return to this issue in the last section. More generally, we see the adjudicating bodies' rejection of the US International Trade Commission methodology as a welcome strengthening of the burden of proof required to demonstrate that a safeguard was imposed as a response to unforeseen developments.

5 ". . . causal link between increased imports . . . and serious injury or threat thereof . . ."

Article 4.2(b) SGA requires

> . . . the existence of the causal link between increased imports of the product concerned and serious injury or threat thereof. . . .

It further specifies that

> [w]hen factors other than increased imports are causing injury to the domestic industry at the same time, such injury shall not be attributed to increased imports.

As discussed above, these requirements are natural components in the attempt to prevent abuse of the Agreement on Safeguards. But they give rise to rather severe problems of interpretation and implementation, also leaving aside the general philosophical problem of the meaning of the term causality. We will in this section touch upon some of these problems. Most of the discussion will concern increased imports as a cause of actual injury, rather than a threat thereof. The issues involved are in any event rather intricate, and the former is conceptually simpler than the latter. An understanding of the former also seems to be a necessary step toward an understanding of the latter.

5.1 The definition of "serious injury"

The appropriate interpretation of the term "serious injury" depends on the objectives of the Member governments. A government that is only concerned with aggregate social welfare might care about aggregate adjustment costs caused by too rapid adjustment to external shocks, and use these costs to measure injury. A government that is more concerned with the situation of particular politically influential groups might judge injury from reductions in the level of production in specific sectors, reduced profitability or financial viability of specific domestic industries, unemployment spells of a significant duration, etc.

Except for a mundane, almost tautological definition of "serious injury" in Article 4.1a SGA,

> ... "serious injury" shall be understood to mean a significant overall impairment in the position of a domestic industry ... ,

the term is not defined in this agreement. For instance, contrary to what is the case in the Anti-dumping or Subsidies Agreements, the Agreement on Safeguards does not contain a *de minimis* standard for import surges (although, *a priori* the term "such increased quantities" seems to address this issue). More problematic is the absence of *de minimis* standards when it comes to injury. It is yet unknown as a matter of WTO positive case law whether a claim by a socially conscious State that laying off a minute percentage of the workforce in a particular field passes the "serious injury" test.

We will not delve into any more elaborate discussion of possible interpretations of "serious injury." The particular choice of measure does not seem to matter for the discussion to follow, as long as it is strictly correlated with domestic production, which we take to be inversely related to injury.

5.2   The choice of explanatory variables

The method typically employed in economics to establish "causality" is to combine a theory for (an understanding of) how the variables are related, with econometric use of actual observations. The theory distinguishes between endogenous and exogenous variables. Endogenous variables are those whose magnitudes are determined within the theory; typical examples are price levels, and levels of production and consumption. The values of the exogenous, or explanatory, variables, on the other hand, are not determined within the theory but are imposed on the analysis. For instance, the standard demand and supply model of a specific market would assume that consumers' incomes influence demand, but would treat these incomes as determined by forces outside the analysis.

More generally, the aim of the theory is to highlight how the exogenous factors contribute to determining the endogenous variables of interest. The theory in this sense predicts how exogenous factors *cause* a particular situation. Clearly, the predictive power of such a theory depends crucially on the choice of exogenous variables. The theory must include all those variables that in actuality are important, since the econometric estimation of the theoretical relationships may otherwise be biased, and thus not trustworthy. For instance, the estimation may exaggerate the contribution to injury of the factors included in the analysis.

5.3 "Increased imports" as cause of injury

Both Article XIX GATT and the Agreement on Safeguards require that unforeseen developments have induced an *increase in imports* which has led to (or threatens to lead to) serious injury, for a safeguard to be legal. This criterion is problematic from an economic point of view: hardly any economic theory would view the volume of imports as an exogenous variable determining, say, domestic employment, or some other indicator of serious injury. Almost any theory would view imports as determined *simultaneously* with domestic employment, and determined by factors that are at least in the shorter run exogenously given to the industry.

If the object of study were imports in a particular industry, exogenous factors included in the analysis would typically be consumer incomes, prices of other products, prices of productive factors, etc. This would be a "partial equilibrium" analysis. If the focus instead were on aggregate imports, the exogenous factors would include consumer preferences, production technologies, national endowments of productive factors, etc.; this would be a "general equilibrium" analysis in which all relevant prices are determined within the model.

It is in our view central to the interpretation of the safeguard provisions in the WTO to see imports as determined simultaneously with domestic variables, such as production and employment. At the risk of offending those with their Economics 101 in fresh memory, but as a service to those who found it useful to reserve this memory slot for other matters, we will therefore in the next subsection lay out a very basic economic analysis of how imports in a particular industry are determined simultaneously with variables closely related to injury.

Generally speaking, imports can be seen as the outcome of the interaction between supply and demand in the importing country, and in the rest of the world. To see how, consider figure 4.1. The right-hand side depicts demand and supply for the product in the domestic economy. At any price less than the price indicated by "a," the demand for the product is larger than what the domestic industry is willing to supply, and for these prices there will be a demand for imports. This demand is illustrated by the downward-sloping curve on the left-hand side. Import demand is thus simply derived by subtracting domestic supply from domestic demand. The position and slope of this curve depends on factors that will be treated

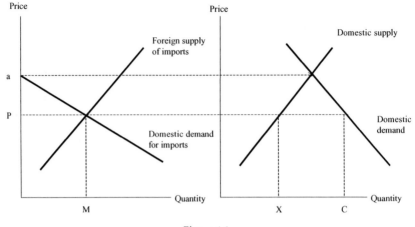

Figure 4.1

as exogenous to the analysis, but that we still might want to include in the analysis, such as domestic income levels, prices of substitute products, and the local cost of production.

In exactly the same fashion one can derive the net behavior of the rest of the world, by subtracting from its supply the volume demanded in the foreign country, for each price. The resulting curve, depicted as the upward-sloping supply curve on the left-hand side of figure 4.1, shows the supply of the import good from the rest of the world at any given price. The imported volume M, as well as the price of the product, is then given by the intersection of the import demand and supply schedules. Having thus established the equilibrium price, the domestic production volume X and the domestic consumption, volume C can be determined on the right-hand side of figure 4.1.

This very simple model illustrates two general points. First, the level of imports is determined *simultaneously* with the price at which trade occurs, and thus also with the amount supplied by the domestic industry. Hence, we might equally well say that domestic production (or some other indicator of injury) causes a certain import volume, as say that imports cause a certain level of domestic production (injury). Consequently, *it is not meaningful to view "increased import" as an exogenous event, since it must be seen as being caused by changes in the underlying determinants of imports,* some domestically determined, others determined in the rest of the world.

Second, we have to distinguish between increased imports that result from a *movement along* the supply curve of imports and increased imports due to a *shift* in this curve. A movement along the import supply curve would occur if only the import demand curve shifted. For instance, a removal of a production subsidy to the domestic industry would reduce domestic supply at any given price, and thus increase the domestic demand for imports. The new equilibrium would then be given at a new intersection point along the import supply curve, and would feature an increased volume of imports. On the other hand, the import supply curve would shift if factors determining import were to change. As an example, reduced consumer income abroad would increase foreign export supply, and thus shift the import supply curve to the right. The consequence would again be an increased volume of imports.

The reason why a movement along the import supply curve needs to be distinguished from a shift in this curve is that both changes would give rise to an increased import volume, and reduced domestic production. The two scenarios thus appear equivalent in this sense. However, the reasons behind the changes are very different. In the first case they stem from changes in the domestic economy, and in the latter from disturbances emanating from abroad.

5.4 When is a change in imports a legitimate ground for a safeguard?

Let us now return to safeguards. As illustrated by the simple framework laid out above, increased imports is not an exogenous development, but the result of more fundamental changes, affecting import demand and/or supply. A fundamental issue when implementing a safeguard regime is therefore the *type* of disturbances that could serve as legitimate grounds for safeguards. Several fundamentally different approaches may be adopted.

A highly permissible standard would be to treat *any* increase in imports, irrespective of the source of the underlying development, as a legitimate ground for a safeguard, provided it is associated with serious injury. This criterion would thus allow not only disturbances emanating from abroad as legitimate grounds, but also those stemming from domestic sources. To see one way in which the effect of increased imports could be disentangled from the direct effect of the cost shock, consider a numerical example.[19]

Suppose that a domestic industry initially produces 10 units, 12 units are imported, and the equilibrium price is 20; this situation is illustrated in

[19] A more general exposition of this line of reasoning can be found in Pindyck and Rotemberg (1987).

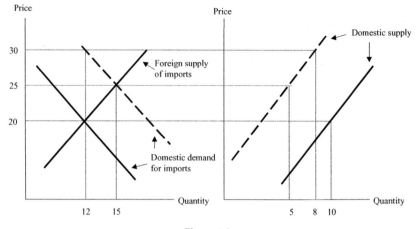

Figure 4.2

figure 4.2. The domestic industry is then hit by an adverse cost shock; this is graphically illustrated by a shift of the domestic import demand to the right (more of domestic demand is directed toward imports) in the panel on the right, and an inward shift of the domestic supply in the other panel. Now, if imports were somehow to remain at 12 units, the price would increase to 30, and local production would fall to 8 units. The resulting injury from this reduction in output would not be a valid reason for a safeguard. However, the higher price induced by the reduced supply will stimulate supply of imports, and in the new equilibrium where the price equals 25, imports will have increased to 15, and domestic production fallen to 5. The fall in domestic production from 8 to 5 induced by the increase in imports *would* then serve as a basis for a safeguard. Hence, according to this criterion, a safeguard could be invoked even though the source of the injury is a domestic shock, but only to the extent that imports "take advantage" of the domestic cost shock.

Consider next a substantially stricter standard. As discussed above, the "unforeseen" criterion can reasonably be interpreted to imply "not being the deliberate cause of." This could be required also with the above more permissible standard, in which case a domestic cost shock could serve as a basis for a safeguard only when it is not caused by the importing country. However, due to the moral hazard-type problems associated with safeguards, it might be argued that safeguards should be reserved for situations where the source of the disturbance is foreign. This would also solve the problem of reckless behavior by domestic private parties. In terms of the analytical framework above, this would amount to a requirement that the shock originates from the foreign import supply, rather than import demand, in order to be a legitimate basis for a safeguard. For instance, an increase in foreign productivity, which would increase the net supply of imports, would be a sufficient reason, while a deterioration of domestic productivity that leads to a higher level of imports through increased import demand, would not qualify.

In our opinion, the possibilities of abuse of the safeguard instrument suggest that the stricter criterion is preferable.[20]

5.5 Methods for attributing injury

If one knew with certainty that the shock to the system had a unique origin, and felt comfortable with the representation of the industry given in the simple framework laid out below, one could deduce whether import demand or supply had changed. In the former case the increase in imports would be associated with an increase in the price, while in the latter case there would be a fall in the price. In practice, however, several disturbances are likely to interact, simultaneously contributing to injury. This fact is acknowledged by the Agreement on Safeguards, which requires that injury shall not be attributed to imports to the extent it has other sources. In order to achieve this, the analysis thus disentangles the various sources of injury.

We will not delve into any more detailed discussion of appropriate econometric/statistical methods for empirically attributing injury – this is a far too complex issue to be addressed in a few paragraphs. Broadly speaking, the literature suggests two possible approaches to the attribution of injury. One is to econometrically estimate the relationship between injury and various possible explanatory variables, using observations on prices, imports, production, etc. The other approach is to use information

---

[20] In the US, safeguards are administered under Section 201 of the 1974 Trade Act. Interestingly, Kelly points out that the legislative history of the Act suggests that domestically induced disturbances were not meant to be legitimate grounds for safeguards in the US:

> The existence of any of these factors such as the growth in inventory would not in itself be relevant to the threat of injury from imports if it resulted from conditions unrelated to imports. Such conditions could arise from a variety of other causes, such as changes in technology or in consumer tastes, domestic competition from substitute products, plant obsolescence, or poor management.
> Senate Report, 1298, 93 Cong., 2nd Session, 20 (1974).

Kelly (1988) adds that "[a]ll these other causes can be characterized as shifts in either the demand or the domestic supply curves."

on demand and supply elasticities, and on changes in injury, to back out what exogenous changes that might have caused the observed injury. We will very superficially describe these below, just to give a feeling for how they work.

5.5.1   Econometric attribution analysis

In order to give some flavor of *one* way an econometric attribution analysis can be done empirically, we will very briefly describe the approach taken by Grossman (1986), who analyzed whether the alleged injury to the US steel industry in the early 1980s in terms of reduced employment, was due to international disturbances, or to domestic factors.[21]

The study is based on a theoretical model that in an important sense is simpler than the model sketched above: whereas in the model above there was an upward sloping supply curve for exports, Grossman assumes that exporters are willing to serve the whole domestic market at a price above a certain threshold, and not serve at all below this value. Graphically, the export supply is thus a horizontal line.[22] This may correspond to a situation where the domestic market is small relative to the world market. Grossman derives an equation that shows how the endogenous variable, domestic employment, depends on the exogenous variables such as prices of various inputs including labor, aggregate production in the US, and the price of imports.[23]

In order to assess the empirical magnitudes of these different influences, Grossman (1986) econometrically estimates the model, using actual data on the endogenous and exogenous variables. The resulting estimated parameters indicate the impact of each of the exogenous factors on employment. These estimates thus summarize the "average" contribution of each of the exogenous factors to employment during the period under consideration.

In order to verify a claim that an import surge has caused serious injury, it does not suffice to look at average relationships, of course. It must be shown that the *particular* instance of alleged serious injury at stake is caused by the factors that determine imports. That is, it must be shown that the injury would not have arisen, had the alleged development not

---

[21] For an alternative approach, see Pindyck and Rotemberg (1987).

[22] By assuming an infinitely elastic supply of imports, Grossman avoids some of the problems discussed above, with the simultaneous determination of import prices, and domestic injury, and can therefore treat the import price as an exogenous variable.

[23] The model is more sophisticated than described here. For instance, it also includes a version where the wage rate is determined endogenously, as well as time trends for various variables.

occurred. In order to investigate this, Grossman (1986) uses the estimated parameter values for counterfactual simulations.

For instance, when assessing the importance of the development of the price of imports for employment, Grossman computes the counterfactual path that the estimated model predicts employment would have followed, had the price of imports remained at the level it had in the early phase of the period, while all other explanatory variables followed their actual paths. By comparing this simulated path for employment with its actual path, one obtains a measure of the contribution of the development of the import price to employment. Similarly, one can simulate the importance of each of the other exogenous factors. Finally, comparing the outcomes of these different experiments, one can derive a measure of the degree to which the import-related variables contribute to the employment development.

It can be argued that this method does not establish more than correlation, being essentially static in its nature. However, Grossman (1986) actually uses a dynamic specification of the model, where delays in the response to exogenous disturbances are taken into account. In this richer model, it is possible to examine whether certain changes in exogenous variables *precede* changes in the level of injury. Such a pattern is usually taken as a requirement for causality to be shown.[24] But we would argue that a pure correlation analysis might also be informative. As mentioned above, if a correlation between the injury measure and (in this case) imports *cannot* be found, a causal relationship seems highly unlikely.

5.5.2 "Injury accounting"

The virtue of the econometric estimation approach is that it can give a detailed understanding of the determinants of injury. But it can often be demanding in terms of data requirements, and it might require a rather sophisticated econometric analysis, in particular when it involves the simultaneous estimation of several equations (such as separate supply and demand relationships).

An alternative approach is proposed by Kelly (1988), and is supported by Irwin (2002). The attractiveness of this approach is that it only requires data that are normally available in safeguard investigations. It builds on the simple supply and demand analysis laid out in figures 4.1 and 4.2 above. Using this model, one can easily derive the predicted relationships between the measure of injury (domestic production) and the exogenous factors

---

[24] One event preceding another related event is not enough for there to be a causality, as the well-known Christmas card example shows: these cards appear before Christmas, and can thus in a statistical sense be shown to "cause" Christmas.

determining import supply and domestic demand. These relationships will depend on demand and supply elasticities, as well as on changes in domestic demand and imports.

One can then decompose the reduction in domestic production in terms of changes in the other variables, given the elasticities. Hence, in a sense the method reverses what normally are the endogenous and the exogenous variables, by asking "given the observed elasticities, how much must the exogenous variables have changed in order to get the changes in the endogenous variable that are actually observed?" These computed changes in imports, and other factors/variables are then compared with actually observed changes. If there is a significant discrepancy between the estimated and the observed variables, the alleged causality from import changes to injury would not seem very plausible.

5.6   Imports as cause of injury threat in US – Lamb

A central issue in the dispute is whether the investigation by the US International Trade Commission adequately attributed the threat of serious injury to imports and to other factors. The procedure employed by the Commission was to identify six factors in addition to imports that might have caused injury, and then to ask whether each of these factors *individually* was more important than increased imports. The Commission found this not to be the case, and hence concluded that increased imports were an important factor threatening injury, and that it was no less important than any other factor. The complainants argued that the US International Trade Commission investigation failed to show the aggregate effects of factors other than increased imports, and that it did not demonstrate a "genuine and substantial relationship" between imports and the injury threat.

According to the Panel, the fact that the threatened injury has to be *serious*, suggests that

> . . . increased imports must not only be *necessary*, but also *sufficient* to cause or threaten a degree of injury that is "*serious*" enough to constitute a significant overall impairment in the situation of the domestic industry. We also note that there is a difference between a sole cause, on the one hand, and a necessary and sufficient cause, on the other. Any sole cause is by definition a necessary and sufficient cause, but obviously not any necessary and sufficient cause is the sole cause, it may coincide with other causes as recognised by the second sentence of SG Article 4.2(b).

(2.238)

... increased imports need *not* be the *sole* or exclusive causal factor present in a situation of serious injury or threat thereof, as the requirement not to attribute injury caused by other factors by implication recognises that *multiple* factors may be present in a situation of serious injury or threat thereof.

(2.239)

... where a number of factors, one of which is increased imports, are sufficient *collectively* to cause a significant overall impairment of the position of the domestic industry, but increased imports *alone* are not causing injury that achieves the threshold of "seriousness" ... the conditions for imposing a safeguard measure are not satisfied ... we cannot see how a causation standard that does not examine whether increased imports are both a *necessary* and *sufficient* cause for serious injury or threat thereof would ensure that injury caused by factors other than increased imports is not attributed to those imports.

(2.241)

In support of its views, the *US – Lamb* panel referred to the panel report on *US – Wheat Gluten*,[25] which was on appeal at the time of the writing of the *US – Lamb* report. The findings on causality in this report were later reversed by the AB.

The AB refers in *US – Lamb* to its findings in *US – Wheat Gluten*, and the AB reverses the *US – Lamb* Panel's causation requirements, arguing that the Agreement on Safeguards

... does not require that increased imports be "sufficient" to cause, or threaten to cause, serious injury. Nor does that Agreement require that increased imports "alone" be capable of causing, or threatening to cause, serious injury.

(170)

The AB still finds fault with the US methodology, however, but on different grounds than the Panel. It first states that the Agreement on Safeguards obliges WTO Members wishing to impose a safeguard measure to determine "whether there is a genuine and substantial relationship of cause and effect between increased imports and serious injury or threat thereof" (179). It further states that

---

[25] *United States – Definitive Safeguard Measures on Imports of Wheat Gluten from the European Communities.* WT/DS166/AB/R. December 11, 2000.

[i]n a situation where *several factors* are causing injury "at the same time," a final determination about injurious effects caused by *increased imports* can only be made if the injurious effects caused by all the different causal factors are distinguished and separated.

(179)

Hence, in the AB's eyes, the US were wrong not because increased imports must be a sufficient cause for injury but rather because the US did not distinguish the effects of factors other than increased imports from the effects that increased imports had on the domestic lamb industry. The AB thus upholds the Panel's conclusion that the US acted inconsistently with the requirement in Article 4.2(b) SGA to show causality between increased imports and the threat of serious injury.

We agree with the AB that the US International Trade Commission attribution analysis was insufficient, due to its methodological deficiencies. As also noted by Irwin (2002), the ruling seems simply based on assertions, and lacks quantitative analysis. An indication in support of the adjudicating bodies' determination that imports had not been shown to cause injury, is Irwin's (2002) observation that in *US – Lamb*, there were simultaneous increases in domestic and import prices and imports, and reductions in domestic consumption and production. These changes are inconsistent with the claim that the dominant effect behind the injury was an increase in import supply, since such an increase would reduce prices in general. Hence, the explanations must instead be sought on the import demand side. Here, reduced domestic demand would not do the trick, since this would not give rise to a price increase. However, reduced domestic supply would give rise to the type of pattern observed. Indeed, the removal of the US Wool Act subsidies that preceded the alleged injury would have had such an effect.

Irwin (2002) also employs the approach proposed by Kelly (1988) to investigate the determinants of reduced domestic output in a number of US safeguard decisions. For the case of *US – Lamb*, Irwin (2002) again finds that the reduction in domestic production resulted from an inward shift in the domestic supply schedule.

While we agree with the AB's dismissal of the USITC's analysis, we find it unsatisfactory that the AB does not explain how a satisfactory analysis is to be done. In order to improve the methods employed by national administrations in safeguard analyses, we would like to see the AB provide some indication to the Members as to how a more thorough quantitative analysis than what is currently being undertaken could be performed.

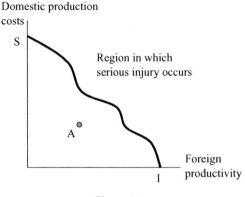

Figure 4.3

5.6.1 Differences in the criteria employed by the US International Trade Commission, the Panel and the AB to determine the legitimacy of safeguards

A situation of serious injury might arise both due to domestic reasons and to reasons clearly beyond the control of the domestic government. The Commission, the Panel and the AB seem to use different criteria for how to weigh the contributions of such internal and external sources. In order to shed some light on differences in these approaches, we will use a simple example where serious injury can result from two developments: increased foreign productivity, and increased costs of domestic production. The former is taken to be a legitimate ground for a safeguard, but not the latter. Thus, in line with the reasoning above we do not view imports as an exogenous factor, even though this analysis might also have been conducted in terms of imports and some external factor.

More importantly, we will assume that the foreign productivity and domestic production costs most of the time take on their "normal" values. But in rare occasions they may increase and possibly cause serious injury. The "normal" value thus serves as a reference point against which deviations in domestic costs and foreign productivity are measured.

The model is graphically illustrated in figure 4.3, which measures foreign productivity on the horizontal axis, and domestic production costs on the vertical axis. Point "A" represents the "normal" value of these exogenous variables. The downward sloping curve "S-I" depicts combinations of foreign productivity and domestic production costs that are sufficiently severe to give rise to "serious injury" according to some agreed-upon criterion. Hence, at any point on this curve or to the "north-east" of it, the industry is experiencing serious injury. This curve is naturally downward

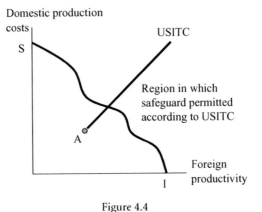

Figure 4.4

sloping, since higher foreign productivity would typically require lower domestic production costs in order for the injury level to remain constant.

We will now try to interpret the criteria employed by the US International Trade Commission, the panel and the AB to determine whether a particular realization of foreign productivity and domestic production costs suffices as a basis for a safeguard. The exposition will be somewhat speculative, in that it rests on our understanding of the different approaches, and we do not always fully understand exactly what is meant. Hopefully, however, the analysis captures salient features of the various criteria, and at the very least demonstrates the virtue of a more formal approach in that it forces a clearer, more explicit statement of the assumptions underlying the analysis.[26]

Let us start with the Commission approach. We interpret it to say that a safeguard is justified if a foreign productivity increase is a more important factor contributing to injury than an increase in domestic production costs, but where the serious injury criterion is evaluated by considering the *combined* effect. Taking the "normal" values of domestic production costs, and of foreign productivity, as a point of reference, there are thus according to this reasoning combinations of foreign productivity and domestic production costs such that the factors contribute equally to injury; let the curve USITC in figure 4.4 depict such combinations. The

---

[26] The analysis here differs from the attribution analysis discussed above, in that the latter is about gaining information about the relative contributions of the various forces to serious injury, whereas the analysis here presumes that these developments are understood. It can thus be seen as comparing criteria used to evaluate the material provided by the attribution analysis.

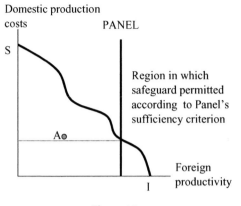

Figure 4.5

US International Trade Commission criterion would hence say that any combination of foreign productivity and domestic production costs such that both are in the "serious injury" region, and to the "south-east" of the USITC curve, would legitimize a safeguard.

Now turn to the Panel. According to (our understanding of) its interpretation, the foreign productivity increase must be both sufficient and necessary to cause serious injury, but need not be the sole cause of injury. Let us consider first the sufficiency part. It should be noted that in order to determine whether a foreign disturbance is sufficient to lead to serious injury, one cannot escape to specify the level of *the other factor(s)* for which the foreign shock is sufficient; as far as we can see, the panel did not specify this level. We will understand the Panel's argument as the requirement that the foreign productivity shock is sufficiently severe that it would lead to serious injury under "normal circumstances." Diagrammatically, this would mean that the foreign productivity and domestic production costs have to be to the "north-east" of the serious injury line, and to the "east" of the vertical line "PANEL" in figure 4.5.

The requirement that the foreign productivity increase is "necessary" for the injury to arise, is harder to understand. It seems to say that in the absence of this shock – which we take to be a situation of "normal" foreign productivity – no negative shock to domestic production costs would suffice to induce serious injury. This does not seem to us to be a sensible criterion; but maybe we have not fully understood the Panel's intentions.

Finally, turn to the AB. As far as we can see, it would allow a safeguard in any situation in the "serious injury" region. The fact that it will

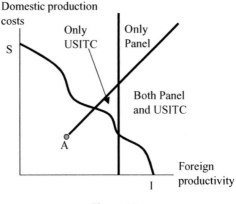

Figure 4.6

decompose the influences of the foreign productivity and the domestic production costs does not seem to hinder the imposition of a safeguard for a disturbance anywhere in this region, but possibly only the magnitude of the measure.

We can now compare the possibility of imposing safeguards using the three different criteria. A first observation is that the AB's criterion is actually more generous to safeguards than both the Panel's and the USITC criterion. In particular, the AB criterion allows for safeguards in cases where the foreign productivity shock is not the main reason for the serious injury.

Secondly, it is not possible to unambiguously rank the Panel's criterion versus that of the US International Trade Commission. On the one hand, like the AB, the Panel does not require that the foreign productivity shock is more important than other factors. On the other hand, the Panel requires (as we interpret it) that the foreign productivity shock must be sufficiently large in absolute magnitude, which is not required according to the Commission criterion. This is illustrated in figure 4.6, where the regions "Only Panel," "Only USITC," and "Both Panel and USITC" illustrate whether a safeguard would be permitted or not.

The differences between the various criteria are due to the fact that the Commission criterion for whether a safeguard is legal is relative, the Panel criterion is absolute, while the AB criterion includes all instances of serious injury.

There are two aspects that are missing from the simple illustration above, however. The first is that the discussion was concerned with a situation where there is only one external factor. Adding factors should not affect the AB's criterion, since it would just require that attribution be done with more factors. However, it is not clear exactly how the analysis should be done with several explanatory factors. But the US International Trade Commission criterion may be more sensitive: this criterion requires the foreign productivity increase to be no less important than *any* other cause. This raises the question of what is *a* cause? It seems as if with the US International Trade Commission method, one could always ensure that the effect due to any particular factor is always smaller than that of the increase in foreign productivity, by disaggregating factors finely enough.

5.6.2 "... threat of ..."

A complicating factor in the present case is the fact that the dispute deals with an alleged *threat* of serious injury, rather than injury. There is in principle nothing wrong with such a use of an escape clause. However, it should only be legal under very special circumstances. It must thus be the case that unforeseen exogenous developments have led to a situation in which the country has not yet suffered injury, but in which the government is able to foresee with a high degree of certainty that serious injury is imminent. There has thus been a drastic change in the government's understanding of the situation in the industry.

Both the Panel and the AB acknowledge the fact that a "threat of" serious injury is distinct from serious injury that has already occurred. The Panel emphasizes the special requirements that the term "threat" imposes:

> ... an examination of the existence of *threat* of serious injury implies a future-oriented analysis of the domestic industry's condition which is distinct from an examination of whether *actual* serious injury exists.
>
> (7.136)

It does think, however, that the method employed in the US International Trade Commission investigation suffices in this regard. The deficiency of the commission "threat of serious injury" – analysis is instead that the data it uses are not representative of the domestic industry. The AB, on the other hand, questions the commission interpretation of the data. It points out that lamb-meat prices actually were higher at the end of the period of investigation than at the beginning of the period, and that the US International Trade Commission without explanation used prices from a period in between the endpoints as the benchmark, a period when prices were high. Furthermore, the Commission did not comment on the fact that prices rose sharply during the last months of the investigation period, a fact that would seem central to the determination of threat of injury:

> Thus, if an industry is *not* yet in a state of serious injury, and that industry has enjoyed rising prices in the most recent past, it is, at least, questionable whether the industry is highly likely to suffer serious injury in the very near future. In such a situation, the competent authorities should devote particular attention to explaining the apparent contradiction between the most recent price rises and their view that the industry is still threatened with serious injury. In this case, the USITC offered no such explanation.
>
> (159)

We agree with the adjudicating bodies that there should be an especially onerous burden of proof in cases of not yet materialized injury. As discussed above, in order to show causality one needs a theory of how external factors threaten to cause injury. Such a theory by necessity has to be dynamic in the context of threat of injury, and this is bound to make it complex. Also, it is neither necessary nor sufficient to verify empirically that the industry presently is suffering injury. Instead a high probability of imminent future injury must be demonstrated.

6 "... necessary ..."

Article XIX GATT requires that the safeguard is *necessary* to prevent serious injury. A central aspect of this is clearly whether the *magnitude* of the safeguard is appropriate. Having found the safeguard unwarranted in the first place, the Panel and the AB reports do not discuss this aspect. We would however like to make a few reflections on this issue.

Consider the framework employed above to highlight the criteria employed by the US International Trade Commission, the Panel, and the AB. Suppose foreign productivity and domestic production costs both increase, and that the new situation is associated with serious injury according to all three criteria. The question is then: how *large* could this safeguard legally be? Article XIX.1.a GATT limits the magnitude by requiring that it is "... to the extent and for such time as may be necessary..." There are several possible interpretations of this term, however.

Consider the graphical illustration in figure 4.7, where the point D represents the situation of injury. Note that a safeguard in the form of a tariff would, from a domestic production point of view, be equivalent to a reduction in the foreign productivity, and would thus essentially shift the point D horizontally inwards. One possibility would be that once

Domestic production
costs

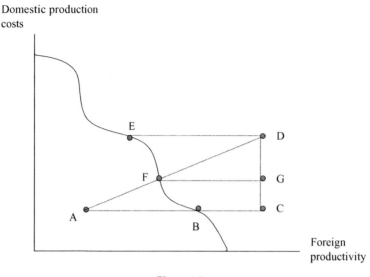

Foreign
productivity

Figure 4.7

permitted, the safeguard could be large enough to just undo the serious injury situation; this would amount to a safeguard equal to the horizontal distance between D and E; the US International Trade Commission criterion seems to be pointing in this direction.

Another possibility would be to argue, perhaps more in line with the AB, that it is only the share of serious injury that is attributable to the foreign productivity increase that should be offset. This attribution can in turn be done in different ways. For instance, decomposing the shift from A to D into a move from A to C, and from C to D, it could be argued that had it not been for the domestic production cost increase given by the distance between C and D, it would have sufficed with a safeguard equal to the distance between B and C. Another possibility might be to argue that when the industry moved from its "normal" state A to state D, it was at point F that the injury became serious. Hence, the share of the "blame" that should fall on foreign productivity is given by the distance between points F and G. In neither of these cases would the safeguard suffice to completely offset the state of serious injury.

It can be noted that, to the extent that our interpretations of the intentions of the US International Trade Commission and the AB are correct, while the Commission has a stricter criterion than the AB for determining whether safeguards are permitted at all, it allows for more trade-restricting measures in cases where they are permitted. Hence, it is unclear which is overall the more stringent criterion.

One might also conceive of other criteria for determining the magnitude of safeguards. The conclusion is thus that the interpretation of the ". . . to the extent . . . necessary . . ." criterion is far from self-explanatory, and that the interpretation might have important effects for the extent to which safeguards can be used.

7   ". . . of the effect of obligations incurred under this Agreement . . ."

Article XIX.1.a requires that unforeseen increase in imports results from ". . . the effect of obligations incurred under this Agreement . . ." This criterion has in case law largely been neglected, and so also in *US – Lamb*. There seem to be quite good reasons for this neglect.

A first problem is the interpretation of the obligations and the Agreement to which the text refers. "This Agreement" is presumably GATT 1947, indicating that liberalization that was effectively undertaken already under previous rounds should not be "counted," since industry has had time to adjust to this earlier liberalization. To take an example: suppose that pre-GATT 1947 the tariff was 30%, that it was reduced to 15% through the rounds before GATT 1994, and that it was reduced further to 10% in the Uruguay Round. In such a case, it is only the cut from 15% to 10% that would serve as the basis for a safeguard. But for how many years after the reduction from 15% to 10% should have been implemented is the Member then allowed to invoke a safeguard? An alternative interpretation, however, is that the alternative to the 10% level is not 15%, but the level that the country would choose, did GATT not exist at all. The former interpretation seems to us to be more reasonable, but the wording of the text is sufficiently ambiguous to allow for both interpretations.

A second problem with the notion of "this Agreement" is that it is not clear that it is warranted, if interpreted as referring to liberalization that has occurred through the agreement on GATT 1994. One can conceive of two main types of situations that this term seeks to address. The first is a safeguard that is invoked in a situation where liberalization has occurred but not under the Agreement, that is, when a Member has liberalized unilaterally. As far as we can see, there is no particular reason not to allow safeguards in these cases. Unilateral liberalization benefits trading partners just as negotiated liberalization (except that it is not "locked in" though an agreement). It would be detrimental to the incentives to undertake unilateral liberalization not to allow safeguards in situations where this liberalization is partly the reason for a situation of serious injury.

More difficult is the question of whether a safeguard should be allowed in a situation where a Member did not make any concession during the most recent round. Intuitively, it might seem doubtful whether a safeguard should be permitted, since the Member was not very forthcoming in the last round. However, in order to determine whether this is a reasonable ground for rejecting the possibility of using a safeguard, one would also have to consider the reasons for this unwillingness to liberalize. The industry at hand is perhaps very sensitive to the Member in question, and the level at which the tariff was bound may as such represent a significant sacrifice to the Member, even if the Member negotiated the same level in the previous round. It is possible that the Member might have chosen a higher bound level, were it not for the possibility to invoke a safeguard, should the threat of serious injury arise.

The reference to obligations incurred under the agreement must be seen as the context for safeguards: what is probably meant through this phrase is that safeguards might prove necessary in a context of trade liberalization. However, the interesting question would be the extent to which safeguard measures should be possible *independently of whether the items are bound or unbound*. There are some good arguments in favor of restricting safeguard actions to the former category only. In such a case, for bound items, Members would have a choice between either raising tariff duties by paying compensation, which would require time-consuming Article XXVIII GATT negotiation, or to unilaterally impose safeguards. The possibility of using quantitative safeguards would then be restricted to the bound items. But on unbound items Members would still have the possibility of responding to adverse developments by raising tariffs to prohibitive levels. They might in principle run the risk of facing a non-violation complaint. Keeping in mind, however, that standing case law has made it clear that such complaints are permissible only if concessions have been exchanged, this does not seem to be a promising perspective legally.

8 Concluding remarks

We believe that the basic verdict in *US – Lamb* – the illegality of the US safeguard – is correct. We also believe that the reason for the ruling – the methodological deficiencies of the US International Trade Commission investigation – is correct as well.

In our view, *US – Lamb* points to two systemic problems. First, the text requires that the cause of serious injury, or the threat thereof, is increased *imports*. But imports are not determined exogenously, they are typically the net result of thousands and thousands of decisions by producers, consumers, and governments. In other words, imports are a *proximate* but not the *ultimate* cause of injury. The Agreement on Safeguards, however, makes it clear that proximate causes suffice for a lawful imposition of safeguards. But allowing safeguards in response to increased imports in general could invite moral-hazard-like problems. To avoid such problems, a basic issue is to determine the sources of disturbances that should be legitimate grounds for safeguards, among all those causing increased imports. This is an issue on which the WTO Agreement is silent, and in this regard, we see a weakness in the *text* governing safeguards.

Second, there are problems relating to the standard of review, and, in particular, to the requirements that should be demanded from a country imposing a safeguard. We believe that some form of quantitative analysis should normally be a necessary but insufficient component to verify "unforeseen developments" and "causality."[27] Such quantification is also required in order to demonstrate the *necessity* of the chosen *magnitude* of the safeguard. It might be argued that the adjudicating bodies are constrained by the material and analysis provided by the parties, and thus are not to be blamed for the unsatisfactory analytical level in this dispute. Furthermore, the AB in this case actually did rule that the US had not shown causality. However, we feel that the adjudicating bodies could have given clearer guidance to the parties concerning the requirements of such an analysis.

One counter-argument to the demand for a more solid quantitative analysis in safeguard cases could be that there are a number of methods that seek to identify and characterize the statistical relationship between endogenous and exogenous variables. Each has its theoretical and practical drawbacks, and no single method can therefore claim to provide *the* test of causality or be *the* tool to use for non-attribution analysis. But, the fact that none of the methods is perfect does not mean that none should be applied, since the lack of quantitative methods is likely to invite even more arbitrariness.

---

[27] Indeed, as the subsequent AB report on Line Pipe itself acknowledged, the attribution exercise is a formidable task, which however has been imposed on all WTO Members. We should note here, however, that the AB made its comments in this respect when dealing with Article 5.1 SG and not with Article 4.2 SG.

Another counter-argument might be that increased requirements for safeguard investigations would disadvantage developing countries, since they might not have the resources to undertake such quantification. This is clearly an argument that needs to be taken seriously. However, we believe that many developing countries have indeed the capacity to undertake at least a basic quantitative analysis. And if a country cannot perform such an analysis, one may wonder, how does it know the source of the injury? Also, whether developing countries would gain or lose from such an increase in the requirements for a safeguard investigation depends not only on how their ability to impose safeguards is affected. It will also depend on the extent to which they will be less exposed to safeguards in their export markets.

Finally, one should not expect econometric or other quantitative methods to provide a "bright line." On the contrary, the systematic introduction of such methods will make the adjudication process more complex, and would make the adjudicating bodies dependent on expert witnesses, as long as such expertise is not incorporated into these bodies.[28] But there is something fundamentally unsatisfactory about a state of affairs where there exists a science that is largely devoted to developing methods for determining causality and attribution, and, at the same time, WTO Members almost completely ignore its existence in their investigations concerning the very same issues. It is the role of adjudicating bodies to sensitize investigating authorities in this respect.

References

Bhagwati, Jagdish. 1981. *Import Competition and Response.* Chicago, IL: University of Chicago Press.

Deardorff, Alan. 1987. Safeguards Policy and the Conservative Social Welfare Function. In Henryk Kierzkowski, *Protection and Competition in International Trade: Essays in Honor of W. M. Corden.* Blackwell: Oxford.

Dixit, Avinash. 1987. Trade and Insurance with Moral Hazard. *Journal of International Economics*, 23: 201–20.

Dixit, Avinash. 1989a. Trade and Insurance with Imperfectly Observed Outcomes. *Quarterly Journal of Economics*, February: 195–203.

1989b. Trade and Insurance with Adverse Selection. *Review of Economic Studies*, 56: 235–48.

---

[28] The WTO Research Division could play an important role in this regard.

Eaton, Jonathan and Gene Grossman. 1985. Tariff as Insurance: Optimal Commercial Policy when Domestic Markets are Incomplete. *Canadian Journal of Economics*, 18: 258–72.

Grossman, Gene. 1986. Imports as a Cause of Injury: the Case of the U.S. Steel Industry. *Journal of International Economics* 121.

Irwin, Douglas A. 2002. Causing Problems? The WTO Review of Causation and Injury Attribution in U.S. Section 201 Cases. Mimeo.

Kelly, Kenneth. 1988. The Analysis of Causality in Escape Clause Cases. *Journal of Industrial Economics*, 37: 187–207.

Mussa, Michael. 1981. Government Policy and the Adjustment Process. Pp. 73–120 in Jagdish Bhagwati, *Import Competition and Response*. Chicago, IL: University of Chicago Press.

Neary, Peter. 1981. Inter-Sectoral Capital Mobility, Wage Stickiness, and the Case for Adjustment Assistance. Pp. 39–67 in Jagdish Bhagwati, *Import Competition and Response*. Chicago, IL: University of Chicago Press.

Newbery, David M. G. and Joseph E. Stiglitz. 1981. *The Theory of Commodity Price Stabilization*. Oxford: Oxford University Press.

Pindyck, Robert and Julio Rotemberg. 1987. Are Imports to Blame? Attribution of Injury under the 1974 Trade Act. *Journal of Law and Economics*, 30: 101–22.

Sykes, Alan. 1990. GATT Safeguards Reform: the Injury Test. In Michael Trebilcock and R. York, *Fair Exchange: Reforming Trade Remedy Laws*. Policy Study 11. C. D. Toronto: Howe Institute.

  1991. Protectionism as a "Safeguard': a Positive Analysis of GATT Article XIX with Normative Speculations. *University of Chicago Law Review*, Winter.

5

EC – Bed Linen
European Communities – Anti-dumping Duties on
Imports of Cotton-Type Bed Linen from India*

MERIT E. JANOW AND ROBERT W. STAIGER

1 Introduction

As comprehensively argued elsewhere in this volume,[1] the WTO's anti-dumping provisions reflect political compromises that mask an underlying lack of consensus on the value and purpose of an antidumping regime at the national level. This is an old story that has been long argued in academic and policy circles. What is noteworthy recently is the significant increase in the use of trade remedies, especially by developing economies. As a result, while the post-Uruguay Round period is generally marked by greater economic openness resulting from various forms of trade liberalization, the use of trade remedies is no longer primarily the province of OECD economies. Indeed, the introduction and use of trade remedies is proliferating around the world.[2]

As we discuss in greater detail herein, it is difficult to make economic sense of the core purposes of the anti-dumping provisions, except in the rare instances of true predation. Of course, there are other non-economic efficiency motivations that may help to explain the rule framework – such as protection of domestic producers, a sense of "unfairness," or the view that this method of helping those hurt by imports is a necessary price or safety valve for nations that are taking steps in the direction of market opening.

* This study has benefited from the suggestions of seminar participants at the Conference on the Principles of Trade Law: The World Trade Organization, held on February 6–7, 2003 in Philadelphia, and especially from the comments of Steve Charnovitz, William Davey, Wilfred Ethier, Gary Horlick, Henrik Horn, Petros C. Mavroidis, Patrick Messerlin, Thomas Prusa, and Donald Regan.
[1] See, Howse and Neven, *Argentina – Ceramic Tiles.*   [2] See, Prusa (2001).

The GATT produced a fairly large number of anti-dumping disputes but few of the panel reports were adopted and implemented.[3] The WTO dispute settlement process has seen a large number of anti-dumping cases brought before it – some forty-five disputes as of this writing, which places anti-dumping as one of the primary areas generating disputes. The WTO anti-dumping rules are highly procedural in nature, designed to give flexibility to varying national practices within a framework that imposes a certain degree of procedural transparency as well as comparability on national dumping and injury methodologies. Put concretely, panels do not investigate *de novo* whether dumping, injury, and causation have occurred but rather review whether or not the national administrating authority has complied with the international obligations contained in the WTO Agreement with respect to those elements of its investigation.

This area of dispute settlement is also one of the handful of substantive areas that has generated a particularly high degree of controversy, not surprisingly within those jurisdictions that have lost in dispute settlement. A specific, but recurring, expression of concern is that the WTO panels have failed to give appropriate deference to national practices, which deference is a key and uniquely highlighted feature of the anti-dumping rules as reflected in the standard of review contained in Article 17.6 therein. Allegations of over-reaching or judicial activism can imply a systemic defect and deserve close scrutiny. Indeed, public perceptions about the WTO dispute settlement system overall have been framed – perhaps disproportionately so – by the anti-dumping cases.

This study summarizes and critically reviews one anti-dumping dispute brought before the WTO concerning the European Communities Anti-Dumping Duties on Imports of Cotton-Type Bed Linen from India, euphemistically referred to herein as *EC – Bed Linen*. This case involves the methodology used by the EC with respect to anti-dumping duties in imports of cotton-type bed linen. The discussion that follows undertakes a three-step analysis. In these three steps we seek to distinguish different levels of economic and legal analysis, beginning with the most general and turning in sequence to the more specific legal and economic issues raised by the *EC – Bed Linen* dispute.

First, we consider the economic basis for the WTO provisions that are at the heart of this dispute. More specifically we ask: What are the underlying

---

[3] According to Horlick and Clark, of seven GATT panels brought under the anti-dumping Code, only three have been adopted and of those only two have been implemented. See, Horlick and Clark (1997), p. 313.

goals of the various WTO provisions touched upon in the Bed Linen case, and are the goals themselves sensible from an economic perspective?

Second, we present and evaluate the key factual and legal elements of the case, focusing primarily on the legal issues raised by the case in its final disposition, e.g. whether at the Panel or the Appellate Body (AB) level, that seem particularly important to understanding the stated legal and economic logic of the case.[4] More specifically we ask: Have the reviewing Panels and the AB applied the law consistently, mindful of WTO precedent? Are the panelists and the AB doing what they state they are doing? Are the judgments well-grounded in legal argument? Is there ambiguity in the applicable law, as drafted? If so, how is it resolved – e.g. with deference to national measures, or through judicial license?

And third, we consider and evaluate the particular legal and economic issues and methodologies raised by the dispute. More specifically we ask: In light of the underlying goals of the relevant WTO provisions, and taking them as given, was the resolution of the substantive economic issues around which the case revolved based on sound economic principles?

2   General economic analysis

The *EC – Bed Linen* case raises several levels of questions from an economic perspective. A first-level question is: What are the goals of the various WTO provisions touched upon in this case, and are the goals themselves sensible from an economic perspective? This is the question that we take up in this section. A second-level question is the following: In light of these goals, and taking them as given, was the resolution of the substantive economic issues around which the specific case revolved based on sound economic principles? This second-level question will be taken up in section 4, after the legal aspects of the case have been fully presented and evaluated in section 3.

What, then, are the goals of the various WTO provisions touched upon in this case? We attempt to answer this question in two steps. First, we consider Article VI GATT itself, within which the basic right of member governments to impose anti-dumping duties is described. Second, we consider the specific articles of the WTO Agreement on Implementation

---

[4] Most recently in November 2002, a 21.5 panel report was released concerning India's complaint that the EC's adjustment measures did not comply with the Dispute Settlement Body's ruling in the original dispute. This report focuses primarily on details of the revised EC methodology for calculating the dumping margins, on cumulation and on injury calculations. It is not discussed in any detail herein.

of Article VI (the Anti-dumping Agreement) that became the key areas of dispute in this case, namely, Articles 2.4.2 and 2.2.2.

Article VI of GATT begins by stating that "the contracting parties recognize that dumping, by which products of one country are introduced into the commerce of another country at less than the normal value of the products, is to be condemned if it causes or threatens material injury to an established industry in the territory of a contracting party or materially retards the establishment of a domestic industry." This statement appears to suggest that the goal of Article VI GATT as it relates to anti-dumping duties (Article VI GATT provides as well for countervailing duties) is, if not to discourage or prevent outright the practice of dumping in international trade, then at the very least to provide governments with the ability to shield their producers from the effects of dumping with extraordinary tariff responses.[5]

The tariff responses to dumping provided for in Article VI GATT are extraordinary not so much because they permit governments to raise tariffs above their bound levels in the face of import-induced injury – there are a variety of other "safeguard" provisions that might be utilized by a WTO member government to achieve this – but because they allow for *discriminatory* tariffs to be imposed and do not provide for the government of the country from which the dumped exports originate to seek *compensation.*

From a standard economic perspective, it is very difficult to make sense of the goal suggested by a reading of Article VI GATT. Unless dumping is truly predatory, which in practice appears rarely to be the case,[6] there is no standard efficiency rationale for the position that dumped imports should be treated any differently by a government than imports that are not dumped. Dumped or not, a given volume of imports will have the same impact on prices and incomes in the domestic economy once it crosses the border: why, then, should a government be permitted to respond to imports that are not dumped in one way (e.g. an Article XIX GATT "safeguard" action) but be granted the use of a special response (anti-dumping duties) when those imports are dumped?[7]

---

[5] The interesting drafting history of GATT's anti-damping provisions are discussed in Jackson (1969), pp. 401–24.

[6] See, for example, Shin (1998).

[7] Hence in standard formal economic models, governments exhibit no special concern for dumped imports as compared to imports that are not dumped, and this is true whether these governments are taken to be interested only in achieving maximum national income or are allowed to be sensitive as well to distributional/political economy concerns (e.g.

Of course, the citizens of a country may decide that dumping is simply "bad" or "unfair" in an ethical sense. These citizens might then ask
their government to prevent such imports from entering the domestic
market, if these dumped imports contribute to overall import volumes
that materially injure producers in the domestic economy. This feature
of preferences, like consumer preferences more generally, would typically
be viewed as sovereign in economic analysis, and so economic arguments
cannot be utilized to so clearly and directly assert that dumped and non-
dumped imports should be treated the same in this case.[8] Indeed, from
this broader perspective, if enough member-governments agree with this
sentiment, then a reason for these governments to provide extraordinary
tariff responses to dumped imports within the articles of the GATT/WTO
could arise.[9] One might interpret the statement at the beginning of Article
VI GATT as reflecting something like this kind of sentiment on the part
of member governments.

To see how this broader perspective could provide a reason for permitting extraordinary tariff responses to dumped imports within the articles
of GATT, let us suppose that member-governments do share this sentiment, but let us suppose further that there were no Article VI GATT. In
this setting, if dumped imports began entering into a country's market
and started contributing to overall import volumes that materially injure
domestic producers, the government of this country might be compelled
(by its citizens) to block the dumped imports at the border. But with no
discriminatory means to do so at its disposal, the government would have
to make use of one of the non-discriminatory safeguard provisions of
the GATT/WTO, and could be compelled to eliminate all injury-causing
imports with a safeguard action, when all it really wanted to do was prevent
the dumped imports from entering its markets. From this broader perspective, the logic of a provision such as Article VI, which provides for

concerns that might give rise to a disproportionate emphasis on producer interests beyond
that implied by economic efficiency).

[8] One might argue that at a minimum a more "cosmopolitan" view should be insisted upon,
so that if dumping into the domestic market is deemed unfair when it is done by a foreign
firm then one should insist that it should also be deemed unfair when it is done by a domestic
firm, and therefore antidumping actions against the former should also consistently apply
to the latter. However, imposing such a cosmopolitan viewpoint on the citizens of a country
goes against the spirit of accepting preferences as sovereign, and so we do not impose it
here.

[9] A similar line of argument might be developed for countervailing duty responses to subsidized exports, though in this regard it is interesting to observe that the language of Article VI
GATT does not "condemn" foreign exports that benefit from foreign government subsidies
in the way that it condemns foreign exports that are dumped.

a discriminatory tariff response in this circumstance, might be understood.[10]

A key question then becomes: Do the particular features of the tariff response allowed by Article VI GATT make sense from this broader perspective? As we have just illustrated, the ability to respond selectively on a discriminatory basis to dumped imports could make sense in this context.[11] But what about the lack of compensation provisions associated with the imposition of anti-dumping duties? As we observed above, this is a second distinguishing feature of anti-dumping duties. As we now argue, this feature is not easily justified even from this broader perspective, and the incentives created by this feature may help to explain an underlying reason for the central problem with anti-dumping actions within the GATT/WTO system, namely, the apparent tendency of member-governments to abuse these actions for protectionist purposes.

The essential point is simple. Compensation provisions in the GATT/WTO play a dual role. On the one hand, these provisions allow member-governments that suffer nullification or impairment as a result of the policy actions of another member-government to achieve some restitution. From this vantage point, it would seem strange to require that a first government compensate a second government for the loss of market access when the former raises its tariffs to prevent the latter's firms from dumping into its markets, given that dumping is viewed as unfair by the member governments.[12] But from the point of view of achieving efficient international policy outcomes, there is a second role for compensation that is potentially important: by seeking compensation, the second

---

[10] The logic of permitting a discriminatory response to dumping might also be understood from the perspective that such a response could help to protect third-country exporters from having their access to a foreign market eroded by dumped competing exports. On the general importance for the GATT/WTO of rules that can prevent the erosion by third parties of negotiated market access concessions, see Bagwell and Staiger (forthcoming).

[11] This is not to say that the ability to impose discriminatory tariffs comes without a cost. There are a number of possible costs associated with deviations from non-discrimination that could be relevant (see, for example, Bagwell and Staiger, 2002, Ethier, 2002, and Horn and Mavroidis, 2001. It is simply that the costs of the discrimination would have to be judged against the possible benefits as described above.

[12] The importance of the distinction between provisions that allow extraordinary tariff measures in response to "fair trade," such as Article XIX, and those that allow extraordinary tariff measures in response to "unfair trade," such as Article VI, is emphasized in the AB report (section IV) on *Line Pipe from Korea*. Our point here is that, while distinct features across these provisions may be warranted along some dimensions (e.g. whether discrimination is permitted), a distinction may not be warranted along the dimension of compensation.

government can force the first government (that takes the original policy action) to face more completely the full costs of its decision. This role for compensation can be important if governments are to face the "right" incentives when making their policy decisions, i.e. the incentives that lead them to make policy choices that are efficient from a world-wide perspective.[13]

Within the context of the GATT/WTO, compensation for the nullification or impairment of a previously negotiated market access concession has generally been interpreted to take one of several forms. The preferred form is the offer of an additional market access concession on other goods, so that the "overall" level of market access is maintained. But when this proves to be not feasible, the fallback is the withdrawal of equivalent concessions by the nullified party, so that the "balance" of market access concessions established by the original negotiation is maintained through measured retaliation.

As a consequence of this line of thinking, it may be argued that a basic problem with the provisions that permit the imposition of anti-dumping duties is that they suspend the general compensation/retaliation principle that otherwise permeates the GATT/WTO.[14] This lack of required compensation may in turn help explain why it is evidently so tempting for governments to find myriad ways to "over-utilize" anti-dumping protection: this is one route to protection where GATT/WTO rules do not require governments to face the full costs of their actions. An implication of this line of argument is that disputes over anti-dumping actions might be mitigated – because the underlying incentives of governments to misrepresent the circumstances that warrant anti-dumping duties would be reduced – if some form of compensation/retaliation rights were created when anti-dumping duties are imposed.[15]

While it may sound far-fetched and impractical to suggest that some form of compensation/retaliation rights should be created when

---

[13] By "efficient from a world-wide perspective," we mean efficient in light of the objectives of each of the member governments. When such efficiency is achieved, there is no further alteration in the policies of the member governments that could serve the objectives of one of them without hindering the objectives of another.

[14] An analogous argument for compensation could apply to countervailing duties. See also note 9 above.

[15] We observe that even the anti-dumping investigation process by itself can offer protection to import-competing producers (see Staiger and Wolak, 1994, and also Prusa, 2001), and so in principle the idea of requiring compensation could be extended to investigations even when they end in a negative finding. In practice however, the argument for compensation would be strongest when anti-dumping duties are imposed.

anti-dumping duties are imposed, when viewed from the perspective of actual anti-dumping practice the suggestion may be less dramatic than it first appears. This is because some compensation is often involved in the resolution of anti-dumping investigations, and so the suggestion above can be restated as a recommendation to make compensation/retaliation a more explicit, calibrated, and systematic feature of the anti-dumping rules.

For example, it can be said that compensation is taken by the exporters when an anti-dumping case ends in a "price undertaking" in which exporters agree to raise prices and no duty is imposed. Similarly, a form of compensation is present when anti-dumping investigations end in the imposition of voluntary export restraints (as in the US steel experience of the 1980s). And finally, one possible interpretation of the proliferation of anti-dumping laws and actions around the world documented by Prusa (2001) is that this new use of anti-dumping actions by the traditional targets of anti-dumping duties represents a blunt instrument for exacting compensation from the traditional users of anti-dumping actions by "retaliating" with anti-dumping actions of one's own.

From this perspective, compensation/retaliation is already and increasingly very much a part of anti-dumping actions. But as the above examples suggest, this compensation/retaliation is not provided for and governed in an explicit, systematic, and calibrated way by GATT/WTO rules. The economic arguments above suggest that, as it has done to great effect in other areas, it is conceivable that the GATT/WTO could harness retaliation and convert it to a tool of international order in the area of anti-dumping actions.

We next consider the specific articles of the Anti-dumping Agreement that became the key areas of dispute in this case, namely, Articles 2.4.2 and 2.2.2. Here we simply observe that these articles represent detailed attempts by the member-governments to spell out the methodologies that are acceptable for determining when anti-dumping actions may be taken and what level of actions are appropriate. Presumably, the reason that member-governments have felt the need to "micro-manage" the methodologies that may be used to determine if anti-dumping actions are warranted and the appropriate level of these actions is that, given the room, governments will find ways to abuse the opportunity to take anti-dumping actions for protectionist purposes.

While these articles (and the other articles of the Anti-dumping Agreement) can therefore be given a sensible interpretation within the context of Article VI, the fact remains that member-governments have evidently not felt the need to spell out to nearly the same degree the conditions under which provisions that permit more reciprocal re-imposition of protection − through the accompanying use of compensation − may be invoked. These provisions include the temporary safeguards provided for in Article XIX GATT as well as the permanent "escapes" provided in the renegotiation provisions of Article XXVIII GATT .[16] Presumably, it is understood that the right of compensation goes a long way toward making the decision to re-impose protection "incentive compatible," thereby obviating to some degree the need for detailed rules covering the circumstances under which such actions may be taken.

3 Factual and legal claims

3.1 Introduction and overview

This case, brought by India, involves the methodology employed by the European Communities with respect to certain anti-dumping duties imposed on imports of cotton type bed linen. The dumping analysis went as follows: the EC undertook a sample of Indian exporters and also created a reserve sample in the event that companies in the sample refused to cooperate. In the sample, one of the five companies was found to have sales in the home markets that were appropriately representative; however, these were outside the ordinary course of trade. As a result, the "normal value" for all of the Indian producers was calculated on the basis of constructed value, which is provided for under Article 2.2.2 of the Anti-dumping Agreement.

The EC based its calculation of administrative, selling, and general costs and of profits on the amounts for the one company that was found to have sales of the same merchandise, although outside the ordinary course of trade. With respect to the injury analysis, the EC undertook a sample of domestic producers comprising seventeen EC companies.

The reviewing Panel concluded that the EC actions were inconsistent with various provisions of the Anti-dumping Agreement. Specifically, the EC was found to have acted inconsistently with its obligations under

---

[16] It is interesting to observe in this regard that the WTO Agreement on Safeguards couples the suspension of compensation rights for the first three years of a safeguard action (Article 8.3) with a more detailed set of rules to which safeguards qualifying for this exemption from compensation must conform, suggesting a trade-off perceived by the member-governments between provisions for compensation and detailed rules for re-imposing protection.

Articles 2.4.4, 3.4 and 15 of the Anti-dumping Agreement in determining the existence of anti-dumping margins on the basis of a methodology that incorporated the practice of zeroing; failing to evaluate all relevant factors having bearing on the state of the domestic industry; considering information for producers not part of the domestic industry; and failing to explore possibilities of constructive remedies before applying anti-dumping duties.[17] The EC appealed and India cross-appealed certain issues.

The AB focused on two sets of issues:

- First, whether the Panel erred in finding that the practice of "zeroing" as applied by the EC, is inconsistent with Article 2.4.2 of the Anti-dumping Agreement; and
- Second, whether the Panel erred in finding that the method for calculating amounts for administrative, selling, and general costs and profits provided for in article 2.2.2(ii) of the Anti-dumping Agreement may be applied where there is data for only one other exporter or producer; and in calculating the amount of profits under that provision, whether a Member may exclude sales by other exporters or producers that are not made in the ordinary course of trade.

3.2   A key issue: the practice of zeroing

Let us first examine the issue of "zeroing" and its consistency with Article 2.4.2 of the Anti-dumping Agreement. Article 2.4.2 explains how domestic investigating officials must proceed when establishing the existence of dumping. It states, in the pertinent part, that

> The existence of margins of dumping during the investigation phase shall normally be established on the basis of a comparison of a weighted average normal value with a weighted average of prices of all comparable export transactions or by a comparison of normal value and export prices on a transaction to transaction basis. A normal value established on a weighted

[17] See AB Report para. 4. In addition, the panel found that the EC actions were not inconsistent with the Anti-dumping Agreement with respect to calculating the amount for profit in constructed normal value; considering all imports from India as dumped in the analysis of injury caused by dumped imports; considering information for producers comprising the domestic industry but not among the sampled producers in analyzing the state of the industry; examining the accuracy and adequacy of the evidence prior to initiation; establishing industry support for the application; and providing public notice of its final determination. There were a number of procedural issues considered by the Panel that were not reviewed on appeal. These are not discussed herein.

average basis may be compared to prices of individual export transactions if the authorities find a pattern of export prices which differ significantly among different purchasers, regions or time periods, and if an explanation is provided as to why such differences cannot be taken into account appropriately by the use of a weighted average to weighted average or transaction to transaction comparison.[18]

Article 2.4.2 therefore establishes two alternative methodologies: (1) that the investigating authorities compare the weighted-average normal value with a weighted average of all comparable export transactions, or (2) by a comparison of normal value and export prices on a transaction basis.

Zeroing, as practiced by the EC, involved identification of the product, which in this case was different models or types of cotton type bed linen, and determining a weighted-average normal value and a weighted-average export price for each *model*. The EC then compared the weighted-average normal value with the weighted-average export price. For some models, the normal value was higher than the export price and in those cases the export price was subtracted from the normal value and a "positive dumping margin" for each model was determined. For some, the normal value was less than the export price, and by subtracting the export price from the normal value for these models, the EC established a "negative dumping margin" for each model. Obviously in this latter category, dumping had not occurred since the export price was greater than the normal price.

When establishing the overall-dumping margin for the product as a whole, the EC undertook a two-stage analysis, and added up the amounts that it calculated as dumping margins. Any negative dumping margin was treated as a "zero." After adding up the positives and the zeroes, the EC would then divide this sum by the cumulative total quantity to come up with the average weighted dumping margin of that product.[19]

A simple example can help to illustrate the broad features of the EC's zeroing methodology. Suppose that, for the purpose of the export transactions under investigation, there are three models, or "types," of bed linen, labeled type 1, type 2 and type 3. Let us call v_1 the weighted-average normal value of type 1, v_2 the weighted-average normal value of type 2, and v_3 the weighted-average normal value of type 3. Similarly, let us call p_1 the weighted-average price of type 1, p_2 the weighted-average price of type 2, and p_3 the weighted-average price of type 3. Finally, let

[18] Para. 50.   [19] Para. 47.

us call e_1 the value of export transactions for type 1, e_2 the value of export transactions for type 2, and e_3 the value of export transactions for type 3.

According to the EC methodology, in a first stage the margin of dumping for each type of bed linen is calculated. Letting d_1 denote the dumping margin for type 1, this is calculated as $d_1 = v_1 - p_1$ for type 1. For types 2 and 3, the analogous calculations are, respectively, $d_2 = v_2 - p_2$ and $d_3 = v_3 - p_3$. If, say, for type 1, the weighted-average price were below the weighted-average normal value, then we would have $p_1 < v_1$ and therefore $d_1 > 0$: in stage 1 the EC would calculate a positive dumping margin for bed linen of type 1. Similarly, if for type 2 the weighted-average price were below the weighted-average normal value, then we would have $p_2 < v_2$ and therefore $d_2 > 0$: in stage 1 the EC would calculate a positive dumping margin for bed linen of type 2. But suppose for type 3 the weighted-average price were *above* the weighted-average normal value: then we would have $p_3 > v_3$ and therefore $d_3 < 0$, and in stage 1 the EC would calculate a *negative* dumping margin for bed linen of type 3.

The issue of zeroing arises in the second stage of the EC methodology, where these type-specific margins are combined in order to calculate an overall margin of dumping for the product under investigation. One approach would be to combine these type-specific margins using export shares as weights to calculate a trade-weighted average of the type-specific margins. Letting D denote the overall margin of dumping calculated under this first approach, we would have

$$D = [(e_1 d_1) + (e_2 d_2) + (e_3 d_3)]/[e_1 + e_2 + e_3].$$

Notice that in the numerator of D, the positive margins for types 1 and 2 (d_1 and d_2) are added together with the negative margin for type 3 (d_3). For this reason, under this first approach, positive dumping margins on some types of the product can be offset by negative margins on other types of the product when calculating the overall margin of dumping for the product under investigation.

But this is *not* what the EC methodology does. Instead, under the EC's "zeroing" methodology negative margins are treated as "zeroes" in this second-stage calculation. Consequently, according to the zeroing methodology, d_3 – which recall is negative – would be set to zero. Letting Z denote the overall margin of dumping calculated under the EC's zeroing approach, we would have

$$Z = [(e_1 d_1) + (e_2 d_2)]/[e_1 + e_2 + e_3].$$

Notice that in the numerator of Z, only the positive margins for types 1 and 2 (d_1 and d_2) are present: the negative margin for type 3 (d_3) is excluded from the calculation (d_3 is set to zero). For this reason, under the EC's zeroing approach, positive dumping margins on some types of the product *cannot* be offset by negative margins on other types of the product when calculating the overall margin of dumping for the product under investigation. As a consequence, in our simple example (but more generally as well, as long as there are some negative margins so that some zeroing takes place), it must be that the EC's zeroing approach leads to a higher calculated overall margin of dumping for the product under investigation than would be calculated in the absence of zeroing (i.e. as a simple statistical matter, it must be that $Z > D$).

The Panel found that the methodology, which included zeroing negative margins, was inconsistent with Article 2.4.2 of the Anti-dumping Agreement.[20] The EC contested this point and argued Article 2.4.2 required a comparison with the "weighted average of prices of all comparable export transactions" which is not the same as requiring a comparison with a weighted average of all export transactions. The EC argument hinged on the term "comparable" and it argued that Article 2.4.2 provides no guidance on how the margins for each type or model should be combined. The EC argued that zeroing takes place at a second stage in the analysis and that the Panel failed to give proper weight to this comparability element in Article 2.4.2.

The AB interpreted the margins of dumping to which Article 2.4.2 refer to be margins of dumping for a product – in this case cotton-type bed linen. It further held that it saw nothing in Article 2.4.2 that suggests a necessary two-stage process nor a distinction between types or models of the same product on the basis of these two stages. It recalled the methodology of Article 2.4 that states the comparison of weighted average normal value will be compared "with a weighted average of all prices of comparable export transactions."

Importantly, the AB agreed with the interpretation of the Panel that by zeroing the negative dumping margins, the EC did not "take fully into account the entirety of the prices of some export transactions . . . Instead, the European Communities treated those export prices as if they were less than they were. This, in turn, inflated the result from the calculation of the margin of dumping." The AB further argued that a comparison between export price and normal value that does not take fully into account the

---

[20] See Panel Report, para 6.119.

prices of all comparable export transactions (including the practice of zeroing) "is not a fair comparison between export price and normal value as required by Article 2.4 and Article 2.4.2."[21] Hence, the AB upheld the Panel's finding that the practice of zeroing "when establishing the existence of margins of dumping as applied by the European Communities is inconsistent with Article 2.4.2."

3.3 Methods for calculating margins under Article 2.2.2 of the Agreement.

Another central issue on appeal had to do with the Panel's interpretation of Article 2.2.2(ii) of the Anti-dumping Agreement. Article 2.2 provides that the margin of dumping for the product may be determined by comparison of the export price of the product with a constructed normal value consisting of the cost of production of the product in the country of origin plus a reasonable amount for administrative, selling, and general costs as well as for profits. Article 2.2.2 sets out how these are calculated.[22]

The first issue under Article 2.2.2(ii) of the Anti-dumping Agreement is whether the method of calculating administrative, selling, and general costs and profits can be applied where there is data for only one other exporter or producer and a second issue reviewed by the AB was whether in calculating the amount for profits, a Member may exclude sales by other exporters that are not made in the ordinary course of trade. India

---

[21] See para 55. On the question of comparability, the AB noted that the product definition was cotton-type bed linen. The EC argued that its interpretation of Article 2.4.2 of the Anti-dumping Agreement was a "permissible interpretation" within the meaning of Article 17.6(ii) of the Anti-dumping Agreement. The Panel disagreed and the AB confirmed their finding.

[22] The Article states: "For purpose of paragraph 2, the amounts for administrative, selling and general costs for profits shall be based on actual data pertaining to production and sales in the ordinary course of trade of the like product by the exporter or producer under investigation. When such amounts cannot be determined on this basis, the amounts may be determined on the basis of:

(i) The actual amounts incurred and realized by the exporter or producer in question in respect of production and sales in the domestic market of the country of origin of the same general category of products; (ii) the weighted average, of the actual amounts incurred and realized by other exporters or producers subject to investigation in respect of production and sales of the like product in the domestic market of the country of origin; (iii) any other reasonable method, provided that the amount for profit so established shall not exceed the profit normally realized by other exporters or producers on sales of products of the same general category in the domestic market of the country of origin.

appealed the findings of the Panel on these two issues and the AB reversed the Panel findings.

On the first issue, the Panel concluded that Article 2.2.2(ii) may be applied where there is data concerning profit and administrative, selling, and general costs for only one other producer or exporter; and further that under this same Article sales not in the ordinary course of trade are excluded from the determination of the profit calculation of a constructed normal value.[23]

As noted, the AB reversed the Panel findings on these two points. Looking at the language of Article 2.2.2(ii), the AB noted that it refers to "the weighted average of the actual amounts incurred and realized by other exporters or producers." In the AB's view, this use of the plural in the article precludes including the singular case. Moreover, the very phrase "weighted-average" cannot be calculated on the basis of only one exporter or producer. In the AB's view, in contrast to the Panel, this weighted-average methodology is the indispensable feature to the calculation method[24] and it is not a concept that is relevant where there is not information from more than one other producer to be considered.

On the question of the exclusion of profits that are not made in the ordinary course of trade, the AB again looked to the language of Article 2.2.2(ii) which states that administrative, selling, and general costs and profits are determined on the basis of "the weighted average of the actual amounts incurred and realized by other exporters or producers" and noted that this does not make exceptions or qualifications regardless of whether those amounts are incurred and realized on production and sales in the ordinary course of trade or not.[25] The AB drew support for this textual interpretation given that the method set out in Article 2.2.2(ii) is one of three alternative methods that can be applied when the administrative, selling, and general costs and profits cannot be determined by the principal method which is set out in the chapeau of Article 2.2.2, which refers to "actual data pertaining to production and sales in the ordinary course of trade."[26] Hence, the AB interpreted this to mean that sales not in the ordinary course of trade are to be excluded when calculating amounts for administrative, selling, and general costs and profits.

By reversing the Panel findings on these two points, the AB concluded that the EC acted inconsistently with Article 2.2.2(ii) of the Anti-dumping Agreement on these points.

---

[23] See para. 6.75 of the Panel Report and para. 6.87.   [24] See para. 75.
[25] See para. 80.   [26] See para. 82.

3.4   Legal and policy questions

In our view, the Panel and the AB got it right that the zeroing methodology as utilized by the EC in this case served to inflate margins and
thus produced results inconsistent with the obligations set out in the
Anti-dumping Agreement. Yet whether one agrees or disagrees with that
conclusion, the legal reasoning utilized by the Panel and the AB to reach
that conclusion deserves some further scrutiny. In particular, we focus on
the treatment of zeroing as well as the deference standard that was applied
in this case.

As discussed above, the practice of zeroing was reviewed in the context
of Article 2.4.2 of the Anti-dumping Agreement. It is interesting to recall
that in the pre-Uruguay Round period, the 1979 Antidumping Code provided fairly detailed guidance on margin calculation methods. It did not
specify however whether comparisons should be made on a transactional
basis, a weighted-average basis or some combination of these methods.
During the Uruguay Round, a number of nations sought to require margin calculations to be made on a consistent basis (e.g. either transaction to
transaction or average to average) rather than a mixture of methodologies
such as weighted averages for home market and individual export transactions for the export market prices. Some GATT members argued that
the mixed methodology of zeroing any individual export transactions that
exceeded the weighted-average normal value resulted in a statistical bias
in favor of finding dumping margins. Defenders traditionally claimed
that transactional review was, however, necessary to prevent "targeted
dumping" aimed at specific types, models, geographic areas, etc.[27]

The resulting Article 2 sets some conditions on the use of transaction price comparisons, but it also retains some ambiguity with respect
to transaction by transaction analysis. It does not specifically mention
the practice of zeroing. As noted, the basic framework requires either
average or transaction price comparisons. Administrators are somewhat
circumscribed in their actions in that the provision does not permit
methodologies to be combined unless there is some evidence of a "pattern"
of export prices that "differs significantly" among different purchasers,
regions or time periods. These terms are not further defined.

The *EC – Bed Linen* dispute actually does not illustrate the specific
problem that informed the crafting of 2.4.2. Instead, it involved the use of
weighted average to weighted average zeroing comparisons but applied a
two-step methodology of zeroing. The AB focused primarily on the point

---

[27] See, Stewart (1993), Kim (2002).

that the EC could not claim that different models of one product are not comparable for purposes of margin analysis and further that it could not exclude some prices when the Anti-dumping Agreement spoke of "all comparable" transactions. In this sense, the AB ruling is not definitive on the issue of zeroing. The AB report seems to hold for the proposition that the EC approach to zeroing prevents a "fair comparison" as required by Articles 2.4 and 2.4.2. We do not read the opinion as stating that zeroing is prohibited.[28] However, the scope for zeroing appears to have been narrowed.

Turning to the question of the standard of review, the EC argued that since the Panel did not find zeroing as such to be impermissible under Article 2.4.2 of the Anti-dumping Agreement,[29] the Panel's determination was inconsistent with the legal standard of review contained in the Anti-dumping Agreement. The standard of review is contained in Article 17.6 of the Anti-dumping Agreement which states that:

(i) in its assessment of the facts of the matter, the panel shall determine whether the authorities' establishment of the facts was proper and whether their evaluation of those facts was unbiased and objective. If the establishment of the facts was proper and the evaluation was unbiased and objective, even though the panel might have reached a different conclusion, the evaluation shall not be overturned;

(ii) the panel shall interpret the relevant provisions of the agreement in accordance with customary rules of interpretation of public international law. Where the panel finds that a relevant provision of the Agreement admits of more than one permissible interpretation, the panel shall find the authorities' measure to be in conformity with the Agreement if it rests upon one of those permissible interpretations.

As is well known, during the Uruguay Round, negotiations over this provision of the Anti-dumping Agreement were especially delicate and have been characterized as a "deal breaker" issue.[30] The resulting compromise was intended by its advocates to constrain the standard of review

---

[28] Indeed, the practice of zeroing has surfaced in another anti-dumping case, *US – Steel*, but in that case Korea did not claim that the zeroing of margins when the subperiods were recombined was a violation of 2.4.2. The *EC – Bed Linen* case also raises an interesting question about the status of zeroing. Having found the zeroing practice as utilized by the EC to be inconsistent with the Anti-dumping Agreement, are other jurisdictions utilizing comparable zeroing techniques also in violation of Article 2.4.2? Are such WTO members under an affirmative obligation to reform their own practices? Since there are a number of other jurisdictions that may deploy an analogous methodology, this question is not merely theoretical. An interesting paper by Natalie McNelis raises and explores this question in some detail. See, McNellis (2002).

[29] See, Panel Report, para. 6.116   [30] See, Croley and Jackson (1996).

applied by a WTO panel and suggest a different and more specific standard than that contained in Article 11 of the DSU.[31]

There are essentially two prongs to 17.6, the first speaks to the standard of review to be applied to the factual features of the case (e.g. requiring the administering agencies to establish facts properly and to evaluate them in an unbiased and objective manner) and the second, 17.6(ii), speaks to the standard of review that should be applied with respect to legal interpretation. The methodology for reaching an interpretative judgment on this second prong is textually ambiguous. Some experts have argued that it bespeaks a two-step process whereby the panel must first consider whether the provision at issue produces more than one interpretation. If not, the panel "must vindicate the provision's only permissible interpretation. If, on the other hand, the panel determines that the provision indeed admits of more than one interpretation, the panel shall proceed to the second step of the analysis and consider whether the national interpretation is within the set of 'permissible' interpretations. If so, the panel must defer to the interpretation given to the provision by the national government."[32] While the operation of 17.6(ii) is not fully clear, it appears to have been introduced to provide a certain additional degree of latitude to national authorities.[33]

In *EC – Bed Linen*, the factual prong of 17.6 was not actively examined by the panel. With respect to the second prong, the panel explicitly noted that it was charged with interpreting the Anti-dumping Agreement in accordance with the customary rules of interpretation of public international law as set out in the Vienna Convention.[34] The AB did not give this issue much in-depth examination. For the AB, given that the Panel had recognized its interpretive responsibility, it deferred to the

---

[31] According to Horlick and Clark (1997), the US made several efforts during the Uruguay Round to significantly narrow the scope of review by a dispute panel with respect to anti-dumping duties. These proposals were strenuously resisted by most other countries and the US eventually had to "relax its position significantly, and, in the end, achieved agreement on language that essentially codified existing panel practice concerning the standard of review," p. 317.

[32] Ibid., p. 200.

[33] Some US anti-dumping advocates have characterized the second part of this legal prong as akin to a "reasonableness" standard, whereby panels are provided an opportunity to defer to an administering authority's interpretation of the Anti-dumping Agreement but are not required to do so. But this "reasonableness" interpretation is not universally accepted among experts and indeed the term itself was advanced by the United States and not accepted during the Uruguay Round negotiations. See, Rosenthal and Vermylen (2000) and Horlick and Clark (1997).

[34] See, Panel Report 6.46.

Panel's reasoning[35] and said that "it appears clear to us from the emphatic and unqualified nature of this finding of inconsistency that the Panel did not view the interpretation given by the European Communities of Article 2.4.2 of the Anti-dumping Agreement as a 'permissible interpretation' within the meaning of Article 17.6(ii) of the Anti-dumping Agreement. Thus, the Panel was not faced with a choice among multiple 'permissible' interpretations, which would have required it, under Article 17.6(ii) to give deference to the interpretation relied upon by the European Communities."[36]

Thus, even though the applicable provision of the Anti-dumping Agreement did not speak of the practice of zeroing as such, the AB concurred with the Panel's interpretation that the EC practice produced results that were inconsistent with the obligations set forth in the Anti-dumping Agreement. This legal reasoning does not suggest to us that the WTO Panel failed to consider whether the interpretation advanced by the EC was within the sphere of a permissible interpretation. The AB's review and treatment of the interpretive standard was not sufficiently detailed in this case, however, to shed much light on how best to operationalize the degree of deference implicated by 17.6(ii). It was considered by the AB in somewhat greater detail in earlier cases.[37]

4 Specific economic analysis

We now consider and evaluate the particular legal and economic issues and methodologies raised by the dispute. More specifically we ask: In light of the underlying goals of the relevant WTO provisions, and taking them as given, was the resolution of the substantive economic issues around which the case revolved based on sound economic principles? The central substantive economic issue of this case concerns the details of measuring the margins of dumping, and in particular the issues of (i) whether the practice of "zeroing" is permissible, and (ii) how the amounts for

---

[35] See, Panel Report Para 6.46.   [36] See, Panel Report 65.

[37] An earlier case, *US – Hot Rolled Steel*, considered 17.6 somewhat more in depth. In that case, the AB held that the 17.6(ii) does not conflict with the DSU Article 11 and explained that the second sentence of 17.6(ii) posits the possibility that under customary rules of interpretation two or more interpretations of an applicable provision would be permissible but that such an interpretation would be considered after applying the rules of the Vienna Convention. See, paras. 58–62. Some experts have suggested that relevant provisions of the Vienna Convention may not allow multiple permissible interpretations, but this is a debate that we cannot fully develop herein. See, Vermulst and Graafsma (2001).

administrative, selling, and general costs and for profits should be measured in calculating the "constructed normal value."

From an economic perspective, the resolution of the issues around which this case revolved appears somewhat twisted. More than anything else, this may illustrate the difficulty of writing rules in an attempt to constrain governments to act "appropriately," but leaving them with the incentive (as discussed in section 2 above) to act inappropriately. In this environment, governments will seek new ways to "game the system," and there is no realistic set of rules that can be written down to prevent this. The Panel and the AB are then left with the difficult task of finding ways to interpret the rules so that they achieve the desired intent, which is to say the Panel or the AB must act to "complete" this incomplete contract. While the findings in this case appear sensible from the point of view of preventing what would seem to most economists to be "abusive" protectionist practices, the arguments offered by the AB to support the decisions can also sound quite arbitrary from an economic perspective.

On the question of whether the practice of "zeroing" is permissible, this appears to be a circumstance in which the explicit rules for calculating dumping margins (as contained in Article 2.4.2 of the Anti-dumping Agreement) leave some ambiguity as to what is permissible. In this case, the EC chose to use a methodology for calculating margins (zeroing) which, while undeniably leading to higher margins than would be calculated if zeroing were not employed (see our discussion in section 3), the EC nevertheless argued was within the permissible methods according to the rules.

On strictly economic grounds, it is difficult to evaluate formally the merits of zeroing, though as we have indicated in section 3 it is clear that, for any given distribution of prices within a product line, as a statistical matter zeroing leads to greater calculated margins than would be calculated in its absence. The difficulty in evaluating formally the economic merits of zeroing can be traced back to the lack of general clarity as to exactly why dumping is to be "condemned" in the first place.

For example, suppose one adopts the perspective that the prevention of predatory pricing is at the heart of anti-dumping actions. Then it might be argued that the practice of zeroing could be justified, because otherwise a firm could engage in "targeted dumping": that is, it could set low predatory prices on some models of a product that were especially close substitutes to the models sold by the local competitors it was attempting to drive out, and then "mask" its predatory pricing ("positive dumping margins") with high prices ("negative dumping margins") on other models of that product that were less-close substitutes with the models sold by its competitors.

As we have described in section 3 above, absent the zeroing methodology, this firm's negative margins would offset its positive margins in the calculation of the overall dumping margin for the product, and by pricing this way a savvy predator might avoid the penalty of anti-dumping duties altogether when zeroing is not permissible. In this case, the practice of zeroing can "unmask" the predator. However, if firms routinely set prices on some models of a product so as to "cross-subsidize" sales of other models of that product, then zeroing would mistakenly identify this normal business practice as dumping. In this case, the practice of zeroing can allow "innocent" (i.e. non-predatory) firms to be made the target of anti-dumping actions.

From this perspective, the problem with zeroing is that, while it could be beneficial in making anti-dumping actions a more effective tool for preventing predatory pricing, it carries with it the associated risk that a firm could be inappropriately penalized with anti-dumping duties even when its product line as a whole is priced so as to earn "its normal value." Therefore, if one adopts the perspective that dumping is to be "condemned" because it is often predatory, and that the prevention of predatory pricing is therefore a serious task of anti-dumping actions, then the merits of zeroing depend on the relative importance of these benefits and risks.

On the other hand, if one rejects this perspective, as many economists do, on the basis of the available evidence suggesting that predatory dumping is rare in practice (see note 6), then the merits of zeroing can be formally evaluated only once an alternative reason for condemning dumping is articulated (as, for example, in the discussion of section 2 above). This is because, in the absence of such an articulation, any formal evaluation of the merits of zeroing would by necessity begin from the position that anti-dumping actions should not be permitted by the WTO in the first place, a starting position that would in large part trivialize the evaluation of the merits of zeroing.

The difficulty, then, is that there is no widely accepted formal framework that implies a role for anti-dumping actions, and that therefore provides a perspective from which the economic merits of zeroing can be formally evaluated. Hence, it is difficult to evaluate formally the economic merits of zeroing, because there is not an accepted understanding of why dumping is to be "condemned" in the first place.

Interestingly, the possibility that the kind of predatory "targeted dumping" described just above might justify the zeroing methodology was considered by the AB (paragraph 62) and dismissed, largely because the AB suggested that ". . . if the European Communities wanted to address, in particular, dumping of certain types or models of bed linen, it could have defined, or redefined, the *product* under investigation in a narrower way" (AB Report, paragraph 62). But the reasoning of the AB on this point may be too simple, because it suggests the possibility that the product under investigation could always be defined narrowly enough to "surgically remove" the targeted dumping. The problem with this possibility is that it suffers from the same basic problem as zeroing: "innocent" (i.e. non-predatory) firms could be made the target of anti-dumping actions, in this case simply by defining the product under investigation in a sufficiently narrow fashion to include only those types or models of the product for which the firm's margins were positive.[38]

In the end, with regard to the EC's practice of zeroing, the AB seems to have found fault with the internal inconsistencies of the EC's defense of its methodology, and in particular with its insistence on seeing ". . . the phys-ical characteristics of cotton-type bed linen in one way for one purpose and in another way for another."[39] A reasonable interpretation of the AB's approach to this determination is that such internal inconsistencies belie an effort to stay within the broader intent of these rules, and indicate in-stead an (awkward) attempt by the EC to pick and choose methodologies for their protectionist effect.

On the question of how the amounts for administrative, selling, and general costs and for profits should be measured in calculating the "con-structed normal value," a central issue was whether a weighted average of administrative, selling, and general costs can be calculated for only one producer. The AB concludes that this is not possible, stating: "First of all, and obviously, an 'average' of amounts for SG&A and profits *cannot* be calculated on the basis of data on SG&A and profits relating to only *one* exporter or producer . . . In short, it is simply not possible to calculate the

---

[38] In fact, in some ways the problem associated with zeroing would be exacerbated under the AB's suggestion, in the sense that the calculated overall margin on this narrower range of models would be higher than the overall margin calculated under zeroing. This can be seen with reference to our example in section 3 above. There we showed that, under zeroing, the overall margin of dumping for the product under investigation was given by $Z = [(e_1 d_1) + (e_2 d_2)]/[e_1 + e_2 + e_3]$. Adopting the AB's suggestion of defining the product more narrowly to include only those models for which the margin was positive, the overall margin (denoted by A) would be calculated as $A = [(e_1 d_1) + (e_2 d_2)]/[e_1 + e_2]$, from which it follows that $A > Z$.

[39] AB Report, p. 19.

'weighted average' relating to only one exporter or producer."[40] Of course, it *is* possible, though trivial, to calculate the weighted average relating to only one exporter or producer: it is defined simply as the amounts for administrative, selling, and general costs and profits for that producer or exporter.

Presumably the underlying logic for why it might be sensible to disallow such calculations when there is only one other exporter or producer is more subtle, and has something to do with the view that data taken from a single other producer or exporter could introduce a large element of idiosyncratic "noise" into the cost calculation, while data taken from a weighted average of a (preferably large) number of other producers or exporters is less likely to reflect the idiosyncrasies of any one producer or exporter. And the more variability there is in the approved methods for calculating costs under the rules, the more room there will be for governments to "game the system" by choosing the approach that best suits their protectionist incentives. In this way, the finding of the AB on this matter may appear sensible, though the particular reasoning by which it supported this decision appears curious.

5   Concluding observations on the legal tests and economic analysis

Let us now consider, in brief, the relationship between the legal rules and economic assessments of the dispute. As noted earlier, there is room for ambiguity in the treaty text that governments can utilize. In a narrow sense, this case suggests that the rules provide a sufficient basis for adjudicators to evaluate whether the particular methodology used by the national authority inflates margins and whether the national procedures are generally consistent with the overall Anti-dumping Agreement. From an economic perspective, however, this case, not unlike certain other anti-dumping cases, points up the conceptual problems of the Anti-dumping Agreement.

This analysis has suggested that one possible approach to shift incentives away from excessive – or unrestrained – use of anti-dumping procedures would be to introduce compensation provisions into the legal texts of the GATT/WTO anti-dumping rules. We have not attempted herein to assess the political feasibility of this or any other reform proposal, but the logic of the basic suggestion follows from a simple economic observation:

[40] Ibid., p. 23.

by having the right to seek compensation, countries can force a government that takes an original policy action to face more completely the full costs of its decision. This is important if governments are to face the "right" incentives when making their policy decisions.

At a broad level, this observation identifies an important role for compensation within the GATT/WTO system. The lack of required compensation may help explain why it is evidently so tempting for governments to find myriad ways to "over-utilize" anti-dumping protection: anti-dumping procedures provide one route to protection where GATT/WTO rules do not require governments to pay the full costs of their actions. While speculative, of course, this suggests that WTO disputes over anti-dumping actions might be mitigated – because the underlying incentives of governments to initiate cases in circumstances that do not warrant anti-dumping duties would be reduced – if some form of compensation were required when anti-dumping duties are imposed.

References

Bagwell, Kyle and Robert W. Staiger. 2002. *The Economics of the World Trading System*. Boston, MA: MIT Press.

Bagwell, Kyle and Robert W. Staiger. Forthcoming. Multilateral trade negotiations, bilateral opportunism, and the rules of GATT/WTO. *Journal of International Economics*.

Ethier, Wilfred. J. 2002. Political externalities, non-discrimination, and a multilateral world. PIER Working Paper no. 02-030, September.

Horlick, Gary N. and Peggy A. Clark. 1997. Standards for Panels Reviewing Antidumping Determinations under the GATT and WTO, in E. Petersham, ed., *International Trade Law and the GATT/WTO Dispute Settlement System*, Dordrecht: Kluwer, at p. 313.

Horn, Henrik and Petros Mavroidis. 2001. Economic and legal aspects of the Most-Favored Nation clause. *European Journal of Political Economy* 17, 233–79.

Jackson, John H. 1969. *World Trade and the Law of GATT*. Bobbs Meredith, pp. 401–24.

McNellis, Natalie. 2002. What obligations are created by WTO Dispute Settlement Reports? World Trade Forum, August.

Prusa, Thomas A. 2001. On the spread of antidumping. *Canadian Journal of Economics*, 34: 591–611.

Rosenthal, Paul and Robert T. C. Vermylen. 2000. Review of key substantive agreements: Panel IIE: Antidumping Agreement and Agreement on Subsidies and Countervailing Measures. *31 Law and Policy International Business*: 871.

Shin, Hyun Ja. 1998. Possible instances of predatory pricing in recent antidumping cases, in Robert Z. Lawrence, ed., *Brookings Trade Forum*, pp. 81–98.

Staiger, Robert W. and Frank A. Wolak. 1994. Measuring industry-specific protection. *Brookings papers on Economic Activity: Microeconomics*, pp. 51–103.

Stewart, Terrence. 1993. *The GATT Uruguay Round: a Negotiating History*, Dordrecht: Kluwer, vol. II, p. 1.

Vermulst, E. and Graafsma. 2001. WTO dispute settlement with respect to trade contingency measures. *Journal of World Trade* 35 (2): 209–28.

6

Mexico – Corn Syrup
Mexico – Anti-dumping Investigation of High Fructose Corn Syrup from the United States, Recourse to Article 21.5 of the DSU by the United States*

ROBERT HOWSE AND DAMIEN J. NEVEN

1 Introduction and summary of main legal issues

The 21.5 AB ruling in *Mexico – Corn Syrup* arises out of a dispute between the United States and Mexico concerning whether the Mexican agency's finding of material injury from dumping was consistent with the Anti-dumping Agreement. The original Panel[1] found that the agency's determination of the existence of a threat of material injury to the domestic industry was made in violation of numerous provisions of the Anti-dumping Agreement. In light of these findings by the panel, the agency made a redetermination and the United States filed a 21.5 complaint, claiming that the redetermination failed to address adequately the defects identified by the original panel.

The 21.5 Panel[2] agreed with the United States that an objective and unbiased agency could not infer the projected increase in imports asserted by the Mexican agency from the evidence on the record, and reached the same conclusion concerning the projections of the effects of these increases on the domestic industry. Here the issue was whether Mexico had analyzed various factors affecting demand for imports and the state of the domestic industry pursuant to Articles 3.4 and 3.7 of the Anti-dumping Agreement and whether the analysis, to the extent that it was done, would allow an objective and unbiased agency to come to the conclusion concerning threat of injury that the Mexican agency did come to.

---

* This study was prepared in the context of the project of the American Law Institute on the Principles of World Trade Law.
[1] *Mexico – High Fructose Corn Syrup*, WT/DS132/R, adopted February 24, 2000.
[2] WT/DS132/RW, June 22, 2001.

These aspects of the dispute engage the considerations in the interpretation of the Anti-dumping Agreement that we discuss in the introduction of our comment on *Argentina – Ceramic Tiles*, including, obviously, the standard of review prescribed in 17.6(i)–(ii) of the Anti-dumping Agreement. However, upon appeal, Mexico raised a number of other issues of a preliminary and procedural nature, including the impact on the panel proceedings of the US failure to engage in consultations, the meaning of the requirement in DSU 3.7 that a Member exercise self-restraint in bringing dispute settlement claims, and the requirement that the Panel give reasons for its conclusions that is contained in Article 12 of the DSU.

2 The analysis of threat of material injury under the Anti-dumping Agreement: the significance of 3.4 and 3.7 and standard of review

2.1 Background

High fructose corn syrup is the product allegedly dumped on the Mexican market by US producers. In its determination, Mexico focused on sugar as the "like" product that would be affected by the imports of high fructose corn syrup. High fructose corn syrup appears to be a substitute for sugar for particular segments of consumers, in particular for soft drink bottlers but also for other industrial users. Soft drink bottlers accounted for 68% of high fructose corn syrup imports in 1996 (the year for which evidence is gathered by the Mexican agency); producers of other beverages accounted for another 13%, whereas other industrial users (outside the drinks industry) accounted for the remaining 19%.

Imports of high fructose corn syrup increased markedly in 1996. Soft drink bottlers as well as other users apparently increased their purchases abroad. It appears however that in 1997 soft drink bottlers reached an agreement with sugar producers such that, in return for favorable sugar prices, they would limit their purchase of high fructose corn syrup, to less than 350,000 tons per year, which would appear to correspond approximately to the level of their purchases in 1996.

In its original determination and subsequent redetermination, Mexico did not dispute the existence of the agreement. Mexico thus claimed that even if the agreement existed and was implemented as of 1997, imports would increase significantly and would cause injury. Mexico still based its expectations of future import growth on the observation of a significant increase in 1996 (a period during which there was no agreement).

Mexico did not provide evidence on the proportion of high fructose corn syrup that was purchased by the soft drink bottlers: the evidence on this matter was only provided in the course of the original Panel proceedings as answers to questions put forward by the Panel (see paragraph 7.176 of the original panel ruling). Mexico did not provide evidence either on the extent to which other producers would be able to substitute high fructose corn syrup for sugar (evidence was also provided during the proceedings, as a result of questions by the Panel). In order to establish injury, Mexico presented the amount of sugar that could be substituted in favor of high fructose corn syrup, as a proportion of the amount of sugar purchased by industrial users. By excluding the final consumption of sugars (sales to final users), Mexico of course obtained a larger figure.

The Panel ruled that Mexico's analysis did not meet the requirement of the Anti-dumping Agreement because the final consumption of sugar should have been considered to evaluate injury and because Mexico should have analyzed the state of the sugar industry more thoroughly. Furthermore, the Panel ruled that Mexico's consideration of the potential effects of the alleged restraint agreement was inadequate. In particular, at paragraph 7.177:

> 7.177 Mexico's contention that users of imported high fructose corn syrup other than soft-drink bottlers could have increased their consumption in amounts sufficient to constitute a substantial increase in imports is in our view questionable. However, even assuming this to be the case, there is no discussion in the final determination of the share of imports and domestic production consumed by soft-drink bottlers, other beverage manufacturers, and other industrial users, and the degree of substitutability of high fructose corn syrup and sugar in their products. Moreover, the alleged restraint agreement affected purchasers accounting for 68 per cent of the imports, suggesting that it would at least slow any further increases in imports. In addition, most other purchasers' ability to substitute high fructose corn syrup for sugar was limited, suggesting that, if the alleged restraint agreement existed, any further increases in imports would be less than they had been in the past. None of these elements is addressed in SECOFI's final determination. We note, moreover, that the final determination states that the alleged restraint agreement does not *rule out the possibility* that bottlers and other users would continue their purchases of imported high fructose corn syrup. However, not ruling out the possibility that imports would continue does not support the conclusion that there is a *likelihood of substantially increased importation*, as provided for in Article 3.7(i).

> (emphasis added)

The Panel was thus concerned that, if the agreement were implemented, imports of high fructose corn syrup would not grow much further in 1997 relative to the level they reached in 1996. Implicitly, the Panel however assumes that the presence of the agreement *does not alter* the benchmark against which increases in imports should be assessed. By comparing levels in 1996 and 1997, and arguing the latter may not grow relative to the former, the Panel assesses them *against the same benchmark*. That is, the Panel does not contemplate the possibility that imports of high fructose corn syrup in the presence of an agreement should be compared to the level of sugar consumption outside the soft-drink industry. It would appear that according to the Panel, the level of imports by users other than soft-drink producers should be considered in relation to total sugar consumption, *including* that of soft-drink producers. The Panel thus rejects an approach whereby the effects of imports are considered segment by segment. The Panel's rejection of segmentation is further underlined by its insistence (see above) that purchases of sugar for final consumption should be considered in addition to purchases by industrial users.

In its redetermination, Mexico addressed the specific points listed by the Panel. In particular, Mexico provided evidence on the share of imports and domestic production, the degree of substitutability and the effects of the restraint agreement. However, Mexico did not provide much further evidence on its essential claim, namely that users other than soft-drink bottlers would continue to shift away from sugar[3].

The compliance Panel thus found that (paragraph 6.23):

> SECOFI's determination that industries other than soft-drink bottlers would undertake a massive shift from sugar use to high fructose corn syrup use, resulting in total consumption of high fructose corn syrup beyond the capacity of the domestic industry to supply, and a consequent significant increase in dumped imports, is not, in our view, one that could be reached by an unbiased and objective investigating authority in light of the evidence relied upon and the explanations given in the redetermination. While in its redetermination SECOFI did set out additional information

---

[3] It is beyond the scope of this comment to fully discuss the evidence submitted by Mexico on this point. However, it would appear that the evidence suffered from very important shortcomings, that were rightly pointed out by the Panel. Mexico appeared to have considered a sample of firms using both sugar and high fructose corn syrup. It had then assumed that the level of overall imports would reflect the proportion observed for these firms but subsequently discounted the overall level by 50 percent. This method appears to be rather arbitrary and does not focus on the right question, namely the extent to which firms have responded to relative prices of sugar and high fructose corn syrup.

concerning the points identified by the Panel as problematic in its original report, SECOFI failed to provide a reasoned explanation of how that information supports the conclusion that there was a significant likelihood of increased imports. We therefore determine that SECOFI's conclusion that there was a significant likelihood of increased importation is not consistent with Article 3.7(i) of the AD Agreement.

In its appellate submission, Mexico claimed that the compliance Panel had erred in relying on a conjecture about the existence of the agreement between sugar and soft-drink producers, whereas Article 3.7 of the Anti-dumping Agreement stipulates that "a determination of a threat of material injury shall be based on facts and not merely on allegation, conjecture or remote possibility."

Effectively, what Mexico seems to argue is that the Panel should not have relied on the same assumption as Mexico (!) with respect to the existence of the agreement and should have assumed that the agreement did not exist. In what follows, we will argue that the Panel failed to properly analyze the effects of the alleged agreement and as a consequence may not have given sufficient credit to the analysis of injury put forward by Mexico.

2.2   The alleged restraint agreement

The alleged agreement between sugar producers should be seen as a decision by sugar producers to discriminate between different buyers of sugar. The emergence of high fructose corn syrup as a substitute for sugar for some industrial uses, and in particular for the preparation of soft drinks, has increased the price elasticity of demand for sugar in those particular segments. In these circumstances, it should be expected that sugar producers will try to discriminate across segments and offer discounts only in those segments that have become more price elastic. Presumably, before the emergence of high fructose corn syrup as a potential substitute, sugar producers did not perceive different price elasticities across segments and charged a single price. Matters changed when high fructose corn syrup was introduced, which only affected demand for a particular segment.

It is not clear why an agreement was necessary[4] in order to implement such price discrimination. In the presence of different demands that can be readily identified, oligopolists can in principle achieve third-degree

---

[4] The legality of this agreement with respect to Mexican antitrust laws would appear to be questionable (the issue was however not raised by the panel and AB rulings).

price discrimination without recourse to an agreement. If indeed the agreement was superfluous to achieve price discrimination, its existence was unimportant to evaluate the change in imports and possibly did not deserve the attention that it was given by the Panel. That is, the normal reaction of sugar producers such that they would offer discounts to those segments for which high fructose corn syrup was an alternative, would have reduced the pace of imports in the absence of an agreement.

However, the presumption that the agreement was superfluous is not satisfactory and the Panel should possibly have considered the matter further. One can only speculate about the circumstances that may have led to the implementation of the agreement but different explanations will entail different consequences for the analysis of potential imports and the analysis of injury. For instance, one hypothesis may be that firms had to reach an agreement in order to avoid arbitrage across segments. Contracts with soft drinks buyers that prevent resale to other users would effectively prevent arbitrage but may not be profitable for each firm taken individually. This may arise if the cost of arbitrage is mainly felt by competitors (who will lose custom as a consequence of the arbitrage). This is particularly likely if there are many firms in the industry and if firms' offerings are not differentiated. In those circumstances, the prevention of arbitrage, which is necessary to enforce third-degree price discrimination, may require the enforcement of an agreement whereby each firm commits to prevent soft-drink buyers from reselling to other users. If this interpretation is correct, the existence of the agreement would affect the analysis of imports since, in the absence of an agreement, discrimination would not have been feasible and imports would have increased further.

There are, however, alternative explanations behind the existence of an agreement, which may not affect the flow of imports, but would still affect the analysis of injury. One alternative hypothesis is that producers may have felt that an agreement was necessary in order to maintain a collusive understanding in the industry. There may have been a concern in the industry that faced with new competition, the ongoing collusive understanding could be jeopardized for instance because individual discounts given to producers of soft drinks could have been perceived as a defection from the collusive understanding. An agreement may thus have served the purpose of providing a new focal point on which firms would coordinate their behavior. It is unclear how the agreement would affect the flow of imports – it all depends on the extent to which the level of discounts may have been coordinated. But the analysis of injury in those circumstances would clearly be affected; in the absence of an agreement, imports of high fructose corn syrup would have destabilized collusion by local firms and arguably may have brought benefits to local consumers and possibly may have increased domestic welfare. Hence, if injury is evaluated in terms of the profits of the domestic firms, the agreement would have reduced injury. But if injury is evaluated in terms of consumer surplus of welfare, the agreement would have increased injury.

2.3   Market segmentation

As discussed in the previous section, it is not clear that an agreement was necessary to undertake third-degree price discrimination but it is likely that third-degree discrimination across different segments would take place as a consequence of the emergence of high fructose corn syrup as a substitute for some industrial uses, including soft-drink production.

This raises a broader question, namely whether the imports of high fructose corn syrup should be assessed relative to the sales of sugar in the segment affected or relative to the overall sales of sugar. As emphasized above, the panel has insisted both the sugar sales for final consumption should be considered in the analysis of injury but also that the level of imports in 1997 (when there was an agreement) should be considered against the same benchmark as those in 1996. That is, the panel has firmly rejected an analysis of the particular segment affected by the substitution in favor of high fructose corn syrup.

Whether a focus on the segment of sugar sales affected by high fructose corn syrup was appropriate could also be interpreted as raising the question of whether the "like" products should not have been defined as the sugar sold in that particular segment rather than as sugar in general.

It would seem that if price discrimination can indeed be enforced, most of the economic effects of the substitution with high fructose corn syrup will be felt in that particular segment. Buyers of sugar in other segments (including final users) will be affected to a much lesser extent: the price that they pay will be affected only in so far as the elasticity that firms will face in those segments will change (assuming constant marginal costs). But if the elasticity that firms faced in the two segments was identical before the introduction of high fructose corn syrup (such that no discrimination was enforced), the elasticity that firms will face in the segments not affected by it will not change. Similarly, the profit that firms make will only be reduced from the sales in the segments affected by high fructose corn syrup. Hence, it would seem that the analysis should be carried out in the segment affected by the syrup and more generally that the "like" product should have been defined as sugar sold in those segments.[5] It would thus appear that the panel erred in insisting that Mexico should have carried out its analysis for the entire sugar market.

2.4 Should the Panel assume that the agreement existed?

As mentioned above, in its appellate submission, Mexico also claimed that the compliance panel had erred in relying on a conjecture, with respect to the existence of the agreement between sugar and soft-drink producers, whereas Article 3.7 of the Anti-dumping Agreement stipulates that "a determination of a threat of material injury shall be based on facts and not merely on allegation, conjecture or remote possibility."

The AB disagreed and emphasized that, in choosing to base its argument on the assumption that the agreement existed, Mexico treated it as a fact. Since Mexico chose to assume the existence of the agreement for the purpose of its analysis, it would, according to the AB, have been "improper for the Panel to have sought, on its own initiative, to go behind the assumptions made by SECOFI."

The attitude of the AB seems appropriate. In general, it would seem reasonable to ask the Panel to give some deference to the agency's assumptions, given 17.6. But here the agency in its actual analysis had relied on the opposite assumption, namely that the restraint agreement *did* in fact exist. In affirming the Panel's decision, the AB here displays a proper understanding of the meaning of 17.6. The correct approach to review agency determinations is not to ask whether the *Panel*, if acting in the place of the agency, could or would properly come to a different or the same conclusion, but rather whether the *actual* analysis done by the *agency* is such as could be made by an objective and unbiased decision maker. Thus the Panel in the first instance must accept the agency's assumptions (provided they are not patently unreasonable) and examine whether, based on such assumptions, the conclusions the agency draws are such as could be drawn by an objective and unbiased decision maker.

2.5 Consultations

Mexico claimed on appeal that the Panel's failure to address the significance of the lack of consultations between the United States and Mexico

---

[5] Market definition in the antitrust field adopts a similar approach. Particular segments are normally considered as separate relevant markets when price discrimination is feasible.

prior to the referral of the dispute to the Panel was an error that was fatal to the panel's jurisdiction or authority over the entire matter. However, as noted by the Appellate Body, Mexico never mentioned this issue in its written submissions to the Panel, and only raised it in oral argument, without actually making any specific claim concerning the legal effect of the failure to engage in consultations. Moreover, when the US submitted a request for a 21.5 Panel to the Dispute Settlement Body (DSB), Mexico not only did not object, but rather stated explicitly to the DSB that it "decided not to oppose the US request at the present meeting" (AB Report, paragraph 39).

As a general matter of procedure the AB held that the Panel was not required to address the issue of lack of consultations because Mexico had simply failed to bring that issue before the panel as a "claim." The AB noted: "The requirements of good faith, due process and orderly procedure dictate that objections, especially those of such potential significance should be explicitly raised. Only in this way will the Panel, the other party to the dispute, and the third parties, understand that a specific objection has been raised, and have an adequate opportunity to address and respond to it" (paragraph 47).

However, as the AB pointed out, even if the parties have not raised any objections, a panel is still required to examine, on its own motion as it were, whether it has jurisdiction or authority over the matter. The AB held that prior consultations were not a condition precedent to the Panel having jurisdiction over the matter, and therefore that the Panel was not required to address the lack of consultations on its own motion. The AB's reasoning here seems to be ironclad: it was able to point to various provisions of the DSU that indicate in certain circumstances the possibility of consultations being waived by consent of the parties. Thus, it cannot be the case that the prior consultations are a pre-condition for the Panel to assume *jurisdiction*, regardless of the conduct and wishes of the parties in regard to consultations.

Because it held that (1) the Panel did not have to address the consultation issue as a "claim" of Mexico since Mexico did not make this claim explicitly; and that (2) the Panel did not have to address it anyway as a threshold jurisdictional issue, the AB never actually got to the underlying interpretive issue of whether under the DSU there is a legal requirement of prior consultations before requesting a 21.5 panel.

Mexico also claimed on appeal that the Panel erred in failing to address the situation that the United States on its request for a panel had failed to explicitly state whether consultations had been held. Article 6.2 of the

DSU provides that a request for establishment of a panel "shall indicate whether consultations were held . . ." The AB held that since Mexico had not stated this issue either as an explicit "claim" to the Panel, and since this issue did not go to jurisdiction either, the Panel was under no obligation to address it. Again, the AB stressed that it did not need to reach the underlying substantive interpretative issue of whether this requirement of 6.2 applied to requests for 21.5 panels.

Does the AB's treatment of the consultations issue tell us anything about how it thinks that the Panel should have dealt with this issue had it been properly before the Panel as a "claim" by Mexico that the United States had violated the DSU? Arguably, the implication of holding that this is not a jurisdictional issue is that, were the Panel to find a violation of this provision of the DSU, it would not dismiss the action, but provide some other kind of relief to Mexico. The obvious form of such relief would be a suspension of Panel proceedings pending the required consultations. Is such relief within the ambit of a Panel's powers?

An alternative view, which is suggested by the fact in this case that at the DSB meeting Mexico did not object to the US request for a Panel, is that enforcement of the consultations requirement appropriately occurs when the DSB has the request for a Panel before it. This would make sense of the requirement in DSU 6.2, discussed above, that in its request, a Member indicate whether consultations have taken place. In the absence of prior consultations, the DSB may not be properly seized of the request for a Panel; since the agenda for a DSB meeting is agreed by consensus, the would-be-defendant could effectively, and with justification, object to the request for a Panel being on the agenda of a particular meeting, given the absence of prior consultations.[6]

2.6   Member self-restraint in recourse to dispute settlement

Article 3.7 of the DSU provides, in part, "[b]efore bringing a case a Member shall exercise its judgment as to whether action under these procedures would be fruitful." The AB held that here too Mexico had not raised the question concerning fruitfulness of dispute settlement

---

[6] This blocking power may not be used in order to frustrate the right to dispute settlement; but the point here is that any such *right* is subject to the condition of prior consultations. Thus, preventing consensus on the agenda in this special situation in order to enforce the condition of prior consultations would arguably be consistent with the letter and spirit of the law.

procedures as a "claim." Such a matter would not go to the jurisdiction of the panel, the AB held, because the notion of exercising one's judgment is inherently self-regulating. Thus – and here the AB cited its ruling in *EC Bananas III* on a similar issue – "Article 3.7 neither requires nor authorizes a panel to look behind that Member's decision and to question its exercise of judgment."

This ruling, while fairly obvious, nevertheless drives home a basic reality of the dispute settlement system overlooked by critics of the Appellate Body and the panels such as Claude Barfield.[7] These critics fault the tribunals for adjudicating claims that are more appropriately left to political negotiations or diplomatic processes in the WTO. These accusations of judicial activism are unfounded, as the law of the DSU as it is written does not provide a basis for the adjudicator second-guessing a Member's decision to go to dispute settlement. A Member has a right to have its claims decided by the tribunal. Given the clarity of the DSU on this point, it would be in fact illegitimate judicial activism for a tribunal to *decline* to adjudicate, on the basis that some other manner of dealing with the dispute would be more fruitful.

At the same time, in considering the legal effect of DSU Article 3.7, the AB did not discuss (and Mexico apparently did not raise) Article 3.10 which provides: "It is understood that requests for conciliation and the use of dispute settlement procedures should not be intended or considered as contentious acts and that, if a dispute arises, all Members will engage in these procedures in good faith in an effort to resolve a dispute." This provision does not have explicit language suggesting that it is exclusively self-policing. Even if it does not go to jurisdiction such that a panel would have to consider the matter on its own motion, does this language nevertheless perhaps confer on the panel a *discretion* to decline to adjudicate, if it believes that dispute settlement is being used as a "contentious act" or that there is bad faith? In other cases, in particular *India – Quantitative Restrictions*[8] and *Turkey – Textiles*[9] the AB has been very disinclined to adopt interpretations of WTO treaties that would limit or qualify a Member's right to go to dispute settlement. It appears to view this right as fundamental to the basic WTO bargain, and thus it would be surprising if

---

[7] Barfield (2001). See also, Roessler (2000).

[8] *India – Quantitative Restrictions on Imports of Agricultural, Textile and Industrial Products*, WT/DS90/AB/R, especially para. 83.

[9] *Turkey – Restrictions on Imports of Textile and Clothing Products*, Report of the Appellate Body, WT/DS34/AB/R, paras. 58, 60.

language as soft as "it is understood . . ." would be considered sufficiently emphatic to qualify such a fundamental right.

2.7   The requirement that the Panel provide reasons

Article 12.7 of the DSU requires that the "report of the Panel shall set out the findings of fact, the applicability of relevant provisions and the basic rationale behind any findings and recommendations that it makes." Mexico maintained that in the Panel's scrutiny of the agency's analysis on redetermination with respect to threat of material injury, the Panel did not link its findings explicitly to discrete violations of Articles 3.4, 3.7, and 3.1 of the Anti-Dumping Agreement, and thus violated the strictures of DSU Article 12.7.

The AB disagreed. It noted that in the original Panel report the Panel had set forth its view of the close relationship between these three provisions and thus that it was relatively straightforward to ascertain how the defects in the agency's analysis identified in the 21.5 report amounted to an application by the agency of those provisions in a manner that fell short of the deferential standards articulated in Article 17.6(ii) of the Anti-dumping Agreement.

The AB is right. In fact, here (just as with its treatment of the assumption about the restraint agreement) the Panel proceeded exactly in the way that is appropriate given Article 17.6 and the nature of the obligations in the Anti-dumping Agreement. That is, it identified the relevant provisions of the Anti-dumping Agreement, and then focused on whether the agency's establishment of the facts was proper and its evaluation of them consistent with the conduct of an objective and unbiased decision maker, and whether the agency's interpretation of the Anti-dumping Agreement is "permissible" under the Vienna Convention on the Law of Treaties rules. In sum, once it identified the relevant provisions and explained why they were relevant to the dispute, it was logical and appropriate that the focus in the Panel's reasons would be on the *actual* analysis of the agency in its application of the provisions, judged against the Article 17.6 standard of review for agency decision making.

2.8   Significance of the Panel's statement that it might be possible to arrive at the result of the Mexican agency on the facts of the case

In paragraph 6.37 of its report, the 21.5 Panel acknowledged that its ruling did not stand for the proposition that "it would not be possible to make

a finding of threat of material injury in the circumstances of this case."
Mexico claimed on appeal that this statement constituted an admission,
as it were, that the Panel was not applying properly the standard of review
in Article 17.6; if indeed a finding of material injury was "possible" in this
case, then the agency must be operating with a permissible interpretation of the Anti-dumping Agreement, Mexico argued, and therefore was
entitled to deference under Article 17.6(ii).

The AB rejected this claim, preferring to interpret the Panel as merely
saying that it was not judging the correctness of the agency's result, but
rather finding fault with the analysis by which it came to that result.
Here, the AB (and indeed the Panel) again for once seem to have grasped
something of the proceduralist nature or focus of agency review under
the Anti-dumping Agreement. In reviewing whether, in the application
of the relevant provisions of the Anti-dumping Agreement, the Agency's
analysis is one that an unbiased and objective decision maker would be
capable of, the panel is not to place itself in the role of an ideal Agency
and actually engage in its *own* analysis of whether it is possible to find,
for instance, a threat of material injury in the circumstances in question.

Examining the entire record *de novo*, it is entirely possible that an
agency could, in applying the relevant provisions of the Anti-Dumping
Agreement, make certain inferences from certain facts and come to a
conclusion of threat of material injury. It is not up to the Panel to speculate
on how that might be done, but only to determine whether the way in
which *this* agency has *actually* drawn inferences from facts is consistent
with the behavior of an objective and unbiased decision maker, applying
the Anti-dumping Agreement in a manner consistent with the Vienna
Convention rules. Again, the AB appears to have grasped the importance
of a panel confining itself to the analysis the agency actually undertook,
rather than the agency asking whether, if the agency itself were to redo
the analysis, it would or could come to the same conclusion as the Panel.

2.9 Parallel proceedings under the NAFTA: a non-issue

In respect of the Mexican redetermination, the United States brought
parallel proceedings under the North American Free Trade Agreement
(NAFTA), chapter 19. Chapter 19 provides for panel review of agency
decisions against the standard of administrative fairness and rationality
that exists in the law of the country to which the agency belongs, in this
case Mexico. Parallel proceedings had also been brought under NAFTA
in respect of the original determination by the Mexican agency, and the

NAFTA panel – albeit applying a rather different legal standard – made similar findings to those of the original WTO panel.

As a general rule, international law is permissive of parallel or overlapping proceedings in the same matter.[10] The existence of the parallel NAFTA proceedings concerning the agency redetermination appears to have had no impact on either the Panel or the Appellate Body 21.5 ruling.

3 Conclusion

From a legal perspective, in its interpretation of the Anti-Dumping Agreement, and particularly the standard of review in Article 17.6, the AB in this decision seems not to have made some of the missteps that we identified in the introduction to our report on *Argentina – Ceramic Tiles*. A proper approach to Article 17.6 requires that the Panel take the analysis of the domestic agency as it finds it, and determine whether the agency's analysis is based on a permissible interpretation of the Anti-dumping Agreement, and conclusions of fact that an unbiased, objective decision maker would be capable of making based on the record in question.

What the AB shows in this ruling is that the correct approach to Article 17.6, while giving deference to the agency's actual decision, may in some circumstances result in an outcome *less* favorable to the defendant Member that has imposed anti-dumping duties – for even in cases where the Panel could itself redo the analysis of the agency to come to a finding of dumping and/or injury *consistent* with the Anti-dumping Agreement, Article 17.6 requires the Panel to limit its examination to whether the *actual* analysis and findings of the agency violate the Agreement. It is ironic and in some sense unfortunate (in terms of public perceptions of the dispute settlement process) that this one case where the AB seems to have properly appreciated the character of Article 17.6 resulted in its application to the disadvantage of the defending government.

From an economic perspective, we have argued that the Panel below erred in not finding it relevant to examine the existence of an agreement on restraint of trade, and analyzing the effects of that agreement (if it existed) on the extent of injury. To return to the legal perspective, however, the Panel and the AB were faced with the actual analysis of the domestic

---

[10] See, for example, *Southern Bluefin Tuna Case – Australia and New Zealand v. Japan*, Award on Jurisdiction and Admissibility, August 4, 2000, Arbitral Tribunal constituted under Annex VII of the United Nations Convention on the Law of the Sea, para. 52.

agency, which had *assumed* the existence of the restraint agreement as a fact.

Finally, from the economic perspective, a panel error not corrected by the AB was to decide that injury analysis must consider the industry in the broadest possible terms, and not take into account market segmentation. As we have argued, isolating the appropriate segment of the market may well enhance the accuracy of an analysis of injury in a case such as this.

References

Barfield, C., 2001. *Free Trade, Sovereignty, Democracy: the Future of the World Trade Organization*, Washington D.C.: AEI Press.

Roessler, F., 2000. "The Institutional Balance between the Judicial and the Political Organs of the WTO", in *New Directions in International Economic Law: Essays in Honour of John H. Jackson*, M. Bronckers and R. Quick, eds., Kluwer Law International, The Hague, pp. 325–46.

7

Argentina – Ceramic Tiles
Argentina – Definitive Anti-dumping Measures on Imports of Ceramic Floor Tiles from Italy*

ROBERT HOWSE AND DAMIEN J. NEVEN

1 Introduction: general considerations on Anti-dumping and WTO law and summary of the legal issues in this case

The WTO rules on dumping and anti-dumping reflect a political bargain, negotiated in the context of a fundamental normative dissensus as to whether dumping is a "wrong" practice and why.

In the GATT, there is an *apparently* strong statement against dumping, which can be defined as the sale of a product in the country of importation at a lower price than in the country of exportation, or at below cost. Dumping, the GATT says, is to be "condemned." However, this is immediately followed by the qualification "*if* it causes or threatens material injury to an established industry in the territory of a contracting party or materially retards the establishment of a domestic injury"(Article VI.1: emphasis added).

Even though dumping with these injurious effects is to be "condemned," the GATT contracting parties obviously did not agree on making dumping illegal in the GATT. Thus, there is no prohibition on dumping in the GATT, however much it may be "condemned," and no remedy available under Article XXIII against dumping. Instead, the GATT permits the unilateral imposition of anti-dumping duties against the dumped products, as long as these do not exceed the margin of dumping.

It is extremely unclear, on any plausible normative theory of multilateral trade liberalization, why price discrimination of the kind "condemned" as dumping undermines the gains from bargained trade concessions. One sort of behavior that is covered by the idea of dumping

---

* This paper was prepared in the context of the American Law Institute Project on the Principles of World Trade Law

is predatory pricing, where goods are priced so low as to drive domestic incumbents out of business, thus paving the way for the firm engaged in predation to become a monopolist. Standard economic accounts of anti-trust law consider predation to be welfare-reducing. However, the GATT bargain does not contain a requirement that Contracting Parties ensure that anti-trust rules apply to the behavior of their firms in world markets. This is simply not part of the kind of bargained cooperative equilibrium implied by the GATT, and therefore, even if dumping *were* a good surrogate for predation, which it is not,[1] there would be no conceptual reason for condemning dumping.

Theories have been advanced, for instance by Jorge Miranda (Miranda, 1996) that "dumping" may reflect other kinds of behavior inconsistent with the GATT cooperative equilibrium, such as the "exportation" of recession or cyclical economic decline to other States. In a recession it might make sense for a producer to sell above marginal cost but below average cost, in order to recoup as much of its fixed costs as possible in a situation of depressed demand. To the extent that such a strategy can capture a greater part of market share abroad, it could reduce demand for domestic products in those markets, and thus theoretically externalize some of the "costs" of recession. However, there is no consensus that such externalization is incompatible with the GATT cooperative equilibrium. To infer such incompatibility would be tantamount to inferring an im-plicit obligation on the part of Contracting Parties to adopt appropriate counter-cyclical policies, so as to avoid such externalization. However, the GATT clearly leaves the problem of negative externalities from inap-propriate macroeconomic policies for the International Monetary Fund (IMF).

Finally, one may understand the function of anti-dumping duties as that of providing some kind of limited reneging from bargained conces-sions in the face of economic and political pressures. It is arguable that without such a possibility for reneging, far fewer concessions would be made in negotiations, and that the pressures in question might even lead to the collapse of the whole bargain. In other words, there is nothing inherently wrong about dumping, but anti-dumping duties provide a necessary "safety valve" (Dam, 2001). While there is an explicit "safety

---

[1] See the empirical work of Hutton and Trebilcock, who examined a large number of anti-dumping cases in the Canadian context and found that in virtually no case was there even the possibility of predation in the facts on the basis of which "dumping" was found (Hutton and Trebilcock, 1990).

valve" in the GATT, that of safeguards or emergency action, it is often viewed as having conditions attached to it that impede its functioning (such as the requirement of compensation, under many circumstances, as well as the application of the duties on a Most-Favored-Nation basis). Set against these controversies at the conceptual level about dumping and anti-dumping, the special legal rules that have evolved through the Tokyo Round Code and which are now reflected in the WTO Anti-Dumping Agreement pose particular problems for a treaty interpreter. Treaty provisions, the Vienna Convention on the Law of Treaties (VCLT) tells us, have to be interpreted in light of purpose and object (Article 31). Many WTO treaties balance multiple purposes, as the Appellate Body acknowledged with respect to the WTO Agreement on Sanitary and Phytosanitary Measures (SPS) in the *EC-Hormones* decision.[2] However, if we take an Agreement like SPS, one can imagine a consensus among WTO Members that all of the purposes are legitimate if not important, including facilitating trade liberalization as well as allowing Members to protect the health of their citizens. There may be disagreement about how such goals should be balanced where they come into conflict in particular situations, but that is a different kind of disagreement.

In the case of anti-dumping, there is no consensus about what purposes anti-dumping duties serve nor which, if *any*, of these are legitimate. A striking contrast between the Anti-dumping Agreement and almost every other major WTO Agreement (except the Subsidies and Countervailing Duties Agreement, which is plagued by similar dissensus about legitimate purposes) is that the Anti-dumping Agreement lacks *any* preamble whatsoever, setting out its purposes and objectives.

In sum, the rules in the Anti-dumping Agreement reflect a bargain or compromise that lacks any Archimedean point of principle as regards the substantive normativity of anti-dumping. Not surprisingly then, many of the rules, including the ones that are at issue in the *Argentina – Ceramic Tiles* case, are of a procedural nature; they purport to ensure that certain evidence is considered by agencies making determinations of dumping and injury, that reasons are provided for decisions, and that the decisions are based on the full available record of pertinent facts.

Proceduralism is often a response to fundamental dissensus about substance. But it is not a solution. Indeed, proceduralism itself may well

---

[2] *EC – Measures Concerning Meat and Meat Products (Hormones)*, Report of the Appellate Body, WT/DS26/AB/R, WT/DS48/AB/R, January 16, 1998, para. 177.

be entangled in complex ways with elements of substantive normativity (Habermas, 1996).

By virtue of the rules in the WTO Anti-dumping Agreement, WTO panels are put in the position of reviewing the decisions of domestic regulatory agencies, with a strong emphasis on the adequacy of procedures. How does one make sense of such a role? If one takes the point of view that anti-dumping is illegitimate, and that its permissibility represents a power-based political compromise lacking normative coherence, then procedural review could be considered as a kind of remote second best; the assumption is that even a substantively unjust regime will cause less injustice when it is applied in a manner consistent with due process and the rule of law.[3] Procedural review is a proper tool to be used, to hem in the effect of rules that owe their existence to power not right.[4]

By contrast, if one believes that anti-dumping constitutes a response to a practice that is unfair in some relevant normative sense, then while on the one hand one will want to make sure that the agency makes positive findings only in cases where there is proof of unfair behavior, one will also not want to overly burden the agency, such that it becomes ineffective in rooting out and addressing the unfair practice in question.

If, to take yet one other possibility, one sees anti-dumping duties as a real-world instrument for constrained reneging from trade liberalization commitments in response to political and economic pressures, even though *dumping itself is not "unfair,"* then one will regard the rules in the Anti-dumping Agreement as simply a bargained dividing line between system-maintaining and/or enhancing reneging and system-threatening reneging. Here, a too rigorous proceduralism, and an especially too rigorous test for administrative rationality, may unduly hinder the agency's discretion to channel the most relief to industries capable of generating the kind of political and economic pressures that justify having a "safety valve" in the first place.[5]

Moreover, a too onerous view of procedural requirements may lead to unnecessary costs in terms of rent-seeking activity. If anti-dumping duties are simply a real world response to political and economic pressures of a certain kind, which the GATT/WTO bargain tolerates in part at least

---

[3] See Dyzenhaus (1991) on the value of the rule of law in Apartheid South Africa.

[4] In the context of review of agency decisions under domestic US administrative law, Cass Sunstein notes the existence of a principle that "[c]ourts should narrowly construe statutes that serve no plausible public purpose and amount merely to interest-group transfers" (Sunstein, 1990, p. 185).

[5] See Sykes (1995) for reflections on the political function of anti-dumping duties.

for good reasons ("a safety valve" that assists regime maintenance and/or development), then it would be desirable to avoid unnecessary costs in the effectuation of the wealth transfer in question – such costs (lawyers, economists, accountants, civil servants, etc.) represent a deadweight loss to the economy. Here, there are equity as well as welfare issues embedded, however. The stricter the interpretation of procedural requirements the more disproportionate burden on Members of the WTO who do not have longstanding administrative and public law frameworks for the application of anti-dumping law, which are mostly developing countries or post-communist countries that are new in the anti-dumping game. Onerous procedural requirements most effectively protect deep pocket defendants, who can afford the legal help necessary to take advantage of them.

Thus, even taking a proceduralist view of the requirements in the WTO Anti-dumping Agreement, one could imagine quite different approaches to standard of review depending on one's view of the meaning and purpose of WTO anti-dumping law. The proceduralist orientation does not solve the problem of a dissensus about what are the legitimate purposes of anti-dumping, and in turn the purposes of regulating the use of anti-dumping.

In these circumstances, the *in dubio mitius* principle applied by the Appellate Body in *EC – Hormones* (para. 165 and accompanying footnote) would suggest that the appropriate standard of review is the most deferential of *any* of the standards suggested by *any* of the plausible theories of the rules. This would represent an overlapping consensus. No Member would have a standard of review applied to its determinations that would be higher, or more restrictive of sovereignty, than that implied by any of the plausible theories of the purpose of anti-dumping law that the Member might hold. This constructed common denominator could also be supplemented by reference to the actual common denominator contained in the negotiating history, where this is discernable. In other words, the negotiating history in some cases may reveal where there is an overlapping consensus about a meaning to a provision, and where the Members simply agreed to disagree, thus requiring that the treaty interpreter resort to the kind of constructed overlapping consensus, described above, which is a minimalist standard of review (Esserman and Howse, 2003).

Article 17.6 of the Anti-dumping Agreement seems aimed at something like this minimalist approach. Article 17.6(i) requires the panel to defer to the agency's establishment and evaluation of the facts if the establishment was "proper" and the evaluation was "unbiased and objective" even though the panel "might have reached a different conclusion". Article 17.6(ii) requires the panel to defer to the agency's interpretation of relevant provisions of the Anti-dumping Agreement as long as that interpretation is one "permissible" reading of the provisions in question. "Permissible" here means permissible under the Vienna Convention rules, which are explicitly referred to in 17.6(ii). Thus, the fundamental question a panel should be asking about an agency's interpretation of provisions of the Anti-dumping Agreement is whether in making the interpretation it has violated any of the rules of treaty interpretation in the Vienna Convention. If the agency has not violated any of those rules, then the reading of the treaty on which it bases its conduct must stand as "permissible."

As a general matter, the Panels and the Appellate Body of the WTO have not applied in any kind of serious or consistent fashion this standard of review.[6] The accustomed role of an adjudicator in an international treaty regime is to make findings of fact and law to determine whether provisions of the treaty have been violated. In the anti-dumping cases, the Panels and Appellate Body have continued to do just this, despite 17.6. They have proceeded to analyze whether, on the law and the facts, the defending Member has violated a given provision of the Agreement.

It is thus not surprising that when the panels and the AB have referred to 17.6, such references appear as obscure or superfluous or both. Given that the panels and the AB have been unable to shift their position from the normal treaty adjudication posture, they have, generally speaking, ended up not knowing what to do with 17.6. (The other dumping case on which we are reporting, *Mexico – Corn Syrup*, is something of an exception: in that case the 21.5 panel and the AB seem to have grasped something at least of the approach that Article 17.6 requires the agency to review.)

In fact, what Article 17.6 does is to ask a different kind of question, or impose a different kind of inquiry. In reviewing agency determinations, the treaty adjudicator is not asked to determine whether the Member or its agency has violated a given provision of the Agreement, but instead whether the reading of the facts by the agency is unbiased, objective, and proper and whether the agency's reading of the WTO anti-dumping law violates the Vienna Convention rules of treaty interpretation. One way of looking at this is affirming that 17.6 constitutes a special rule of State responsibility: in respect of agency determinations (as opposed to the actual contents of its domestic anti-dumping legislation), a Member's responsibility is not *pacta sunt servanda* as such; its responsibility is to

---

[6] For a comprehensive and persuasive review, see Tarullo (2002).

ensure that, in applying the law, the agency's analysis of the facts and law reaches a certain minimum standard of administrative rationality and fairness.

Argentina – Ceramic Tiles is an example of the failure to apply the kind of standard of review suggested by 17.6; the panel ends up flailing about, lacking guidance in how it should approach agency discretion, either from the purpose and object of the treaty (which as we suggest are not agreed), or from the negotiating history. In the end, willy nilly the Panel ends up imposing a maximalist rather than minimalist standard of administrative rationality and fairness, one that is probably consistent with only one view of the purpose of WTO anti-dumping rules – the view that they are a second best to the prohibition of anti-dumping law, which is normatively justified but politically infeasible.

There are four main issues that the panel ruling in *Argentina – Ceramic Tiles* addresses, most of which have a procedural character. First, the EC challenged the decision of the Argentinian agency to rely in its determination on price information supplied by the petitioners, "facts available," and to ignore that provided by the respondents. Second, the EC argued that the Argentinian agency had failed to meet the obligation imposed in Article 6.10 of the Anti-dumping Agreement to calculate an individual margin of dumping for each exporter, even taking into account the limits of that obligation. Third, the EC argued that the agency had not taken into account differences in physical characteristics between products in making its price comparison in order to determine whether imports were being sold in the export market at lower prices than in the home market, as was required by Article 2.4 of the Anti-dumping Agreement. Finally, the EC claimed that in failing to indicate that it was going to rely on facts available, the agency violated its obligation in Article 6.9 to provide to the parties, prior to a final determination, disclosure of any essential facts upon which it relies.

2 "Facts available": Article 6.8 of the Anti-dumping Agreement

The EC challenged the decision of the Argentinian agency to rely in its determination on price information supplied by the petitioners and to ignore the information provided by the respondents. Under Article 6.8, an agency may rely on "facts available" where "any interested party refuses access to, or otherwise does not provide, necessary information within a reasonable period or significantly impedes the investigation . . ." This is subject, however, to the requirement in Annex II(6) that, where information is not accepted, the supplying party has to be informed of the reasons "forthwith" and have an opportunity to provide "further explanations within a reasonable period."

Argentina provided four reasons why the respondents' information was rejected and the determination was based instead on "facts available": (1) the failure of respondents to provide adequate non-confidential summaries of confidential information; (2) the lack of supporting documentary evidence provided by the respondents; (3) the failure to comply with the formal requirements of the agency's questionnaire; (4) and some of the information provided by the respondents was not provided in a timely fashion.

The Panel's analysis of the consistency of the agency's actions with Article 6.8 illustrates virtually a complete confusion about the meaning of standard of review in the Anti-dumping Agreement. The Panel began with the fantastical jurisprudential step of turning Article 17.6, which compels *deference*, into a new, additional *obligation* on the agency. Thus, in paragraph 6.24, the Panel interprets Article 17.6 as if it impose, beyond any other provision in the Anti-dumping Agreement, a requirement on an agency to give reasons in its determination to rely on "facts available" and to ignore information supplied by the petitioner.

The Panel thus uses Article 17.6 to read into Article 6.8 a requirement that 6.8, or Annex II, does not impose on the agency. Moreover, now that it has turned the deference clause against the agency to make its burden heavier, the Panel interprets the requirement of giving reasons in a non-deferential way. Even though the main factors that led to the agency's decisions to rely on available facts *were explicitly mentioned* in its final determination, in particular the absence of non-confidential summaries and of supporting documentation, this does not suffice to meet the Panel's conception of the requirement to give reasons.

Moreover, in using 17.6 to impose procedural obligations to provide reasons in excess of those contained in Article 6, the Panel simply flouted the AB ruling in *Thailand – H Beams*, where the AB made it clear that 17.6 was not to be used in this manner. There the AB stated: "The aim of 17.6.(i) is to prevent a Panel from 'second-guessing' a determination of a national authority . . . Whether evidence or reasoning is disclosed or made discernible to interested parties by the final determination is a matter of procedure and due process . . . comprehensively dealt with in other provisions, notably Articles 6 and 12 . . ." (paragraph 117). The Panel used as an excuse for flouting this ruling the notion that it referred to final determinations, whereas the concern of the Panel was whether reasons for the agency's decisions were recorded in any document. But the AB's *general* point was of course that 17.6 is simply not *about* imposing additional procedural obligations on the agency – *tout au contraire.*

The Panel went on to consider whether the Argentinian agency's actions were consistent with 6.8. Having used 17.6 to impose a new burden on the agency, it naturally ignored 17.6 in examining the agency's conduct against 6.8, and thus showed the agency no deference.

With regard to the absence of non-confidential summaries, the Panel summarily rejected this concern as a ground for ignoring the respondent's information. The reasoning of the Panel is another good illustration of utter confusion about what is involved in review of agency decision making under the Anti-dumping Agreement. The Panel pointed to provisions of the Anti-dumping Agreement that permit an agency to make determinations based on confidential information, in order to make the argument that it was not reasonable for the agency to reject information because it was not in such a form as was appropriate for a public process. But, of course, the fact that the Agreement *permits* a Member's agency to rely on confidential information does not in the least mean that it should be read so as to frustrate the *domestic* administrative law framework of a Member, where that framework requires or implies the requirement of publicity. Assuming that the agency was acting in a manner consistent with Argentine public law values, it should have been accorded deference, under 17.6, when it decided that it could not use information that could not be properly presented publicly as a basis for its findings.

One of the considerations that led the Panel astray is that the WTO Anti-dumping Agreement itself requires that non-confidential summaries be provided of certain confidential information (6.5.1). The Panel opined that this requirement is aimed not at the possibility of public justification (not at the values of administrative democracy) but rather at ensuring that interested parties can defend themselves adequately (paragraph 6.38). That may well be true, but because the non-confidential summaries provided by the respondent may be adequate for these purposes, it does not follow that it was unreasonable for the agency to consider them inadequate for the legitimate purposes of publicity in Argentinian public law. Under an appropriate standard of deference, necessary information surely includes information that is necessary to conduct agency decision making in a manner consistent with domestic public law values.

With respect to the agency's second concern about lack of supporting documentary evidence, the agency questionnaire clearly stated that the respondent must reply "as precisely as possible, attaching supporting documents for its replies . . ." (quoted by the Panel at paragraph 6.60). A further instruction to the respondent in the questionnaire states explicitly that information must be given with regard to sources used and corresponding documentation attached. Furthermore, Argentina provided evidence that supporting documents were requested at later points in the process, by means of a letter to the petitioner.

The Panel, astonishingly, concluded that this language was not sufficiently clear to constitute notice to the respondent that supporting documentation was required, and therefore, if not provided, it could result in rejection of the information in the petitioners' answers in the questionnaire.

By what twisted reasoning did the Panel arrive at such an absurd conclusion? The Panel affirmed that "the exporters were never informed that in the absence of a certain number of supporting documents their information was going to be rejected . . ." The petitioners are presumably adults, represented by lawyers. It is an obvious inference that when an agency requests supporting documentation as an answer to its question, the consequence of being unable to support the answer with documentation is that the agency *may* ignore the answer. The language used in the questionnaire did not say that it would be nice if the respondent provided the supporting documentation, or helpful. It made supporting documentation a *requirement* with respect to every answer, where documentation was available.

A further notion invoked by the Panel in coming to its conclusion was that under the Anti-dumping Agreement the burden is on the agency to verify the information provided by interested parties (Article 6.6). The implication of this burden is not, as the Panel suggests, a presumption that a respondent's information will be relied on without supporting documentation, but just the reverse! The Panel suggests that it was *open* to the agency to engage in verification by on-site inspection of documents at the premises of the respondent in Europe. But the existence of such a possibility could hardly create a reasonable expectation that the agency would not reject answers in a questionnaire unsupported by documentation clearly requested. At its discretion an agency might reasonably choose to address the problem by conducting on-site verification. But agency resources are limited.

There is nothing in the Anti-dumping Agreement to suggest that the agency must cure the failure of the petitioner to provide requested documentation to support its answers. The Panel's suggestion (paragraph 6.6) that the request in the questionnaire for documentation was vague, because it did not specify what kind of supporting documents were required in light of the agency's methodology, is utterly tendentious. The questions being asked are obviously those concerning prices and sales. Any half-competent lawyer or accountant would be able to figure out what sort of invoices, etc., would constitute supporting documentation in such circumstances.

With respect to Argentina's third concern, namely, the failure to comply with formal requirements of the questionnaire, at one level the failures in question seem trivial, such as not providing certain figures in US dollars, or not translating balance sheets. Certain of the respondent's firms simply did not answer one or other questions on the questionnaire as well.

The Panel is right when affirming that these defects would not justify an agency in disregarding all relevant information submitted by the respondent. But the Panel fails to place these defects in the context of Argentina's other concerns and to consider the possibility that, cumulatively, the shortcomings in the respondent's provision of information suggest a lack of diligence and serious responsiveness to the agency's concerns that, given scarce agency resources, might justify a recourse to alternative sources of information. The same could be said about Argentina's fourth concern, late submission of information. Here, the conduct of the respondent does not seem egregious, when taken in isolation. But, cumulated with the other examples of lack of diligence and responsiveness, it lends support to the notion that the agency was not exercising its discretion unreasonably in coming to an overall implicit judgment that the respondent was inadequately cooperative and forthcoming, thus justifying recourse to other sources of information.

3 Failure to calculate individual margins of dumping

Article 6.10 of the Anti-dumping Agreement provides that: "The authorities shall, as a rule, determine an individual margin of dumping for each known exporter or producer concerned of the product under investigation." However, where the number of exporters is too large to make such individual determinations practicable, the agency may limit itself to a "reasonable number of exporters," using samples that are statistically valid.

Again, here, the Panel used Article 17.6 to impose on the agency a requirement of giving reasons not contained in the relevant provisions of the Anti-dumping Agreement. Thus, there is nothing in Article 6.10

that requires an agency to provide a reasoned justification for its decision that the number of exporters is too large. The correct approach would be to assess whether under 17.6 the agency's decision not to calculate individual margins was based on the relevant facts, i.e. a large number of exporters making individual calculations impracticable. Obviously, this impracticability standard itself implies some sort of deference. An agency will assess practicability on the basis of its knowledge of its resources, the complexity of the individual case, and so forth. As for any appropriate understanding of deference, it would ill behoove a panel to second guess such a judgment, unless it appears manifestly unreasonable and arbitrary.

But the Panel could not leave its reading into the Anti-Dumping Agreement of obligations that do not exist in the Agreement as just being non-existent. The Panel also read into the Agreement an obligation, when using a sample instead of making determinations of margins for all exporters, to make an individual determination of margins for each exporter in the sample. But no such requirement is contained in the language of 6.10, which sets out two procedures, the preferred method of making individual determinations of dumping margins for *all* exporters, and the alternative of constructing a single margin for *all* exporters.

Such an interpretation is unsupported by the text of 6.10, and it leads to inequity in the treatment of different respondents. Some respondents will be able to have individual margins of dumping applied to them, by virtue of the contingency of being singled out as part of a statistical sample, whereas others will have margins applied to them that are constructed based on the information from the sample group.

But even if the Panel's interpretation is not explicitly *contradicted* by 6.10, and even if *arguendo* this was allowed under the Vienna Convention, it would still surely be a case where 17.6.(ii) would apply such as to also render the agency's reading "permissible," since there is no text in 6.10 that explicitly imposes a requirement that when a sample is used, individual margins of dumping be attributed to those respondents in the sample.

4   Adjustments for differences in physical characteristics

Article 2.4 of the Anti-dumping Agreement provides that: "A fair comparison shall be made between the export price and the normal value . . . Due allowance shall be made in each case, on its merits, for differences which affect price comparability, including . . . physical characteristics." The Panel found that while the agency identified and took into consideration some physical characteristics that could affect price comparability, it did not take into consideration other characteristics such as tile quality. Argentina had argued that there was a very large variety of tile models with many variances and different properties, and that the information provided by the respondents was inadequate for purposes of identifying differences for purposes of a fair price comparison.

The Panel's rejection of this explanation is based on the language in the final sentence of Article 2.4, which requires the agency to "indicate to the parties in question what information is necessary to ensure a fair comparison . . ." The Panel also noted that in its final determination, the agency acknowledged that there were significant price differences depending on the model of tile, not just the size category. Here the Panel's ruling appears sound. The agency was aware, and indeed any competent agency should be aware, that a factor like quality, as well as size, will affect price comparability; to the extent that the information supplied was inadequate for purposes of its analysis, 2.4 clearly provided the agency with the means to obtain the precise information needed from the parties.

5   Article 6.9: requirement of disclosure of facts on which the agency relies

Article 6.9 of the Anti-dumping Agreement provides that the authorities "shall, before a final determination is made, inform all interested parties of the essential facts under consideration which form the basis for the decision whether to apply definitive measures. Such disclosure should take place in sufficient time for the parties to defend their interests."

The Panel interprets this provision in such a way as to find that the agency violated it by not disclosing to the respondents that it would be relying, in its determination, on facts other than those provided in the respondents' questionnaires.

This seems an obvious misreading of Article 6.9, which does not require disclosure of the agency's interpretation of the facts, or its approach to them, but disclosure by the agency of the facts themselves. In this instance, the facts on which the agency relied were made aware to the respondents – they formed part of the record. Respondents were not told, however, that, in terms of the entire record, the agency was going to base its determination on these facts, as opposed to other assertions *on the record*. All that 6.9 requires is that, if a fact is going to be used as a basis for the determination, it needs to be disclosed. An agency could hardly be expected to tell the parties in advance which sub-sets of facts on the record it was going to use to make which set of findings.

In addition to having no textual basis, the thrust of the Panel's interpretation may have negative incentive effects. The Panel is basically affirming that a respondent may fail to provide information clearly requested, but that the respondent nevertheless has a right to be put on notice that the failure may result in reliance on other sources. If this were so, then respondents would have incentives to be unforthcoming where doing so might advantage them or frustrate the investigation, knowing that they can avoid any prejudice to their case from lack of disclosure at the last minute, so to speak, since the agency will have to let them know if their behavior is going to result in reliance on alternative sources.

6 Conclusion

From a legal perspective, we have argued that the panel's treatment of the legal issues displays a failure to understand and apply properly the deferential standard of review in Article 17.6 of the Anti-dumping Agreement, as well as a misreading of certain specific operative provisions of the Agreement. More generally, the panel's approach displays lack of sensitivity to the challenges faced by an administrative agency seeking the best evidence but at the expense of reasonable administrative costs, and within a limited time period.

From an economic perspective, since anti-dumping is generally not an efficient instrument, either for addressing anti-trust concerns such as predation (were they to exist), or for dealing with adjustment costs, an intrusive approach such as that adopted here by the panel could enhance efficiency, if it discourages the award of anti-dumping duties. However, if the micromanagement of agency procedures exemplified by this decision does not result in fewer or lower anti-dumping duties being levied, its effect may simply be to increase the deadweight losses involved in administering protection (legal costs, and agency resources, etc.).

If we adopt a political economy perspective, and see the relative ease of anti-dumping as providing a safety valve that allows WTO Members to make greater concessions in negotiations, and reduces pressures to renege in more fundamental ways on treaty commitments, then an interpretation such as that of the panel in this case which makes imposition of anti-dumping duties more costly or difficult than the text of the Anti-dumping

Agreement would seem to require might well be undesirable from an economic perspective.

References

Dam, K. W., 2001. *The Rules of the Global Game: A New Look at US International Economic Policymaking.* University of Chicago Press, Chicago, IL.

Dyzenhaus D., 1991. *Hard Cases in Wicked Legal Systems: South African Law in the Perspective of Legal Philosophy,* Clarendon Press, Oxford.

Esserman, S. and R. Howse, 2003. "Judges and Global Politics: Has the WTO Gone Too Far," *Foreign Affairs,* vol. 82/1, pp. 130–141.

Habermas, J., 1996. *Between Facts and Norms: Contributions to a Discourse Theory of Law and Democracy.* The MIT Press, Cambridge, MA.

Hutton S. J. and M. J. Trebilcock, 1990. An Empirical Study of the Application of Canadian Anti-dumping Laws, *Journal of World Trade,* vol. 24, pp. 123–146.

Miranda, J., 1996. Should Anti-dumping Laws be Dumped? *Law and Policy in International Business,* (1996), 255ff.

Sunstein, C., 1990. *After the Rights Revolution: Reconceiving the Regulatory State,* Harvard University Press, Cambridge, MA.

Sykes, A., 1995. The economics of injury in anti-dumping and countervailing duty case, in *Economic Dimensions in International Law: Comparative and Empirical Perspectives,* J. Bhandari and A. Sykes, eds., Cambridge University Press, Cambridge, pp. 83–125.

Tarullo, D., 2002. The Hidden Costs of International Dispute Settlement: WTO Review of Domestic Anti-Dumping Decisions, unpublished manuscript, Georgetown Law Center, 2002.

8

US – Lead and Bismuth II
United States – Imposition of Countervailing Duties on Certain Hot-Rolled Lead and Bismuth Carbon Steel Products Originating in the United Kingdom: Here Today, Gone Tomorrow? Privatization and the Injury Caused by Non-Recurring Subsidies*

GENE M. GROSSMAN AND PETROS C. MAVROIDIS

1 Facts of the case

In 1993, the US Department of Commerce began to levy countervailing duties on imports of certain leaded bars from the United Kingdom. The United States applied tariffs to goods imported from British Steel Engineering Steels, a subsidiary of British Steel plc. Following investigations by the US Department of Commerce and the United States International Trade Commission, the US authorities held that the imposition of duties was both required by Section 701 of the Tariff Act of 1930 (as amended) and not in violation of any of the country's obligations as a member of the World Trade Organization.

In its investigation of the domestic industry's petition for countervailing duties, the US Department of Commerce determined that British Steel Engineering Steels was the owner of assets that originally belonged to British Steel Corporation, a former state-owned company in the United Kingdom. According to the US Department of Commerce, British Steel Corporation received equity infusions and outright grants from the British government totaling £7 billion between 1977 and 1986 that were used to develop capacity for producing leaded bars.

* This study was prepared for the American Law Institute project on "The Principles of WTO Law." We are grateful to Richard Diamond, John Ragosta, Don Regan, and the participants in the ALI conference held in Philadelphia, PA on February 6–7, 2003 for their comments on earlier drafts.

In 1986, British Steel Corporation joined with the privately owned Guest, Keen, and Nettlefolds to create a joint venture known as United Engineering Steels Limited. Both British Steel Corporation and Guest, Keen, and Nettlefolds contributed assets to United Engineering Steels Ltd., including the assets for producing leaded bars that were formerly held by British Steel Corporation. In 1988, the British government privatized British Steel Corporation by first ceding all of its property, rights, and liabilities to British Steel plc and then selling its shares in that company on the equity market. The US Department of Commerce did not dispute the British government's claim that its sales of British Steel plc shares took place at arm's length and for fair market prices. Still, it ruled that the benefits that British Steel Corporation had garnered from the equity infusions and cash grants had "traveled" to its successor company, British Steel Engineering Steels.

Under US trade law, an equity infusion by a government on terms different from those that would be required by a private investor is considered to be a *non-recurring subsidy*. When such a subsidy causes or threatens to cause material injury to a domestic industry, the law allows for the imposition of a countervailing duty. Since the US Department of Commerce ruled that the subsidy that had been granted to British Steel Corporation had "passed through" to British Steel Engineering Steels upon the change in asset ownership, it deemed a countervailing duty on imports from British Steel Engineering Steels to be appropriate. The US Department of Commerce computed the size of the tariff by first allocating a portion of the grants made to British Steel Corporation to the production of leaded bars and then assessing the useful life and depreciation pattern of the assets that were purchased by British Steel Corporation with the funds contributed by the British government.

2   Issues raised before the WTO Panel

The European Communities complained to the panel that the United States had failed to act in conformity with its obligations under the WTO Agreement on Subsidies and Countervailing Measures (hereinafter, the SCM Agreement) when it imposed countervailing duties on imports of leaded bars from the United Kingdom following administrative reviews in 1995, 1996, and 1997. The European Communities did not dispute the legality of the countervailing duties originally imposed by the United States on imports of leaded bars, although it could have done so on grounds similar to those elaborated in its complaint.

The dispute between the United States and the European Communities arose because the latter – which were legally entitled to represent British Steel plc/British Steel Engineering Steels before the WTO – disagreed with the US Department of Commerce determination that a benefit from a non-recurring subsidy had passed through to British Steel Engineering Steels upon the change in ownership of the capital used to produce leaded bars. In the judgment of the European Communities, the current owners of British Steel Engineering Steels could not have "benefited" from any subsidy to British Steel Corporation, because the British government sold its holdings in British Steel plc at fair market prices.

The European Communities argued that the US actions were inconsistent with a series of provisions of the SCM Agreement, most notably Article 21, Article 19 (which, in the opinion of the European Communities, provides the context for Article 21), Article 10, Article 1, Article 2, as well as Article VI.3 of the GATT. Article 21 of the *SCM Agreement* governs the duration and review of countervailing duties.

The WTO Members agree that a countervailing duty shall remain in force only for as long as is necessary to counteract the effects of a subsidy that causes material injury to an industry in the importing country. In Article 21.1 (which is of particular relevance to the dispute at hand), the WTO Members agree that

> if as a result of the review under this paragraph, the authorities determine
> that the countervailing duty is no longer warranted, it shall be terminated
> immediately.

Article 19.1 of the SCM Agreement dictates that countervailing duties must be levied in accordance with the provisions of the SCM Agreement and Article 19.4 further stipulates that no countervailing duty

> shall be levied on any imported product in excess of the amount of the
> subsidy found to exist.

Article 10, echoing Article 19.1, makes it clear that the imposition of countervailing duties shall only occur in accordance with the relevant provisions of the SCM Agreement and in its footnote 36 clarifies that the purpose of a countervailing duty is to offset a subsidy, as provided in Article VI.3 GATT.

Finally, Articles 1 and 2 of the SCM Agreement provide the agreed definition of a subsidy. According to Article 1.1 and Article 2.1, a subsidy can be deemed to exist only if a government makes a payment that confers a benefit to a specific enterprise or industry (or group of enterprises or industries). The European Communities argued that neither British Steel plc/British Steel Engineering Steels nor any other enterprise or industry in existence at the time of the administrative reviews undertaken by the US Department of Commerce could have benefited from any subsidy that might have been paid in the past, because a fair market price had been paid for all assets used to produced leaded bars. According to the European Communities, the United States should not have continued its countervailing duties upon administrative review, because one of the pre-conditions for a countervailing duty – namely, the existence of a subsidy that confers a benefit – was not satisfied.[1]

In the hearings before the Panel, the United States did not dispute the EC allegation that the assets of British Steel plc once held by the British government had been sold at a fair market price. Rather, the United States maintained that, even if this indeed was the case, the benefit of the original subsidy had passed through to the acquiring entity and thus the goods produced with the subsidized capital could be lawfully subject to countervailing duties.

3 Decision of the Panel

In its report, *United States – Imposition of Countervailing Duties on Certain Hot-Rolled Lead and Bismuth Carbon Steel Products Originating in the United Kingdom* (WT/DS138/R), the Panel sided with the European Communities, concluding that

> . . . by imposing countervailing duties on 1994, 1995 and 1996 imports of leaded bars produced by UES and BSplc/BSES respectively, the United States violated Article 10 of the SCM Agreement.
>
> (Panel Report, para. 7.1)

The Panel reached this conclusion because, in its view,

> . . . the USDOC should have examined the continued existence of "benefit" already deemed to have been conferred by the pre-1985/86 "financial contributions" to BSC, and it should have done so from the perspective of UES and BSplc/BSES respectively, and not BSC.
>
> (Panel Report, para. 6.70)

---

[1] The European Communities did not request a retroactive remedy (that is, reimbursement of duties perceived to be illegal) in case the Panel would agree with its argument. Since the Panel was not confronted with such a request, it was required, in accordance with the maxim *non ultra petita*, to confine its findings to the issue invoked by the European Communities.

Moreover, the Panel noted that

> . . . fair market value was paid for all productive assets, goodwill etc. employed by UES and BSplc/BSES in the production of leaded bars imported in the United States in 1994, 1995 and 1996. In these circumstances, we fail to see how pre-1985/86 "financial contributions" bestowed on BSC could subsequently be considered to confer a "benefit" on UES and BSplc/BSES during the relevant periods of review.
>
> (Panel Report, para. 6.81)

This reasoning led the Panel to conclude that the countervailing duties imposed by the United States on leaded bars were illegal under the WTO Agreement.

4 The US appeal and the Appellate Body's decision

The United States raised two issues in its appeal to the Appellate Body (AB).[2] First, the United States argued that the Panel did not apply the correct standard of review when evaluating the lawfulness of the US Department of Commerce actions: the Panel applied the review standards outlined in Article 11 of the Understanding on Rules and Procedures Governing the Settlement of Disputes (the DSU) whereas, in the view of the United States, the appropriate standard was that outlined in Article 17.6 of the Agreement on Implementation of Article VI of the General Agreement on Tariffs and Trade 1994 (the Anti-dumping Agreement).

Second, the United States argued that the panel had erred in ruling that the US Department of Commerce should have focused its administrative review on whether a benefit had accrued to the owners of British Steel plc/British Steel Engineering Steels following the privatization of British Steel Corporation. Rather, the United States argued, it was enough for the US Department of Commerce to consider whether a subsidy had conferred a benefit to industry production. The United States felt that the Panel further erred in finding that United Engineering Steel Ltd. and British Steel plc/British Steel Engineering Steels had gained no benefit from the British government's financial contributions to British Steel Corporation.

The AB rejected both of the US claims. The AB ruled that the Panel had applied the correct legal standard in reviewing the case and upheld the Panel's finding that the focus of the US administrative review should

---

[2] The AB report mentions three issues (see WT/DS138/AB/R at para. 43). However, items (b) and (c) in para. 43 of the report refer to the same underlying issue, namely the "pass through" of the benefits of the non-recurring subsidy upon the change in asset ownership.

have been on whether the subsidy had conferred a benefit on a particular legal entity and not on production *per se*. Furthermore, it found that no such benefit had been conferred on any existing legal entities, because the previously subsidized assets were sold by the government at market prices (para. 75).

5 The standard of review

The WTO regulates the standard of review that adjudicating bodies must apply when examining the conformity of actions taken by Members with the WTO contract. The review standards are discussed in two separate places in the WTO Agreement. First, Article 11 of the DSU discusses the general standards to be used in all disputes brought to the WTO except those covered by a specific rule. Second, Article 17.6 of the Anti-dumping Agreement provides specific rules governing the review of disputes arising from the application of antidumping policies. Article 17.6 is the only specific rule thus far included in the WTO contract that might be interpreted as an exception to Article 11 of the DSU.

The WTO has yet to clarify the operational differences between the standards of review required in disputes arising under the Anti-dumping Agreement and those to be applied in other disputes. But the wording of Article 17.6 of the Anti-dumping Agreement suggests that the Members may have wished the adjudicating bodies to adopt a more deferential attitude toward the actions of Members taken in response to perceived dumping than those taken for other reasons. In particular, Article 17.6(ii) of the Anti-dumping Agreement requires that when a panel

> finds that a relevant provision of the Agreement admits of more than one permissible interpretation, the panel shall find the authorities' measure to be in conformity with the Agreement if it rests upon one of these permissible interpretations.

In other words, if more than one interpretation of a term appearing in the Anti-dumping Agreement is possible, and if the domestic authority investigating the dumping claim adopted one of the admissible interpretations, then the ensuing actions should not be ruled illegal even if the WTO Panel would have preferred another interpretation of the ambiguous term. In contrast, Article 11 of the DSU, *prima facie*, does not seem to offer the same latitude. The article instructs a panel to

> . . . make an objective assessment of the matter before it, including an objective assessment of the facts of the case and the applicability of and conformity with the relevant covered agreements.

Arguably, this clause may require the WTO adjudicating bodies to decide on a single interpretation of terms in the WTO Agreement (outside of the antidumping area) and to outlaw all actions by domestic authorities that run counter to the preferred interpretation.[3]

Also germane to the US appeal is the Declaration on Dispute Settlement Pursuant to the Agreement on Implementation of Article VI of the General Agreement on Tariffs and Trade 1994 or Part V of the Agreement on Subsidies and Countervailing Measures (the Declaration), which the WTO Members adopted in Marrakesh in the discussions that led to the conclusion of the Uruguay Round; and the Decision on Review of Article 17.6 of the Agreement on Implementation of Article VI of the General Agreement on Tariffs and Trade 1994 (the Decision), which perhaps constitutes an attempt by the parties to give operational content to the Declaration. The Declaration advises the Ministers from the Member countries to

> [r]ecognize, with respect to dispute settlement pursuant to the Agreement on Implementation of Article VI of GATT 1994 or Part V of the Agreement on Subsidies and Countervailing Measures, the need for the consistent resolution of disputes arising from anti-dumping and countervailing duty measures.
>
> (italics in the original)

while the Decision instructs that the

> . . . standard of review in paragraph 6 of Article 17 of the Agreement on Implementation of Article VI of GATT 1994 shall be reviewed after a period of three years with a view to considering the question of whether it is capable of general application.

Apparently, the Declaration advises that disputes arising under the SCM Agreement should be adjudicated similarly to those arising under the Anti-dumping Agreement, and the Decision specifically requests that the WTO Members address the possibility of "exporting" Article of

---

[3] Inasmuch as the WTO has not been called upon to clarify the practical differences between Article 17.6 of the Anti-dumping Agreement and Article 11 of the DSU, it is mere speculation that the former grants greater leeway to investigating authorities when responding to alleged instances of dumping than the latter clause leaves to such authorities in other matters.

17.6 of the Anti-dumping Agreement to disputes arising under the SCM Agreement.

The United States argued, in its appeal to the AB, that when the Members issued their Declaration calling for "consistent resolution of disputes," they meant to impose similar standards of review for disputes over countervailing duties and those concerning antidumping actions. The AB rejected this claim on four grounds. First, inasmuch as the language of the Declaration is hortatory, the AB argued that it has little if any legal significance, especially since it does not prescribe any particular course of action that should be followed in order to achieve the stated objective. Second, the failure of the WTO Members to take the action envisaged in the *Decision* within the indicated three-year time period suggested that the Members did not intend Article 17.6 of the Anti-dumping Agreement necessarily to be the standard of review in disputes involving countervailing duties.

Third, Article 1 of the DSU makes it clear that the rules reflected in that agreement, including its Article 11, should apply to all disputes brought to the WTO adjudicating bodies unless special or additional rules and procedures are spelt out in its Appendix 2. Whereas Appendix 2 of the DSU does in fact make reference to Article 17.6 of the Anti-dumping Agreement as an exception, it does not mention any special or additional rules that should regulate the standard of review of disputes arising from the SCM Agreement. Fourth, the AB argued that a precedent had been established in prior WTO jurisprudence to treat Article 11 of the DSU as the appropriate standard of review "for all but one of the covered agreements."

The decision reached by the AB on the issue of the appropriate standard of review seems to us to be the correct one. As the AB first noted in its report on *United States – Standards for Reformulated and Conventional Gasoline* (WT/DS2/AB/R of April 29, 1996) the WTO adjudicating bodies lack discretion as to the methods they can use when interpreting the WTO contract: the Members removed such discretion in Article 3.2 of the DSU, which requires the dispute settlement system of the WTO to interpret provisions of the various WTO agreements "in accordance with customary rules and interpretation of public international law." The customary rules of public and international law have been codified in Articles 31 and 32 of the Vienna Convention on Laws and Treaties (VCLT), which state that a treaty must be interpreted in accordance with the ordinary meaning of its terms in their context, taking into account the objectives of the treaty, any subsequent treaties or practice, and, when justified by the rules spelt out in Article 32 of VCLT, the preparatory work performed when the treaty was negotiated.

The ordinary meaning of the terms used in the Declaration, which was cited by the United States in its argument that Article 17.6 of the Anti-dumping Agreement ought to apply to the review of disputes arising under the SCM Agreement, supports the conclusion reached by the AB. First, the Declaration indeed is couched in hortatory language, and is, therefore, not legally binding. Where the Declaration states that the "Ministers *recognize the need* for the consistent resolution of disputes" (emphasis added), it clearly does not endorse or mandate any particular course of action. At most, the quoted phrase in the Declaration might be seen as a best-endeavors clause; that is, it might reveal the Members' intention to provide in subsequent actions the means to ensure consistency in the resolution of disputes under the Anti-dumping Agreement and the SCM Agreement.

An absence of legally binding language does not, however, immediately imply that there are no legal ramifications. Indeed, were the AB to interpret the Declaration outside of its context, it might have been forced to ask itself whether the Declaration provides sufficient normative guidance as to what actions are expected from the Members under the best-endeavors clause. However, the need for the AB to address this issue is obviated by the context of the Declaration itself.

The context of the Declaration includes at least the entirety of the WTO Agreement.[4] Thus, the Decision discussed by the AB in its report forms part of the context in which the Declaration must be interpreted. Since the WTO Agreement does not dictate any hierarchy of the two legal instruments, it is their terms and subject matter that must be used to determine which, if any, has priority. But we note that only the Decision prescribes specific actions that the Members should take to achieve the aims described in the Declaration. Moreover, the Decision discusses explicitly the possible "export" of Article 17.6 of the Anti-dumping Agreement to the SCM Agreement, whereas the Declaration does not.

Consequently, we consider it appropriate to regard the Decision as the procedural vehicle that the Members intended to be used in order to help realize the objectives expressed in the Declaration. The AB was correct to turn to the Decision for normative guidance. But when it did so, the AB

---

[4] It has sometimes been argued that other treaties relating to a similar subject matter, especially if they include as signatories more or less the same set of partners, can also form part of the legal context. The merits of this argument are irrelevant for the present analysis.

recognized that the specific action prescribed by the Decision for dealing with the possible use of Article 17.6 of the Anti-dumping Agreement in disputes arising under the SCM Agreement had not occurred within the specified time period. From this, the AB inferred that the Members did not intend to accomplish (at least for the time being) the aims spelled out in the Declaration, at least insofar as the application of identical standards of review, in disputes arising from the two different agreements concerned. We concur with this conclusion. Since the Members failed to review within three years the question of whether Article 17.6 of the Anti-dumping Agreement is capable of more general application, they could not have meant the objective of similar standards of review in the two types of disputes to be realized immediately.

When the Members failed to take specific actions to ensure identical standards of review, their lack of action warranted a resort to the status quo. But the status quo in this case is provided by Article 1 of the DSU, where it states that all rules in the DSU should apply to all disputes brought to the WTO adjudicating bodies unless special or additional rules and procedures are prescribed by Appendix 2. Since no new rule was articulated in the Declaration, the Decision, or in any subsequent legal instrument issued by the WTO Members, it follows that Article 11 of the DSU remains the relevant provision governing the standard of review in disputes arising under the SCM Agreement. The AB finding to this effect is well justified.

6   The "pass through" of non-recurring subsidies

The SCM Agreement allows a WTO Member to take countervailing action against imports when a foreign government provides a subsidy to its local producers and certain further conditions are met. The SCM Agreement defines a subsidy to be any financial contribution by a government to a specific enterprise, industry, or group of enterprises or industries that confers a benefit to the recipients. It allows countervailing measures when a Member can establish the existence of a subsidy so defined and can show that subsidized goods sold within its borders have caused or threaten to cause injury to a domestic industry.

As previously noted, the European Communities did not challenge the US claim that a (non-recurring) subsidy had been paid by the British government to British Steel Corporation at the time when the latter was a state-owned company. Nor did the United States contest the EC allegation that the divestiture of assets formerly owned by the British government was conducted at fair market prices. The contentious issue in this case has to do with the appropriate interpretation of the word "benefit" in the Agreement's definition of a subsidy. Does British Steel Engineering Steels now benefit from the equity infusions that were formerly granted to British Steel Corporation when the latter was a state-owned company?[5] If so, then the United States might be legally justified in levying a countervailing duty on imports of leaded bars from that company. If not, then no such countervailing measures are allowed.

In order to interpret the meaning of the word "benefit" in the context of the SCM Agreement, it is necessary to consider first the *raison d'être* of the Agreement itself.[6] Only by understanding the objectives of the Agreement and what behaviors it is meant to discourage can we discern how it ought to be applied in circumstances that are not explicitly discussed. We therefore begin with a discussion of why Members have decided to tolerate countervailing duties in response to certain subsidies, and why the imposition of such duties has been linked to the occurrence (or threat) of injury in a domestic industry.

6.1   Objectives of the SCM Agreement

Like any trade agreement, the SCM Agreement is meant to discourage governments from taking unilateral actions that would harm their trading partners. The presumption in international relations is that governments

---

[5] Recall that the United States argued in its appeal that the Panel should have considered whether a benefit was conferred to productive operations rather than to a legal or natural person. The AB rejected this claim, noting that Article 14 of the SCM Agreement refers to a "benefit to the recipient" and that prior jurisprudence by the AB has made clear that a benefit cannot exist in the abstract, but only if enjoyed by a beneficiary (i.e. a specific recipient). We will argue, however, that the distinction proposed by the United States between benefit to productive operations and benefit to a specific entity is of no legal consequence, once the term "benefit" is appropriately interpreted. In particular, we will argue that it is appropriate to consider a producer as having received a benefit anytime its production is competitively advantaged. With this definition of benefit, it makes no difference whether we look for benefit to productive operations or to specific producers. In either case, it is necessary to ask whether British Steel Engineering Steels enjoys any competitive advantage from the subsidies previously paid to British Steel Corporation, considering that the current owners of British Steel Engineering Steels purchased the assets of British Steel Corporation at fair market prices.

[6] As previously noted, Article 31 of the VCLT requires that the terms in an international treaty be interpreted in, and not independent of, their context. In its past decisions, the AB routinely has endeavored to interpret the terms of the WTO Agreement in their context; see, for example, the AB report *United States – Definitive Safeguard Measures on Imports of Circular Welded Carbon Quality Line Pipe from Korea* (WT/DS202/AB/R of February 15, 2002) at § 165.

can do as they choose with regard to policies whose effects are confined within their borders. But many policies – domestic as well as trade policies – impinge upon the interests of foreign citizens and corporations. In the absence of any agreements, governments might have little reason to take these "international externalities" into account when setting their national policies.

Policies that are set without regard to their potentially adverse effects abroad are bound to be globally inefficient, in the sense that an alternative set of policies could be found that all governments would agree is preferable to the chosen ones. To further global efficiency, a trade agreement makes it costly for a government to choose policies that inflict harm on trading partners. Countervailing duties are the primary instruments in the SCM Agreement for imposing costs on a government that chooses to invoke subsidies.

Why do the Members of the WTO wish to discourage certain subsidies? This question is the same as asking "in what ways might a subsidy inflict 'harm' on another Member country?" The answer to this question depends, of course, on the interpretation of the word "harm." The appropriate application of the treaty – including, for example, to situations in which subsidized assets have undergone a change in ownership – should be one that helps to avoid the sort of harm that was of concern to the signatories.

One possibility would be to associate harm with a loss of aggregate economic welfare. That is, we might assume that the parties to the SCM Agreement wished to discourage subsidies, because they feared that such policies would reduce the sum of consumer surplus, producer surplus, and government revenue in other Member countries. If this indeed were the objective of the treaty, then the application of countervailing measures should be sanctioned only for cases in which a subsidy can be shown to inflict a welfare loss on another Member. We argue, however, that an interpretation of the SCM Agreement that associates harm with a loss in aggregate economic welfare cannot be sustained in the light of the manner in which the Agreement was structured.[7]

---

[7] Goetz, Lloyd, and Schwartz (1986) and Diamond (1989) consider the rationale for countervailing duty law and conclude that these laws are best understood as a means to protect an entitlement of domestic producers from the harmful effects of foreign subsidies rather than as a means to promote global economic efficiency. Our understanding of the SCM Agreement is quite similar. We do not mean to imply, however, that a welfare standard for injury tests would be the wrong standard to use. To the contrary, we believe that an alternative injury test that looked for harm to aggregate welfare would better serve the objective of promoting international efficiency than the test required in the SCM Agreement as it now stands. We come back to this point in section 6.3.6, when we discuss the desirable changes to the SCM Agreement that are suggested by this case.

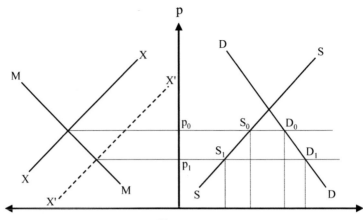

Figure 8.1

As is well known, if product and factor markets are competitive and well-functioning, then a foreign subsidy to production of a good cannot reduce aggregate welfare in an importing country. This point can be seen with the aid of figure 8.1. In the figure, the left side shows the world market for the good before and after the subsidy is introduced. The curve XX is the original excess supply curve in the country that implements the subsidy. This curve gives, for each world price, the amount that the country's firms produce in excess of what is demanded by local consumers. This corresponds to the volume of its exports at the given price. The curve MM is the aggregate excess demand curve of the rest of the world; it is the excess of world demand outside the subsidizing country over the aggregate production at each price. The world equilibrium without subsidies is found at the intersection of the two curves, where the excess supply of the one country matches the total excess demand of the others. The no-subsidy world price is p_0.

A subsidy typically encourages production in the subsidizing country.[8] Thus, at each price, local firms are willing to produce more output when subsidized than otherwise. It follows that the subsidy shifts the excess supply curve of the subsidizing country to the right, as depicted for example by X'X'. As can be seen in the figure, the effect of the subsidy is to reduce the world price of the subsidized good.

The right side of the figure shows the impact of the subsidy in a country that imports the good. The effects of the subsidy are transmitted to the

---

[8] We will clarify this point below, distinguishing in particular between recurring and nonrecurring subsidies.

importing country via the fall in the world price. The demand curve in the importing country is labeled DD, while the supply curve is labeled SS. At both p_0 and p_1, the quantity demanded exceeds the quantity supplied, which implies that the good is imported from abroad.

We can now find the effects of the subsidy on aggregate welfare in the importing country. First, consumers benefit from the lower price. The gain in consumer surplus is given by the area of the trapezoid $p_0 p_1 D_1 D_0$. It includes both the savings to consumers on the D_0 units that they consumed before the subsidy was introduced, and the difference between their willingness to pay for the $D_1 - D_0$ extra units they purchase after the price decline and what those units cost them.

Producers, meanwhile, are hurt by the fall in price. The loss in producer surplus is equal to the area of $p_0 p_1 S_1 S_0$. This includes both the loss of revenue on the S_1 units that they produce after the subsidy is in place but sell for a lower price than beforehand, and the surplus relative to marginal cost that they earned on the units that no longer are produced once the subsidy is introduced. The figure shows that the harm to producers can never be as large as the benefit to consumers; in total, the country gains surplus equal to the area of $S_0 D_0 D_1 S_1$. If markets were competitive and well-functioning in the importing countries and governments were concerned only about aggregate economic welfare, then importing countries would be thankful when a trading partner introduced a subsidy, and would have no reason to discourage such subsidies with the threat of countervailing actions.

Of course, it is not true that a subsidy always enhances aggregate welfare in all Member countries. It is simple to see, for example, that a subsidy will reduce welfare in a country that exports products that compete with the subsidized good. Figure 8.2 reproduces the left side of figure 8.1, but shows on the right side the effects of the subsidy in a country that exports a good in competition with the country that has implemented the subsidy. In such a country, consumers gain an amount equal to the area of $p_0 p_1 D_1 D_0$ while producers lose an amount equal to the area of $p_0 p_1 S_1 S_0$. Here, the producer loss outweighs the consumer gain.

Aggregate welfare losses might sometimes occur in an importing country as well. Let us reconsider, for example, the situation depicted in figure 8.1, but suppose this time that wages are rigid (or sticky) in the country that imports the subsidized good. In other words, instead of a "well-functioning market" we imagine that there are imperfections in the importing country's labor market. Then the reduction in output induced by the foreign subsidy will be accompanied by an increase in unemployment in the importing country. As usual, the supply curve SS gives the

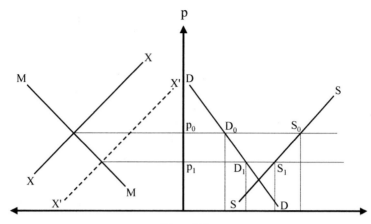

Figure 8.2

private marginal cost of production in the importing country, including the entirety of the wage bill. But, with wage rigidities, the social cost of output is less than the private cost, because the workers in the industry do not have the opportunity to earn a similar wage elsewhere in the economy. Since the social cost is less than the private cost, $p_0 p_1 S_1 S_0$ represents an understatement of the loss in producer surplus caused by the foreign subsidy. If the social loss is large enough, it can outweigh the benefit to consumers.

A foreign subsidy can also reduce aggregate welfare in an importing country when a few large firms dominate the industry. In such circumstances, the firms (foreign and domestic) may exploit their market power by charging prices in excess of marginal production costs. As Brander and Spencer (1985) have shown, subsidies can have strategic effects on firm behavior in markets with imperfect competition. If a subsidy causes foreign firms to sell more output than otherwise, the optimal response of competitors in the importing country may be to reduce the volume of their own sales. But this will spell a loss of monopoly profits for the domestic firms, which will offset and perhaps outweigh the net benefit depicted in figure 8.1.[9]

---

[9] A predatory subsidy is an extreme example of a strategic subsidy. The intent of such a policy is more than just to induce firms outside the subsidizing country to cede market share, but actually to drive them from the market. Like strategic subsidies, predatory subsidies can reduce aggregate welfare in an importing country, both because the local producers that leave the industry forfeit their prospective profits, and because the consumer price may rise once the local competitors exit.

We conclude that the effect of a subsidy on aggregate welfare in another Member country is *a priori* ambiguous. Therefore, if the Members had intended the SCM Agreement to discourage actions that would inflict welfare losses on others, they would have directed the "test" for actionable subsidies toward identifying conditions where aggregate loss is most likely to occur. For example, an external welfare loss is more likely to occur when a government subsidizes firms that sell in an imperfectly competitive market. So the test for an actionable subsidy might have made reference to the competitive conditions of the subsidized industry. Similarly, a welfare loss is more likely when wages are sticky in the importing country than when they are flexible; so the Agreement might have made reference to the labor-market conditions there. The Agreement might also have allowed for countervailing measures in Member countries that export goods in competition with the subsidized good, inasmuch as these countries are quite likely to suffer welfare losses as a result of a foreign subsidy.

In fact, the SCM Agreement does not confine the use of countervailing duties to situations in which an importing country has established the presumption of a welfare loss. The Agreement makes no reference to labor-market conditions, to market structure, or even to consumer welfare. And the Agreement makes no allowance for countervailing measures in countries that export the subsidized good, where the presumption of welfare losses surely exists.[10] Rather, countervailing measures are permitted only when there has been (or threatens to be) injury to a domestic industry in an importing country.

The observation that injury to import-competing interests provides the sole basis for countervailing action points to a different interpretation of the objective of the SCM Agreement. Evidently, the signatories meant to discourage certain policy actions that would harm competing *producer*

---

[10] Although the Agreement recognizes the possibility of serious prejudice to the interests of another Member that may arise due to the displacement of exports of a like product to the market of the subsidizing member or to a third-country market, it does not allow serious prejudice to exporting interests to be a basis for countervailing action. Rather, in such cases, the Agreement calls for consultations between the Member that is granting or maintaining a subsidy and the complaining Member, followed by a panel review in the event that consultations do not result in a mutually agreed solution. Only after a report by a panel or Appellate Body has been adopted in which it is determined that a subsidy has resulted in adverse effects to the interests of another Member and the subsidizing Member has failed to take appropriate steps to remove the adverse effects of the subsidy may the complaining Member take such countermeasures as have been authorized by the Dispute Settlement Body (see Articles 7.8 and 7.9 of the SCM Agreement).

interests in the importing country. This objective is understandable in the light of recent literature on the political economy of trade policy, which has emphasized that governments often set their trade policies with objectives other than the maximization of aggregate economic welfare in mind. The policies that are chosen typically reflect a compromise among competing constituent interests. Moreover, some interests – especially those that are relatively concentrated – receive more weight in the political process than others. Less concentrated groups are not so successful in the political arena, in part because they have difficulty in overcoming the free-rider problems that plague collective political action (Olson, 1965). Thus, governments often are induced by political pressures to give more weight to producer interests than to consumer welfare when making their decisions about trade policy.

Our interpretation that the main objective of the SCM Agreement is to discourage subsidies that might harm producers in importing countries finds support in many other provisions of the Agreement. For example, Article 12.9 specifies that the domestic producers of a like product *must* be invited by the investigating authority to offer their views about an alleged subsidy and proposed countervailing measures, whereas the authority has discretion to decide whether or not to allow consumers of the subsidized good to do so. Article 15.1 requires that "a determination of injury . . . shall be based on positive evidence and involve an objective examination of both (a) the volume of the subsidized imports and the effect of the subsidized imports on prices in the domestic market for like products and (b) the consequent impact of these imports on the domestic producers of such products." And Articles 14 and 19 require the size of the countervailing duty to be set so as to just offset the adverse effects of the subsidy on conditions in the domestic industry. This latter provision can only be understood as an attempt to restore competitive conditions in the industry to what they would have been had the subsidy been absent.

6.2   Subsidy benefits and changes in ownership

We return now to the central issue in *US – Lead and Bismuth II*, which concerns the appropriate interpretation of the term "benefit" where it is used in Article 1.1(b) of the SCM Agreement in the definition of an actionable subsidy. Bearing in mind that the objective of the SCM Agreement is to discourage governments from enacting policies that might harm producer interests in importing countries, the definition of a subsidy must be one that helps to identify policies that would inflict such harm. Accordingly, "benefit" must be evaluated in terms of the effect of the policy on the competitive position of the firm or firms that (directly or indirectly) received the government's contributions, rather than in terms of the effect of the contributions on the profits or wealth of the owners of those firms.

In *US – Lead and Bismuth II*, the AB was called upon to decide the legitimacy of continued US countervailing duties following a change in ownership. The European Communities claimed that, because the current producers in the United Kingdom had acquired the assets of British Steel Corporation at fair market prices, they could not have received benefits from any prior subsidies. The United States countered that the original subsidy continued to favor British production of the exported products, even if the current owners of the assets had not profited personally from the purchase of those assets.

As previously noted, the AB ruled in favor of the European Communities on this central issue in the case. It found that the "financial contributions" to British Steel Corporation had conferred no "benefit" to United Engineering Steels Ltd. or to British Steel plc/British Steel Engineering Steels and that, in consequence, the US application of countervailing duties on the lead bar products was inconsistent with its obligations under the SCM Agreement. In particular, the AB argued that

> [t]he question whether a "financial contribution" confers a "benefit" depends, therefore, on whether the recipient has received a "financial contribution" on terms more favorable than those available to the recipient in the market. In the present case, the Panel made factual findings that UES and BSplc/BSES paid fair market value for all the productive assets, goodwill, etc., they acquired from BSC and subsequently used in the production of leaded bars imported into the United States in 1994, 1995 and 1996. We, therefore, see no error in the Panel's conclusion that, in the specific circumstances of this case, the "financial contributions" bestowed on BSC between 1977 and 1986 could not be deemed to confer a "benefit" on UES and BSplc/BSES.

We find this ruling to be wholly misguided, inasmuch as the Appellate Body's interpretation of the treaty text fails to accord with the clear intentions of the signatories of the SCM Agreement. Because the SCM Agreement fails to provide an explicit definition of the term "benefit," the adjudicating bodies are left to interpret the term on a case-by-case basis. But each such interpretation must be consistent with the overall objectives of the Agreement. We have already described the nature of those objectives; i.e. the Members wished to discourage governments from invoking subsidies when such policies would bring harm to producer interests in an importing country.

Since the signatories wished to avoid potentially adverse effects of a subsidy on producers in an importing country, then surely the appropriate question to ask in this case is whether the US producers continue to be disadvantaged relative to what would have been their competitive situation *but for* the subsidies paid to British Steel Corporation. This perspective provides the necessary guidance for interpreting the term "benefit" in this case; a benefit existed in the period under administrative review if and only if the British producers of leaded bars enjoyed a privileged position in the industry thanks to some enduring effects of the government's contributions.

We note that a change in ownership – at fair market prices or otherwise – has no bearing on competitive conditions in the world market for leaded bars. The British supply of exports is the difference between the British industry's supply of leaded bars and the local demand for those products. The industry supply, in turn, reflects the producers' marginal costs of production. Whereas the existence of the assets transferred by British Steel Corporation to United Engineering Steels Ltd. and then sold to British Steel plc/British Steel Engineering Steels may have affected the conditions of British supply in the periods under review, the amount that was paid in each transaction affected only the distribution of wealth among shareholders. Evidently, the AB interpreted "benefit" in the sense of "adding to wealth": the owners of British Steel plc/British Steel Engineering Steels are no wealthier today than they would have been had no contribution been made to British Steel Corporation. But the interpretation of the term "benefit" as an addition to wealth cannot be sustained in the context of the SCM Agreement. Accordingly, the observation that the assets were divested by the UK government at fair market price is irrelevant to the determination of whether the original subsidy conferred a benefit to the current producers of leaded bars that continues to impact adversely the producers of like products in the United States.[11]

---

[11] David Palmeter has made an additional excellent point to us in private discussions. If a change in ownership at fair market prices were sufficient to extinguish the benefits of a subsidy under countervailing duty law, then not only privatization but also equity sales between private citizens would have this effect. Since many shares of publicly traded firms change hands each year, a government's legal right to countervail against foreign subsidies would quickly be eliminated by such private changes in ownership.

6.3   Administrative review of non-recurring subsidies

The fact that the AB misinterpreted the term "benefit" in its ruling on *US – Lead and Bismuth II* does not, however, validate the US claim that it fulfilled its obligations under the SCM Agreement when it conducted its administrative reviews of the countervailing duties on leaded bars. Even with an appropriate interpretation of benefit as anything that provides a competitive advantage to foreign producers, it is incumbent upon the importing country to review periodically the ongoing need for a countervailing duty (see Article 21.2 of the SCM Agreement).

Here, the Agreement calls for the authorities, where requested, to "examine whether the continued imposition of the duty is necessary to offset subsidization, whether the injury would be likely to continue or recur if the duty were removed or varied, or both." In other words, the investigating authority must review whether the exporting entities continue to reap benefits from the subsidy, within the meaning of this term that we have already discussed. In fact, the investigating authorities in the United States made no effort to examine this issue when they conducted their administrative reviews in 1994, 1995, and 1996. Accordingly, they failed to establish the legality of continued imposition of countervailing duties on leaded bars from the United Kingdom.

What obligations did the SCM Agreement impose on the US investigating authorities when they conducted their administrative reviews of the countervailing duties on leaded bars? In order to answer this question, it is necessary for us to elaborate the essential differences between a recurring subsidy and a non-recurring subsidy, a topic to which we now turn.

6.3.1   Market effects of recurring subsidies

A recurring subsidy is one that provides for ongoing financial transfers from the government, often in relation to some economic activity or variable. Examples include fiscal incentives for employment or output and public provision of goods and services at below market prices.

It is easy to see how a recurring subsidy can promote exports, and how the subsidized exports can cause harm to a domestic industry in the importing country. Take, for example, the case of a fiscal inducement to production. Under such a scheme, foreign firms producing the subsidized product receive an amount s per unit of output from their government in addition to the price p they collect from the sale of the products. In the left panel of figure 8.3, we show the pre-subsidy supply and demand curves for

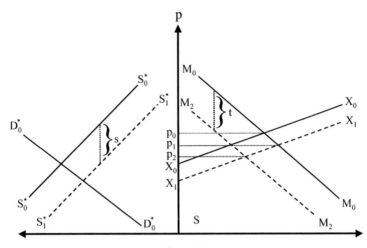

Figure 8.3

the subsidized product in the foreign country, $S_0^* S_0^*$ and $D_0^* D_0^*$, respectively. The subsidy shifts the foreign supply downward by an amount s, because foreign firms are willing to sell a given quantity at a lower international price when a subsidy is offered in view of the extra compensation they will receive from their own government. The supply curve that prevails with the subsidy in effect has been labeled $S_1^* S_1^*$ in the figure.

The effect of the subsidy on the world price is depicted in the right side of figure 8.3. Export supply at any world price p is the difference between supply and national demand at that price. The foreign country's pre-subsidy export supply curve is depicted by $X_0 X_0$, whereas the subsidy causes the curve to shift to $X_1 X_1$, with a vertical displacement that is less than or equal to s. The curve typically shifts by less than s, because the output subsidy serves to promote foreign production whereas an equivalent fall in the price p would both reduce foreign supply and boost foreign demand.[12] The subsidy induces a decline in the world price and an increase in the volume of exports, as we have noted previously.

The fall in world price spells injury to competing industries in the importing countries. But the injurious effects of the subsidy can be offset with a countervailing duty. Consider, for example, a per-unit tariff of size t, where t is set equal in magnitude to s. A tariff of t would shift the import demand vertically by an amount t, so that the import demand curve with the countervailing duty in place would be the one depicted by $M_2 M_2$. The

---

[12] The vertical displacement of the export supply curve would be exactly equal to s if foreign demand for the product were totally unresponsive to price.

figure shows the new (net of tariff) world price as p_2, where $p_2 \geq p_0 - s$. The gross price in the importing country is $p_2 + t$, which therefore exceeds p_0. Thus, a countervailing duty set equal in size to the per unit subsidy to foreign output is (more than) enough to restore a domestic price in the importing country greater to what it would have been *but for* the subsidy. It follows that a countervailing duty of size t leaves the domestic industry in the importing country at least as well off as it would have been without the foreign subsidy.[13]

It is apparent that a continuing countervailing duty would be needed to offset the ongoing benefit to foreign firms of a recurring subsidy. Were the duty to be removed at any time while the subsidy remained in place, the equilibrium world price would revert to p_1 and producers in the importing country would fare worse than at p_0, the price that would prevail in the absence of a subsidy.

6.3.2   Market effects of non-recurring subsidies

A non-recurring subsidy, by contrast, is a government contribution that is paid only once or perhaps a limited number of times. Usually, such contributions are used to finance wholly or partially the acquisition of fixed assets such as technology, plant, and equipment. Contributions that fall into the category of non-recurring subsidies include cash grants, loan guarantees, equity infusions, and government loans at below market interest rates. The SCM Agreement does not draw any legal distinction between recurring and non-recurring subsidies. It allows for countervailing duties when a Member establishes the existence of a subsidy of any sort and shows that subsidized imports are causing or threaten to cause injury to a domestic industry producing like products. The Agreement stipulates that the duties should not exceed the full amount of the subsidy, calculated as the benefit received by the exporting firm or industry per unit of the subsidized and exported product.

The countervailing duties at issue in *US – Lead and Bismuth II* were imposed, as we have indicated, in response to non-recurring subsidies. The US Department of Commerce found that the British government had provided equity infusions and cash grants to British Steel Corporation totaling £7 billion between 1977 and 1986. According to the United States, these contributions were used to finance investments by British

---

[13] If there were more than a single importing country, this conclusion would be strengthened, because then the aggregate world import demand curve would shift with the tariff by an amount less than s.

Steel Corporation that allowed the company to develop capacity for producing leaded bars. The United States has made no claim that the British government continues to make contributions to the firms or industry on an ongoing basis.

According to our discussion above, the investigating authorities in the United States are obliged under the terms of the SCM Agreement to show that the current producers of leaded bars in the United Kingdom are benefiting from the subsidies that were paid to British Steel Corporation. With our interpretation of "benefit" as anything that gives foreign firms a competitive advantage, the investigating authorities should have asked how (if at all) the industry competition differed in the review period from what would have been the competitive situation *but for* the earlier payment of the non-recurring subsidies.

To see the issues involved, we discuss the impact of a non-recurring subsidy on subsequent industry competition and show how a countervailing duty can be used to offset the adverse effects of such a subsidy on competing interests in an importing country. First, let us consider a non-recurring subsidy that is offered to help finance fixed-scale investments by one or more foreign firms. A fixed-scale investment is one in which the firms face a dichotomous decision; they can either choose to undertake a project of some predetermined size or to forego it entirely. Examples of such investments might include an R&D project to design a new product or a project to build a new manufacturing facility at minimum efficient scale.

Under such circumstances, the subsidy will change competitive conditions in the industry, at least initially, if one or more of the firms in the industry that would not have undertaken the project absent the subsidy decides differently in response to the government's contribution. Clearly, the subsidy can cause more foreign firms to be active in the industry than would otherwise be the case, or it can cause them to produce at greater scale. The initial effects of such a non-recurring subsidy, which were depicted in figure 8.1, include an increase in exports and a fall in the world price of the subsidized good. The fall in world price may well cause injury to firms in the domestic industry.

Next we consider the initial effects of a non-recurring subsidy that is used to help finance investments that may vary in size. For such investments, firms must choose not only whether to pursue the indicated projects, but also at what level to invest. For example, when a firm installs capital equipment, it must decide how much machinery to purchase, perhaps trading-off the fixed cost of the machines against the potential savings in labor costs. In a simple example, the government might offer to pay a fraction of firms' investments in machinery and equipment.[14] Firms then would choose their levels of investment to maximize profits net of investment costs. The benefits would come in the form of reduced labor costs. The smaller is the fraction of the total investment cost that the firms must bear themselves, the greater will be the scale of investment that equates marginal benefit with marginal cost (to the firm). The direct effect of a non-recurring subsidy is to increase the scale of investment, which in turn has an indirect effect of lowering firms' marginal production costs. Since profit-maximizing firms supply output up to the point where the marginal cost is equal to the market price, they will supply more output at a given price level and their marginal costs will be lower. It follows that a non-recurring subsidy that induces extra investment also shifts the foreign industry supply curve, ultimately reducing the world price of the subsidized good. Again, producers in the importing country who must compete with the subsidized good may suffer as a result.

6.3.3   Injury determination

Having established that a non-recurring subsidy can cause harm to a domestic industry in an importing country producing a like product, we proceed now to discuss the conditions that must be met before a country can introduce a countervailing duty order and (in the next subsection) the requirements under the SCM Agreement for periodic review of such orders.

As previously noted, the SCM Agreement requires an injury determination before any countervailing duties are imposed. Article 15.1 mandates:

> A determination of injury for purposes of Article VI of GATT 1994 shall be based on positive evidence and involve an object examination of both (*a*) the volume of the subsidized imports and the effect of the subsidized imports on prices in the domestic market for like products and (*b*) the consequent impact of those imports on the domestic producers of such products.

Article 15.5 further stipulates:

> It must be demonstrated that the subsidized imports are, through the effects of subsidies, causing injury within the meaning of this Agreement. The demonstration of a causal relationship between the subsidized imports and the injury to the domestic industry shall be based on an examination of all the relevant evidence before the authorities.

---

[14] Loan guarantees, loans at below market rates of interest, and infusions of equity that would not be forthcoming from private investors work similarly.

US trade law calls on the US International Trade Commission to conduct an investigation in which it must determine whether an industry in the United States has been materially injured or threatened with material injury *by reason of imports of the subsidized merchandise*.[15]

Evidently, the SCM Agreement requires the investigating authority to resolve a question of causality. To do so, it must invoke a hypothetical comparison between the various indicators of industry health – output, employment, profits, etc.[16] – and what the situation in the industry would have been had the non-recurring subsidy never been granted. The authority can only determine that the subsidy has caused injury if it finds that investments have taken place that would not have occurred but for the foreign government's policies, that the investments have improved the competitive position of the subsidized producers, and that the resulting shift in the foreign supply has been responsible for a deterioration in the performance of the US industry that produces a like product.[17]

6.3.4   Administrative review

The requirements for an administrative review are similar. According to Article 21.1 of the SCM Agreement,

> A countervailing duty shall remain in force only as long as and to the extent necessary to counteract subsidization which is causing injury.

Clearly, it is not enough for an investigating authority to have shown that a non-recurring subsidy caused injury sometime in the past. Rather, the use of the present tense in the subordinate clause obliges the investigating authority to demonstrate continuing injury that can be attributed to the subsidy.

The first and most difficult question that should be raised in any such review of a non-recurring subsidy is whether the level of capital (physical

---

[15] See Subtitle A of title VII of the Tariff Act of 1930, as added by the Trade Agreements Act of 1979 (19 U.S.C. § 1671 et seq.) and subsequently amended.

[16] Article 15.4 of the SCM Agreement stipulates that "the examination of the impact of the subsidized imports on the domestic industry shall include an evaluation of all relevant economic factors and indices having a bearing on the state of the industry, including actual and potential decline in output, sales, market share, profits, productivity, return on investments, or utilization of capacity; factors affecting domestic prices; actual and potential negative effects on cash flow, inventories, employment wages, growth, ability to raise capital or investments . . ."

[17] Goetz, Granet, and Schwartz (1986) and Diamond (1989) also have stressed the need for counterfactual analysis in determining whether foreign subsidies have caused injury to domestic producers.

and intangible) invested in the industry remains higher than it would have been but for the subsidy. The current US practice, which involves no such inquiry, implicitly assumes that the extra investment induced by a subsidy will remain "marginal" – that is, above and beyond what would have occurred without the subsidy – no matter how industry conditions evolve subsequently. But this assumption is not justified. Events in an industry may cause investments that were marginal at the time they were made to become inframarginal thereafter.

We illustrate with an example. Suppose a foreign government has provided a low-interest loan to finance the construction of a new plant. Suppose further that the investment would not have been economically justified without the government's contribution, i.e. the discounted profits that the producer could expect to derive from the plant were insufficient to cover the private cost of the investment at the time of construction. Surely, in the period just after the new plant came on line, the foreign industry had a greater level of output than would have been the case but for the subsidy. For this reason, the subsidy may well have caused some injury to a US import-competing industry.

But now suppose that consumer demand for the industry's output grows in the following years at a rate that exceeded the original expectations. The increased demand may have caused industry conditions to improve to such an extent that it would have been profitable for a foreign producer to build the extra plant even without the inducement of the subsidy. When that happens, it is no longer true that the subsidy is responsible for competitive conditions different from those that would have prevailed in the hypothetical, but-for world. A plant that was marginal at the time of its construction can become inframarginal in the light of subsequent events.

An administrative review of a countervailing duty order for a non-recurring subsidy routinely should ask the question "is the foreign production advantaged in the review period relative to what it would have been had the subsidy never occurred?" Answering this question in the current case would require a counterfactual analysis of what investments would have taken place in the years since British Steel Corporation received its grants and equity infusion from the British government. If the foreign export supply of the lead bar products remains greater (at a given price) than it would have been but for the subsidy, then the United States would be well justified in continuing to countervail its adverse effects on the US industry. But if the "benefits" from the subsidy to British production have evaporated over time due to changed economic conditions in the steel industry, then the countervailing duty ought to be eliminated.

6.3.5   Where did the Appellate Body go wrong

As we have argued earlier, the Appellate Body erred in its interpretation of the word "benefit." Had it been correct to understand the word benefit to mean an increase wealth, then it also would have been correct to examine whether the current owners of the British Steel Corporation assets had acquired these assets at fair market prices. But with the appropriate understanding of benefit as a boost to the British firm's competitive position, the relationship between the price paid by the current owners for the British Steel Corporation assets and the fair market price is not germane to the analysis. It is possible that the current owners paid a fair price for the British Steel Corporation assets and still the firm has benefited in regard to its competitive condition, because the investment remains inframarginal in the sense that the capital stock would not be the same today had there never been a subsidy. Conversely, it would also be possible in other circumstances for private agents to acquire once-subsidized assets from the government at below market prices, and yet the assets could be seen as causing injury to a domestic firm, because the assets no longer can be considered as inframarginal.

We illustrate these points with a pair of constructed examples. Suppose first that a government G made equity infusions in 1990 into a publicly owned company C. The company used the capital so contributed to purchase 1,000 Euros-worth of machinery. Suppose further that, had a profit-maximizing private company faced a similar commercial opportunity, it would only have invested 500 Euros in view of the prevailing market cost of raising capital. Clearly, the subsidy initially was responsible for an extra 500 Euros of investment. The extra machinery presumably meant extra output, and potentially caused harm to a competing industry in an importing country.

Now suppose that market conditions remain exactly the same between 1990 and 1995 and that machines purchased by C suffer no depreciation. In 1995, these machines are worth 800 Euros, less than the 1,000 Euros that C paid for them. Now if C sells the machines to a private buyer B for the market price of 800 Euros, this transaction does not negate the benefit to B from the original subsidy. Had there never been a subsidy, only 500 Euros of investment would have taken place. Then B would only have been able to purchase the 500 Euros-worth of machinery from C in 1995. Since the subsidy caused an extra investment of 500 Euros, the competitive position of B in the world market is better in 1995 than it would have been absent the subsidy. And firms in the importing country may still be suffering injury as a result.

The facts of our second illustrative example are similar as concerns the initial subsidy and investment in 1990. But now we suppose that between 1990 and 1995 there has been robust growth in demand for the output of Company C and other firms selling like products. By 1995, additional investments have taken place in the industry, and the original investment of 1,000 Euros has been justified by subsequent market developments. In other words, a private company that would have invested only 500 Euros in 1990, would by 1995 have purchased the additional machines in response to the subsequent market growth. Indeed, in our example, the machinery purchased by C in 1990 has a market value of 1,500 Euros in 1995, thanks to the improved conditions in the industry. Now, even if we observe that B has purchased the machines from C in 1995 at the below market price of 1,000 Euros, there is no injury to competing firms in the importing country that can be attributed either to the original equity infusion or to the subsidized sale of the public assets. Absent these subsidies, market conditions in the industry and the sales, profits, and employment of competing firms would have been much the same as they are in reality. Therefore, the importing country would not be justified in continuing its countervailing duty following an administrative review in 1995.

6.3.6   Must the SCM Agreement be modified?

In principle, WTO Panel and Appellate Body reports are directed only to specific addressees, namely the parties to the dispute.[18] However, the WTO adjudicating bodies do often cite prior case law to support the reasoning they have used to reach a decision. Thus, AB reports do sometimes set precedents that – although not legally binding – have real effects on subsequent dispute resolution.

The WTO adjudicating bodies have, on several occasions, ruled that the resale of subsidized assets at arm's length and at fair market prices

---

[18] In Article 19 of the DSU, the parties have agreed that "where a panel or the Appellate Body concludes that a measure is inconsistent with a covered agreement, it shall recommend that the Member concerned bring the measure into conformity with that agreement." This language would seem to suggest that the panel and Appellate Body decisions are not binding on other parties with seemingly similar circumstances.

extinguishes the benefits of a non-recurring subsidy.[19] We believe that these adjudicating bodies have repeatedly misinterpreted the meaning of the term "benefit." We have supported our case not with arguments about what the text "should have said" but rather with reference to the text of the SCM Agreement itself, and its intended meaning. Accordingly, we do not believe that any modification of the existing legal instrument is necessary in order that the adjudicating bodies apply an interpretation of the term benefit that is consistent with the economic principles embodied in the Agreement.

However, we do favor a modification of the SCM Agreement that would render the injury test in subsidy cases more in line with the principles of welfare economics. As we have noted previously, the text of the Agreement leaves little room for interpreting the requisite injury test in welfare-economic terms. The wording of the Agreement is quite clear that, to invoke a countervailing duty, a Member must show that subsidized imports are causing injury to domestic producers of a like product, and nothing further. In our view, the SCM Agreement would better serve the objective of promoting efficiency in trade relations if Members were limited in their application of countervailing measures to circumstances in which they demonstrated that foreign subsidies have been damaging to aggregate economic welfare. In cases where a foreign subsidy does no such harm but does adversely impact certain interests in the importing country, it ought to be the responsibility of the importing country to effect the domestic redistributions that make the losers whole.

7 Conclusions

In this review, we have argued that the AB applied a faulty interpretation of the term "benefit" in its report on *US – Lead and Bismuth II*. The AB ruled that a company that purchases assets at fair market value cannot benefit from a subsidy that was paid at an earlier time to facilitate the acquisition of those assets. Although we agree that the acquiring company cannot *profit* by purchasing assets at a fair market price, its competitive position in the industry nonetheless can be advantaged relative to what it would have been "but for" the subsidy. The signatories of the SCM Agreement were concerned with injury caused by subsidies. Accordingly, an interpretation

---

[19] Most recently, in *United States – Countervailing Measures Concerning Certain Products from the European Communities* (see WT/DS212/R), the Panel ruled that a privatization at arm's length and for fair market value extinguishes the benefit to the privatized producer of a subsidy that was paid to the original owner of the privatised assets (July 31, 2002).

of "benefit" as something that improves a firm's or industry's competitive position is more consistent with the intentions of those who signed the agreement.

Our conclusion regarding the AB ruling does not exonerate current US practice in its administrative reviews of countervailing duty orders. An administrative review that is consistent with the obligations imposed by the SCM Agreement should pose the counterfactual question, is the importing-competing industry injured relative to what its economic health would have been "but for" the non-recurring subsidy? Since the AB ruled, in effect, that there was no continuing subsidy after the privatization of the British Steel Corporation assets, it did not address the question of what injury test should be used in an administrative review of a non-recurring subsidy.

We summarize our conclusions as follows:

(i) The AB ruled correctly that the Panel applied an appropriate standard of review according to Article 11 of the DSU.
(ii) The AB ruled incorrectly that a change in ownership of assets at fair market value provides per se evidence of an absence of subsidy, because it precludes "benefit" to the acquiring firm.
(iii) A consistent interpretation of the SCM Agreement calls for a "but for" test for continuing injury from a non-recurring subsidy. The authorities in the importing country should periodically review whether its domestic producers of like products are suffering harm relative to what would be their economic condition but for the prior non-recurring subsidy. To effect this test, the authorities must ask whether or not the subsidized investments have become inframarginal in the light of subsequent events in the industry.
(iv) No modification of the existing legal instrument is needed for the *Agreement* to be interpreted in a manner consistent with the economic principles raised by this case.

8   Postscript

Subsequent to its ruling in *US – Lead and Bismuth II*, the WTO Appellate Body reversed its position that a government's sale of assets at fair market prices necessarily extinguishes the benefits from a non-recurring subsidy. In its report on *US – Countervailing Measures on Certain EC Products*, the Appellate Body ruled (see para. 7.127) that the Panel erred in concluding that "[p]rivatizations at arm's length and for fair market value must lead to the conclusion that the privatized producer paid for what he got and thus did not get any benefit or advantage from the prior financial contribution bestowed upon the state-owned producer." Privatization at arm's length and for fair market value may result in extinguishing the benefit. Indeed, we find that there is a rebuttable presumption that a benefit ceases to exist after such a privatization. Nevertheless, it does not necessarily do so. There is no inflexible rule requiring that investigating authorities, in future cases, automatically determine that a "benefit" derived from pre-privatization financial contributions expires following privatization at arm's length and for fair market value.

However, the Appellate Body did not reason, as we have, that the price at which a privatization of public assets takes place is irrelevant to the existence or not of a continuing benefit from a prior non-recurring subsidy. Rather, the AB argued that the market price of an asset need not reflect the "actual exchange value of the continuing benefit of past non-recurring financial contributions," because the government may be able to manipulate private market valuations by changing or threatening to change the policy environment in which the assets operate.

References

Brander, James A. and Spencer, Barbara J. 1985. Export Subsidies and International Market Share Rivalry. *Journal of International Economics* 18: 83–100.

Diamond, Richard. 1989. Economic Foundations of Countervailing Duty Law. *Virginia Journal of International Law* 29: 767–812.

Goetz, Charles J., Granet, Lloyd, and Schwartz, Warren F. 1986. The Meaning of "Subsidy" and "Injury" in the Countervailing Duty Law. *International Review of Law and Economics* 6: 17–32.

Olson, Mancur. 1965. *The Logic of Collective Action*. Cambridge, MA: Harvard University Press.

9

US – Export Restraints
United States – Measures Treating Export
Restraints as Subsidies*

MERIT E. JANOW AND ROBERT W. STAIGER

1 Introduction

This study examines the dispute brought before the World Trade Organization (WTO) concerning the *United States – Measures Treating Export Restraints as Subsidies* (WT/DS 194), euphemistically referred to herein as *US – Export Restraints*. In this dispute, Canada challenged the US treatment of export restraints under US countervailing duty law and practice. The principal legal focus was therefore on the WTO Subsidies and Countervailing Measures (SCM) Agreement. This is one of a handful of WTO cases where the complainant (Canada) was not challenging the application of a governmental measure (by the US here) but rather the WTO consistency of existing legal measures. Essentially, Canada claimed that certain US legislation along with established practice by the US Department of Commerce constitute a violation of US obligations under the SCM Agreement.

The GATT has long recognized that subsidies can serve as a non-tariff barrier to international trade. Export subsidies were targeted as an early priority. Establishing more robust rules to cover subsidies became a priority during the Tokyo Round of multilateral trade negotiations and resulted in the 1979 Subsidies Code, which like other GATT codes only applied to its signatories. According to many analysts, the Code had proven inadequate

* This study has benefited from the suggestions of seminar participants at the Conference on the Principles of Trade Law: The World Trade Organization, held on February 6–7, 2003 in Philadelphia, and especially from the comments of Steve Charnovitz, William Davey, Wilfred Ethier, Henrik Horn, Robert Howse, Petros C. Mavroidis, and John Ragosta. We are particularly indebted to Robert Hudec for extensive comments on earlier drafts of this study.

for a number of reasons – including the ability of parties to engage in forum shopping between the Code and Article VI – and the negotiation of a more comprehensive set of disciplines covering subsidies and the application of countervailing duties remained a priority during the Uruguay Round. Agreement on the definition of a subsidy was one of a number of highly contentious features of the negotiations.

The discussion that follows undertakes a three-step analysis. In these three steps we seek to distinguish different levels of economic and legal analysis, beginning with the most general and turning in sequence to the more specific legal and economic issues raised by the *US – Export Restraints* dispute. First, we consider the economic basis for the WTO provisions at the heart of this dispute. More specifically we ask: What are the underlying goals of the various WTO provisions touched upon in the *US – Exports Restraints* case, and are the goals themselves sensible from an economic perspective?

Second, we present and evaluate the key factual and legal elements of the case, focusing primarily on the legal issues raised by the case in its final disposition that seem particularly important to understanding its legal and economic logic. We ask: Have the reviewing Panels and the Appellate Body (AB) applied the law consistently and mindful of WTO precedent? Are the Panelists and the AB doing what they state they are doing? Are the judgments well grounded in legal argument? Is there ambiguity in the applicable law, as drafted? If so, how is it resolved – e.g. with deference to national measures, or through judicial license?

And third, we consider and evaluate the particular legal and economic issues and methodologies raised by the dispute. Here, we ask: In light of the underlying goals of the relevant WTO provisions, and taking them as given, was the resolution of the substantive economic issues around which the case revolved based on sound economic principles?

2   General economic analysis

The *US – Export Restraints* case raises several levels of questions from an economic perspective. Here, we first consider the question: What are the goals of the various WTO provisions touched upon in this case, and are the goals themselves sensible from an economic perspective? A second-level question is the following: In light of these goals, and taking them as given, was the resolution of the substantive economic issues around which the case revolved based on sound economic principles? This second-level question will be taken up in section 4, after the legal aspects of the case have been fully presented and evaluated in section 3.

What, then, are the goals of the various WTO provisions touched upon in this case? The case centers on the question of whether export restraints can qualify as subsidies within the definition of a subsidy provided in the SCM Agreement. Given the fundamental nature of this question, all the provisions of the SCM Agreement are potentially affected by its resolution.

According to the panel in *Brazil – Aircraft*, ". . . the object and purpose of the SCM Agreement is to impose multilateral disciplines on subsidies which distort international trade." In broad terms, the SCM Agreement attempts to accomplish this by: defining the notion of a subsidy and drawing a distinction between a general subsidy and a subsidy which is "specific" (Part I);[1] prohibiting certain kinds of specific subsidies (Part II); requiring that most other kinds of specific subsidies, while not prohibited, must be maintained in a manner that does not cause adverse effects to any other WTO member (Part III); and spelling out the procedures for imposing countervailing duties (Part V).[2]

As this broad description indicates, the SCM Agreement consists of a complex and varied set of provisions, and a systematic evaluation of the economic logic of this Agreement is far beyond the scope of this paper. Nevertheless, we may make a number of general observations about the economic logic of these provisions.

2.1 Part II of the SCM Agreement

Article 3 of Part II of the SCM Agreement prohibits two kinds of subsidies. Export subsidies are prohibited in 3.1(a), while subsidies contingent upon the use of domestic over imported goods are prohibited in 3.1(b). As we discuss below, the economic basis for 3.1(a) is difficult to articulate, while the economic basis for 3.1(b) can be given a relatively straightforward interpretation.

---

[1] As noted in the Introduction, agreement on the very definition of a subsidy was a challenging feature of the negotiations, and the resulting definition requires a financial contribution and a benefit conferred thereby.

[2] As a provisional measure (now no longer in force), Part IV of the SCM Agreement permitted a third kind of subsidy to be maintained even when the subsidy does cause adverse effects to another WTO member. Except in special circumstances, Part IV disallowed the use of remedies covered in the SCM Agreement against these subsidies.

2.1.1   Article 3.1(a)

The prohibition of export subsidies contained in Article 3.1(a) serves to complement and clarify the treatment of export subsidies in section B of Article XVI GATT. The rationale for limiting export subsidies is contained in paragraph 2, section B of Article XVI GATT: "The contracting parties recognize that the granting by a contracting party of a subsidy on the export of any product may have harmful effects for other contracting parties, both importing and exporting, may cause undue disturbance to their normal commercial interests, and may hinder the achievement of the objectives of this Agreement." From an economic perspective, the conditions that would give rise to *importing* governments viewing export subsidies in this way are not obvious.[3]

In our companion essay in this volume on *Canada – Dairy*, we evaluate in some detail the underlying logic in the GATT/WTO on export subsidies. We shall not repeat that discussion in total herein. However, the essential point of that discussion is that, for export subsidies to actually harm an importing government, economic arguments indicate that the importing government would have to (a) be concerned about the injury to domestic producers caused by the increased exports resulting from the foreign subsidy, *and* (b) lack the ability to use tariffs or other policy instruments to respond to this injury.

As the discussion of exporter versus importer interests in section 2.1 of our companion essay on *Canada – Dairy* explains, even in a world of bound tariffs importing nations have some tools under the WTO to respond to the perceived adverse effects of export subsidies – e.g. through the imposition of countervailing duties or renegotiation of tariffs. Thus, additional prohibitions on export subsidies do not factor in the full economic interests of all importing nations. Moreover, from a worldwide perspective, it can be argued that governments that choose to subsidize their exporters in the absence of international agreements should be encouraged to subsidize *more* under international agreements, not less. This conclusion runs counter to the long history of efforts in the GATT/WTO to eliminate export subsidies, but it is derived from formal economic thinking under standard arguments.[4]

---

[3] See Bagwell and Staiger (2002), chapter 10.

[4] See ibid. This conclusion follows provided that the goal of the WTO is to serve the interests of its member governments, and that those interests are represented at the WTO bargaining table.

The fundamental point is that the standard economic rationale for the purpose of negotiations over trade policy is that trade volumes are inefficiently low when governments set their trade policies unilaterally. As a consequence, from this perspective, the central task of trade negotiations is to expand trade volumes beyond their unilateral levels to more efficient levels. Since agreements to restrict export subsidies are agreements to restrict trade volumes below unilateral levels, it may be concluded that such agreements appear to run counter to the essential purpose of international trade agreements. Any economic argument in support of international agreements to restrict export subsidies must overcome this basic dilemma.

We have offered two interpretations of this conclusion in our companion essay on *Canada – Dairy*. A first interpretation emphasizes the limits of existing formal economic reasoning in this instance, and casts doubt on the ability of existing formal economic models to adequately capture the role that international agreements can play in limiting export subsidies. According to this interpretation, it is important to seek and develop further alternative modeling approaches that might better reflect some critical feature associated with the issue of export subsidies that the standard models have failed to capture. For example, it is possible that modeling approaches which see international agreements as helping governments make commitments to their own private sectors – rather than to other governments – may point the way to a more complete understanding of the role that international agreements adopted in order to limit export subsidies can play.[5]

A second interpretation would place more weight on the presumptions implied by the standard economic arguments. This second interpretation casts doubt on the rationale for international agreements to limit export subsidies. At the least, this conclusion reflects the need for further articulation of the rationale for the treatment of export subsidies within the GATT/WTO. At most, the GATT/WTO's approach to export subsidies might benefit from a fundamental overhaul.

2.1.2   Article 3.1(b)

The prohibition of subsidies for the use of domestic over imported goods contained in Article 3.1(b) can be given a fairly straightforward

---

[5] For a recent review of the commitment approach to the study of trade agreements, see Bagwell and Staiger (2002, chapter 2).

interpretation in economic terms. Such subsidies can be shown to be equivalent in economic terms to a direct subsidy for the production of the domestic good. Hence, the prohibition of the subsidies described in 3.1(b) can be seen to close a "loophole" that might otherwise exist for getting around the disciplines on production subsidies contained in Part III of the SCM Agreement.

To see the logic underlying the claim that a subsidy for the use of a domestic over an imported good is economically equivalent to a production subsidy for the domestic good, let us suppose that domestic users of good y must pay the price charged by foreign exporters, p^*, to use an imported good, and must pay the price charged by domestic producers, p, to use the domestic good. However, owing to the subsidy for use of the domestic over the imported good, which we denote in ad valorem terms as s, the effective price to domestic users of buying the domestic good – net of the subsidy payment they receive – is $p(1 - s)$. As long as the subsidy program is not so generous as to wipe out altogether the use of the imported good in the domestic economy, the domestic users must be indifferent between using the imported good at price p^* and using the domestic good at the effective price $p(1 - s)$. Assuming that these goods are "perfectly substitutable" in their intended use, we then have as an implication of this indifference the arbitrage condition that $p(1 - s) = p^*$, or equivalently $p = p^*/(1 - s)$.

Let us now suppose that the domestic economy is "small" on world markets, so that from this economy's perspective p^* is effectively fixed.[6] The first expression derived above, $p(1 - s) = p^*$, indicates that the users of good y in the domestic economy will face a user cost for this good which is tied down by p^*, and is therefore unaffected by the subsidy program. The second (equivalent) expression derived above, $p = p^*/(1 - s)$, indicates that domestic producers of good y will enjoy a higher price for their product as a result of the subsidy program (i.e. when $s > 0$). In this way, the effect of the subsidy program just described is equivalent to a direct production subsidy paid to domestic producers of good y. This equivalence follows, because such a direct production subsidy program would have the effect of raising the subsidy-inclusive price received by domestic producers of good y while leaving the price paid by domestic users of good y to be determined by the competitive conditions of foreign exporters (i.e. p^*) and therefore unaffected. As a consequence, a production

---

[6] The argument presented above is simplified by the "small country" assumption, but the point extends as well to the "large country" case.

subsidy rate could then be chosen to exactly replicate the economic effects of a subsidy for the use of a domestic over an imported good.

By this logic, it may be argued that the prohibition contained in Article 3.1(b) helps to make more comprehensive the disciplines on production subsidies contained in Part III of the SCM Agreement.

2.2 Part III of the SCM Agreement

Simple economic principles raise a basic question about the internal consistency of provisions that give governments the right to challenge specific subsidies under Part III of the SCM Agreement and the coexisting fundamental right of WTO members to maintain tariffs at their bound levels. The point is, the economic effects of any particular (non-prohibitive) tariff on any particular import good y can be exactly replicated by removing the tariff and replacing it with the dual policies of (i) a tax on domestic consumption of good y, and (ii) a subsidy to domestic production of good y, both applied at the same rate as the tariff. As we explain below, this basic equivalence between different combinations of policy instruments gives rise to the possibility that the right to take actions under Part III of the SCM Agreement can interfere with the ability of tariff bindings to serve as the instrument by which governments make market access commitments.

The observation that a tariff is equivalent to a combined policy of consumption tax/production subsidy can be understood intuitively as follows. If an importer of a product must pay an import tariff on that product, then the importer's costs of acquiring that product and delivering it to domestic consumers will typically rise, and a competitive importer will have to pass the added costs of doing business on to domestic consumers in the form of a higher domestic price for the imported good. If there is a competing domestic product that is similar to the imported good in the eyes of domestic consumers, then domestic consumers will tend to shift their purchases toward this domestic product in response to the rising price of the imported good, and this consumer response will in turn tend to raise the price that domestic producers of the import-competing product receive.

The upshot, then, is that the imposition of an import tariff on y has two effects on the prices prevailing in the domestic economy: (i) it raises the price paid by domestic consumers for the imported good y and for the domestically produced "versions" of y; and (ii) it raises the price received by domestic producers who produce versions of y. The first effect is identical to the effect of a consumption tax placed on domestic consumers

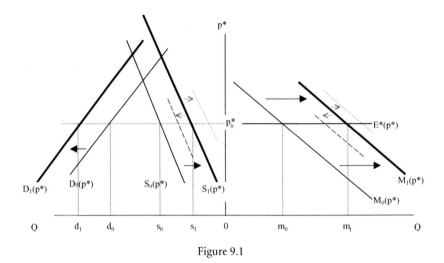

Figure 9.1

who consume y (in any of its versions, imported or domestic). The second effect is identical to the effect of a production subsidy paid to domestic producers who produce (any version of) y.[7]

2.2.1   Subsidies and the relationship between tariff bindings and market access

This basic link between tariffs and production subsidies raises an important question for the GATT/WTO, because the treatment of subsidies is evidently a critical ingredient in determining the nature of the relationship between negotiated tariff bindings and the implied market access. We may illustrate this with the use of figure 9.1.

Let us consider a country that imports good y. Let us suppose further that this country offers domestic producers of good y an ad valorem subsidy r, and applies an unbound tariff T to imports of good y from abroad. In the right-hand quadrant of figure 9.1, the foreign exporter price of good y, denoted p^*, is measured on the vertical axis while the quantity of good y is measured on the horizontal axis. The downward sloping curve labeled $M_0(p^*)$ depicts the domestic country's import demand for good y

---

[7] A final question concerns what is to be done with the tax revenue collected as a result of the consumption tax, and the tax revenue needed to fund the production subsidy. If the production subsidy is funded by the tax revenue collected under the consumption tax, there will be an amount of tax revenue left over after the production subsidy has been funded which will be exactly the amount that would be collected as tariff revenue under the equivalent tariff.

as a function of the foreign exporter price, p^*, given the domestic tariff and subsidy policies T and r, respectively. The horizontal line labeled $E^*(p^*)$ depicts the export supply of good y from the foreign country as a function of the foreign exporter price p^*.[8] The implied import volume and foreign exporter price at the tariff and subsidy policies T and r are depicted in the right-hand quadrant of figure 9.1 as m_0 and p_0^*, respectively.

In the left-hand quadrant of figure 9.1, the foreign exporter price of good y is again measured on the vertical axis while the quantity of good y is measured on the horizontal axis, but the left-hand quadrant of figure 9.1 depicts the underlying demand and supply curves for good y in the domestic economy. The domestic demand curve is labeled $D_0(p^*)$, because domestic demand for good y is a (decreasing) function of the domestic price of good y, which we denote by p, and the domestic and foreign exporter price of y are related through the tariff T by the arbitrage condition $p = (1 + T)p^*$.

Hence, for a given T, an increase in p^* implies by the arbitrage condition a proportional increase in p, allowing domestic demand to therefore be written as $D_0(p^*)$. The domestic supply curve is labeled $S_0(p^*)$, because domestic supply for good y is an (increasing) function of p (and hence of p^*, given T), and also depends (positively) on the production subsidy level r. Given the tariff T and production subsidy r, the positions of the domestic demand and supply curves are pinned down in the left-hand quadrant of figure 9.1, and at the foreign exporter price of p^*_0, they determine the domestic quantity of good y demanded (labeled d_0) and supplied (labeled s_0), whose difference corresponds to m_0.

Suppose, now, that the domestic country binds its tariff in a GATT/WTO negotiation at the level t where t < T. Figure 9.1 depicts the implications of this tariff binding with the bold curves. In the left-hand quadrant of figure 9.1, the domestic demand curve shifts out to the curve labeled $D_1(p^*)$ while the domestic supply curve shifts back to the curve labeled $S_1(p^*)$. Intuitively, as we have observed above, a tariff is equivalent to a consumption tax and production subsidy, and so cutting a tariff is equivalent to cutting a consumption tax (which would shift the domestic demand curve out) and cutting a production subsidy (which would shift the domestic supply curve back). In the right-hand quadrant of figure 9.1, the domestic country's import demand curve shifts out to the

---

[8] The horizontal foreign export supply curve reflects the simplifying assumption that the domestic country is "small" on world markets. This assumption simplifies the exposition, but is inessential to the point being made.

curve labeled $M_1(p^*)$, reflecting the shifts in domestic demand and supply just described. At the (unchanged) foreign exporter price, the domestic country's tariff binding results in an expansion of the quantity of good y demanded in the domestic country to d_1, a contraction of the quantity of good y supplied by the domestic country to s_1, and a consequent expansion of import volume to m_1.

As figure 9.1 illustrates, the act of binding a tariff implies an offer of market access to foreign exporters, where market access is understood to reflect the competitive relationship between imported and domestic products. In terms of figure 9.1, this competitive relationship is embodied in the position of the domestic country's import demand curve, and so the offer of additional market access is captured in the right-hand quadrant by the outward shift of the domestic country's import demand curve induced by the bound tariff reduction. At a most basic level, the relationship between tariff bindings and market access rests at the heart of GATT/WTO operations. At the same time, we have observed above that there is a basic link between the economic effects of tariffs and production subsidies, and figure 9.1 suggests that the treatment of subsidies will be a critical ingredient in determining the nature of the relationship between negotiated tariff bindings and the implied market access.

We next illustrate with figure 9.1 how the right to take actions against production subsidies under Part III of the SCM Agreement can have important consequences for the ability of tariff bindings to serve as the instrument by which governments make market access commitments. We consider a first example in which this right can help to strengthen – by which we mean tighten or maintain – the relationship between tariff bindings and market access, and we consider next a second example in which this right can weaken – by which we mean loosen or disrupt – the relationship between tariff bindings and market access. We then identify an operational distinction between these two examples, and suggest that economic arguments could support introducing such a distinction into Part III of the SCM Agreement.

2.2.2   Challenging a "new" subsidy under Part III of the SCM Agreement

Consider, then, a first example in which, subsequent to binding its tariff at the level t in a GATT/WTO negotiation, the domestic country introduces a new production subsidy on good y at a rate R where $R > r$. In the left-hand quadrant of figure 9.1, the higher production subsidy rate R will shift the domestic supply curve out from the bold curve labeled $S_1(p^*)$ to the dashed curve. In the right-hand quadrant of figure 9.1, the implied reduction in market access is captured by the inward shift of the domestic country's import demand curve, from the bold curve labeled $M_1(p^*)$ to the dashed curve. Evidently, as reflected by the inward shift of the domestic import demand curve, the introduction of this new production subsidy has in effect reduced the level of market access from the level that was implied by the tariff binding at t given the original production subsidy level r.

If the exporting country which negotiated the tariff binding with the domestic country is unable to seek redress for the loss of market access implied by the introduction of this new subsidy, then the value of the tariff binding as a means to secure market access is diminished. This diminished value arises because the foreign exporting country has no means of preventing the market access implied by a domestic tariff reduction from being systematically offset by subsequent increases in the domestic production subsidy. And as a consequence, governments are less likely to see negotiated tariff bindings as a meaningful way to secure access to foreign markets for their exporters.

We may conclude that the relationship between tariff bindings and market access would be strengthened – that is, tightened – and the value of tariff bindings as a means to secure market access would be thereby enhanced, if it were possible to challenge the introduction of the new production subsidy in this circumstance. It might therefore be said that, by providing an avenue for this possibility, the right given in Part III of the SCM Agreement can serve to strengthen the relationship between tariff bindings and market access in this circumstance.

2.2.3   Challenging an "existing" subsidy under Part III of the SCM Agreement

Consider next a second example in which, subsequent to binding its tariff at the level t in a GATT/WTO negotiation, the domestic country is confronted with a challenge to its existing production subsidy r under Part III of the SCM Agreement. Assuming this challenge is successful, the domestic country must eliminate the production subsidy (i.e. set r = 0). In the left-hand quadrant of figure 9.1, the elimination of the production subsidy r will shift the domestic supply curve back from the bold curve labeled $S_1(p^*)$ to the dotted curve. In the right-hand quadrant of figure 9.1, the implied increase in market access is captured by the outward shift of the domestic country's import demand curve, from the bold curve labeled $M_1(p^*)$ to the dotted curve. Evidently, as reflected by the outward shift of the domestic import demand curve, the successful challenge to the domestic country's existing production subsidy has in effect increased the level of market access from the level that was implied by the tariff binding at t given the original production subsidy level r.

In this circumstance, it can be argued that the value of the tariff binding as a means to secure market access is diminished by the right to challenge the existing production subsidy under Part III of the SCM Agreement. This diminished value arises because the domestic importing country has no means of preventing the market access implied by a bound domestic tariff reduction from being systematically augmented by subsequent legal challenges to its domestic production subsidy. And as a consequence, governments are less likely to see negotiated tariff bindings as an acceptable way to offer foreign exporters access to their markets.

We may conclude that the relationship between tariff bindings and market access is weakened – that is, loosened – and the value of tariff bindings as a means to secure market access is thereby diminished, when the existing production subsidy in this circumstance can be challenged. It might therefore be said that the right given in Part III of the SCM Agreement can serve to weaken the relationship between tariff bindings and market access in this circumstance.

2.2.4   Part III of the SCM Agreement and the relationship between tariff bindings and market access

We may now identify an operational distinction between these two examples. In the first example, it was a new subsidy that was challenged under Part III of the SCM Agreement. In the second example, it was a subsidy that existed at the time of the tariff binding that was challenged under Part III of the SCM Agreement. The logic we have described above supports the position that a distinction between "new" and "existing" subsidies could be usefully introduced into Part III of the SCM Agreement, and that only the former should be considered actionable.

In fact, this position could be interpreted as a statement that economic arguments would support the elimination of Part III of the SCM Agreement and a return to the use of "non-violation" nullification-or-impairment claims against domestic subsidies. In this regard, the first example represents a circumstance in which Article XXIII.1(b) GATT could be used to invoke such a claim. The second example represents a circumstance in which claims under Article XXIII.1(b) GATT would not apply, because such claims would fail the requirement that the production subsidy could not have been reasonably anticipated by the exporting country at the time of the negotiation of the original tariff binding.

2.2.5 Agreements to limit subsidies and "efficient" trade agreements

Thus far we have emphasized that the treatment of subsidies will be a critical ingredient in determining the nature of the relationship between negotiated tariff bindings and the implied market access, and have evaluated Part III of the SCM Agreement from this perspective. A more complete economic analysis might characterize the efficient design of international agreements when governments make choices over both tariffs and subsidies.[9] In such an analysis, a key question is whether agreements to limit subsidies (along the lines of Part III of the SCM Agreement) would be part of this characterization. As it turns out, the answer is generally "No": it can be argued that an agreement to limit subsidies is generally not part of an efficient overall international agreement.[10] Hence, under this more complete economic analysis, the economic case against a provision such as Part III of the SCM Agreement is even stronger.

Intuitively, the reason is that, when government policy choices are extended beyond tariffs to include subsidies as well, the standard economic rationale for the purpose of international negotiations continues to take a simple form: trade volumes are inefficiently low when governments set their (subsidy and trade) policies unilaterally. As a consequence, from this perspective, the central task of international negotiations is to expand trade volumes beyond their unilateral levels to more efficient levels. This task can be accomplished through negotiated tariff bindings alone, leaving subsidies to be determined unilaterally by each country, provided that something like Article XXIII.1(b) GATT is in place to prevent the introduction of new subsidies from offsetting the market access implied by tariff bindings. Moreover, any limits placed on the permissible levels of subsidies by an international agreement would tend to reduce efficiency directly, for the simple reason that subsidies can often (in fact, according to the "targeting principle," almost always) achieve a given government objective more efficiently than tariffs, and so placing limits on subsidies in this context simply restricts governments to a less efficient set of policy instruments.

---

[9] Efficiency in this instance would be measured relative to the objectives of the WTO Member governments as those objectives are represented at the WTO bargaining table.
[10] See Bagwell and Staiger (in process).

2.2.6   Interpretation

As was the case with the treatment of export subsidies in Article 3.1(a), the observation made here regarding the treatment of subsidies in Part III of the SCM Agreement invites at least two possible interpretations. A first interpretation emphasizes the limits of existing formal economic reasoning in this instance, and casts doubt on the ability of existing formal economic models to adequately capture the role that international agreements to limit subsidies can play. According to this interpretation, it is important to seek and develop further alternative modeling approaches that might better reflect some critical feature associated with the issue of subsidies that the standard models have failed to capture.

For example, as we mentioned in the context of export subsidies, it is possible that modeling approaches which see international agreements as helping governments make commitments to their own private sectors – rather than to other governments – may point the way to a more complete understanding of the role that international agreements to limit subsidies can play. In any event, under this first interpretation, the wisdom of GATT/WTO efforts to restrain the use of subsidies is not really in doubt. A second interpretation would place more weight on the presumptions implied by the standard economic arguments reviewed above, and this second interpretation casts doubt over the rationale for international agreements to limit subsidies.

2.3   Part V of the SCM Agreement

As we observed in section 2.1.1 above, countervailing duties represent one way that an importing government can respond to foreign exports that are subsidized. But among the various options for response that the importing government might consider under GATT/WTO rules, countervailing duties are exceptional in that they (i) are discriminatory and (ii) imply no compensation/retaliation rights for the exporting/subsidizing government. Here we simply observe that the discriminatory nature of the countervailing duty response might be supported with economic arguments on the grounds that, as a feature of the underlying preferences of the citizens represented by their governments at the WTO, subsidized exports are considered "unfair." However, the lack of compensation/retaliation rights for the exporting/subsidizing government is more difficult to support with economic arguments, due to the incentives for "over-utilization" that this feature of countervailing duty law creates. We develop these observations further in the related context of anti-dumping duties in our companion essay in this volume on *EC − Bed Linen*.[11]

2.4 Summary

More broadly, the point is that the SCM Agreement is, as it was described above, an attempt to ". . . impose multilateral disciplines on subsidies which distort international trade," and some (though not all) of these disciplines admit a natural economic efficiency-enhancing interpretation. As noted previously, the fundamental inefficiency associated with unilateral policy choices is insufficient trade volume. To the extent that the provisions of the SCM Agreement operate to reduce export subsidies and, ultimately, export volumes, they tend to work against efficiency. Moreover, to the extent that the provisions of the SCM Agreement create ambiguity about the market access implications of tariff commitments and thereby interfere with the ability to negotiate greater market access, they tend to work against efficiency.

On the other hand, to the extent that the provisions of the SCM Agreement provide disciplines on the use of (new) subsidies that help governments negotiate more effective market access agreements through tariff commitments and achieve greater trade volumes, then these provisions may be interpreted as contributing to efficiency from an economic perspective.

3   Facts of the case and legal issues before the panel

3.1   Introduction.

As noted in the introduction, this dispute between the United States and Canada has to do with the treatment of export restraints under US

---

[11] A distinction between anti-dumping duties and countervailing duties in the context of the potential desirability of compensation/retaliation rights is that there does not exist an agreement within the GATT/WTO to limit dumping, whereas with regard to subsidies the SCM Agreement represents just such an agreement. It might then be argued that countervailing duties can play a useful role in restricting the use of subsidies, and thereby can be seen as helping to enforce the provisions of the SCM Agreement, and that the idea of permitting such actions to lead to compensation/retaliation rights by the affected exporting governments would work against this enforcement purpose. However, against this reasoning it can be argued that the SCM Agreement already provides for remedies in the case of violations of the Agreement, and that countervailing duty actions can therefore be logically separated from enforcement actions for the purposes of considering the potential desirability of the addition of compensation/retaliation rights.

countervailing duty law and practice.[12] The US, as a preliminary matter, requested the case to be dismissed because the measures at issue were discretionary and therefore did not oblige WTO inconsistent action, which was nevertheless not applied in this case. Canada argued that the US measures *obliged* the US to treat export restraints as a "financial contribution" under the SCM Agreement Article 1.1, which interpretation is inconsistent with the subsidies agreement. We shall come back to this question of sequencing, which we believe had significant implications for the resolution of the case.

The specific US measures at issue included: (1) section 771 (5) of the Tariff Act of 1930; (2) the Statement of Administrative Action (SAA) which accompanied the Uruguay Round Agreements Act; (3) the US Department of Commerce's (DOC) Explanation concerning the CVD Final Rules and (4) the US "practice" concerning the treatment of export restraints.

The mandatory/discretionary nature of the US measures is an important part of this case. However, we first focus on the substantive question of whether export restraints can constitute a subsidy and then turn to the question of whether the US measures require the DOC to treat export restraints as subsidies.

3.2   The purpose of the SCM Agreement and the treatment of export restraints under the SCM: is this a financial contribution?

As we see below, under Article 1.1 of the SCM Agreement, the definition of a subsidy has two elements: (1) a financial contribution, which can be provided through various means as specified in four sub-paragraphs, (2) which thereby confers a benefit.

Article 1.1 of the SCM Agreement defines a subsidy as follows:

> A.   1.1 For the purpose of this Agreement, a subsidy shall be deemed to exist if:
>
> (a)(1) there is a financial contribution by a government or any public body within the territory of a Member (referred to in this Agreement as "government"), i.e., where:
>
> > (i) a government practice involves a direct transfer of funds (e.g., grants, loans and equity infusion), potential direct transfers of funds or liabilities (e.g., loan guarantees);

---

[12] Specific provisions invoked included Articles 1.1, 10, 11, 17, 19, and 32.1. Canada also invoked certain other provisions of the SCM Agreement and the WTO, which the Panel did not address, such as Article XVI.4 and Article 32.5 of the SCM Agreement.

(ii) government revenue that is otherwise due is foregone or not collected (e.g., fiscal incentives such as tax credits);

(iii) a government provides goods or services other than general infrastructure, or purchases goods;

(iv) a government makes payments to a funding mechanism, or entrusts or directs a private body to carry out one or more of the type of functions illustrated in (i) to (iii) above which would normally be vested in the government and the practice, in no real sense, differs from practices normally followed by governments;

or

(a)(2) there is any form of income or price support in the sense of Article XVI of GATT 1994; and

(b) a benefit is thereby conferred.

The key specific issue in this dispute was whether export restraints can constitute a "financial contribution" and whether the US treatment of export restraints under its measures is consistent with the SCM Agreement. The parties agreed that an export restraint could confer a benefit hence the Panel focused solely on the question of whether an export restraint could constitute a "financial contribution."

The SCM Agreement itself does not define the term export restraint nor does it specifically clarify whether and under what circumstances it could be deemed to constitute a financial contribution. The parties disagreed on both dimensions. Canada defined an export restraint as "a border measure that takes the form of a government law or regulation which expressly limits the quantity of exports or places explicit conditions on the circumstances under which exports are permitted. Such measures could also take the form of a government-imposed fee or tax on exports of the product calculated to limit the quantity of exports."[13]

The United States took a broader view to encompass "any action or an act that holds back or prevents exports." The US also argued that it was neither practicable nor desirable for the panel to come up with a new definition of an export restraint since the SCM Agreement itself did not define the term. The Panel agreed with this latter view and chose to go with the definition as proposed by the United States rather than attempting to define an export restraint anew.

In the US view, an export restraint can constitute a financial contribution within the meaning of SCM Agreement 1.1(a)(1) since a limitation or prohibition of exports could be functionally equivalent to an entrustment

---

[13] See para. 8.16.

of or direction to a private body to provide goods domestically.[14] In Canada's view, however, the government must explicitly and affirmatively instruct the private entity to provide the goods in order to come under the SCM Agreement, Article 1.1(a)(1)(iii) and (iv). An export restraint as such, Canada argued, does not authoritatively instruct or commission producers of the restrained good to do anything; instead it limits their ability to export.[15] Hence, in the Canadian view, an export restraint cannot satisfy the definitional standard under Article 1 of the SCM Agreement.

3.3   The Panel's interpretation of the SCM Agreement

The Panel held that the SCM Agreement's use of the term "entrustment" or "direction" in subparagraph iv of Article 1.1 refers to a situation where the government is executing a particular policy by operating through a private body. Further, it says that the action of the government must therefore be an explicit and affirmative act, be it through delegation or command; addressed to a particular party, and the object of which is a particular duty.[16] All three of these elements must be present in order for the act of either "entrustment" or "direction" to have occurred. In this way, an explicit and affirmative action of delegation or command is deemed to be critical.

As a result, the Panel found the US approach that centers on the "effect" of an export restraint to be overbroad, and potentially resulting in a determination that any government measure that had the effect or caused an increase in the domestic supply of a good would constitute a government entrusted or directed provision of goods and hence a financial contribution (8.36). It noted and analogized from the reasoning of the Appellate Body in *Canada – Aircraft Credits and Guarantees* that "the focus of the SCM Agreement's obligations is on the granting government." Here, for the "entrusts and directs" standard to be met, i.e. for there to be a financial contribution in the sense of sub-paragraph (iv), the government action must be the focus, rather than the possible effects of the action on, or the reactions to it by those affected, even if those effects or reactions are expected.[17] The SCM Agreement, the Panel argued, was concerned

---

[14] See para. 8.22.   [15] See para. 8.26.   [16] See para. 8.29–8.30.

[17] See para. 8.42. Another issue between the parties had to do with the definition of "private body" as used in Article 1.1(a)(1)(iv). On this point, the Panel held that the term was a counterpoint to "government" or "public body" and hence any entity that is neither a government nor a public body would be a private body.

about subsidies as *defined* in the agreement, which includes the notions of financial contribution, benefit, and specificity.

To further clarify and amplify this point, the Panel undertook an examination of the negotiating history of the inclusion of the "financial contribution" requirement in the Agreement. This negotiating history contained a longstanding difference between the United States and Canada as to the extent to which the existence of a benefit conferred by any government could be considered a subsidy that is subject to countervailing measures. The Panel concluded that the definition that was ultimately arrived at during the negotiations rejected the US approach of defining subsidies as a benefit resulting from any government action by requiring that the government action be a financial contribution, as set out in an exhaustive list.[18] In a word, the Panel found that the negotiating history of a subsidy, which required both a financial contribution and a benefit, limited the countervailability of benefits from any sort of government measures to a finite list of measures that would, if they confer benefits, constitute subsidies.

For these reasons, the Panel concluded that an export restraint as defined by Canada in the dispute cannot constitute government entrusted or directed provision of goods in the sense of sub-paragraph (iv) and there was not a financial contribution in the sense of Article 1.1(1) of the SCM Agreement.[19]

3.4   Mandatory versus discretionary actions

The US had requested that the claims be dismissed in that the US legislation, as well as the practice at issue, were discretionary in nature and do not *require* the US to treat export restraints as subsidies. Absent such a requirement, the mere discretionary authority to interpret export restraints as subsidies would not be actionable as a violation of the WTO.[20]

---

[18] See para. 8.69.

[19] The panel went to some pains to reiterate that it was only referring to the definition of an export restraint as used by Canada and it was not making any judgment as to the WTO consistency of any other measures that Members may label export restraints or that fall outside the bounds of the Canadian definition. See para. 8.76.

[20] The US also raised certain other procedural claims that it believed should result in a dismissal of claims. For example, the US claimed that the DOC "practice" with respect to its interpretation of the applicable US rules does not constitute a governmental measure and therefore should not be a matter for review by the dispute settlement panel. See para. 4.1, 4.17 and 8.1.

Canada agreed that no violation could be found if the measures at issue were discretionary. However, Canada argued that even if the statute was discretionary, section 771(5) as "interpreted by" the Statement of Administrative Action and the Preamble constitute mandatory legislation that require the Department of Commerce to violate its obligations under the SCM and further that the Statement and preamble "curtail the discretion" of the Department of Commerce to act in a WTO-consistent fashion.

The Panel rejected the US request to dismiss the case. It argued that the issue of whether the measures are mandatory or discretionary "goes to the substance."[21] It relied on certain GATT/WTO precedent for the proposition that "only legislation that *mandates* a violation of a WTO/GATT obligation can be found as such to be inconsistent with those obligations."[22] Discretionary legislation, on the other hand, cannot be challenged, only its specific application. This was identified as the "classical test," and one agreed by the parties to be applicable in this case.

The Panel decided to apply the classical test to this dispute[23] to help determine whether the US law is mandatory with respect to the treatment of export restraints as "financial contributions" in the countervailing duty investigation. By choosing to apply the classical test, the Panel stated that this had "longstanding historical support" that had been recently employed by the Appellate Body.[24] Further, that it served a rational objective in ensuring "predictability of conditions for trade" in that parties will know to challenge legislation that will "necessarily result in action inconsistent with GATT/WTO obligations, before such action is actually taken."[25] These issues are considered more directly in section 3.7 below.

3.5   US measures

In making its determination whether US law requires that export restraints be treated as financial contributions, the Panel looked at the language of the US measures and analyzed each of the US measures separately to determine whether any or all of the measures had a functional life of its own[26] as well as whether "taken together" they had a required character. We turn now to briefly review the challenged US measures.

---

[21] See para. 8.2.   [22] See para. 8.4.
[23] With respect to this classical test, the panel cited the Appellate Body language in *US – 1916 Act* as well as the GATT Panel Report in *US – Tobacco*. See paras 8.3–8.6.
[24] See para. 8.9.   [25] See para. 8.9.   [26] See para. 8.85.

Section 771 (5). The Panel also examined the legislative history of pre and post WTO US law. It noted that the relevant provisions of US law as to what constitutes a subsidy (section 771(5)(D)), which in turn requires a financial contribution and the conferring of a benefit, essentially mirror the language of the SCM Agreement. The statute does not explicitly address export restraints. The Panel argued that the statute read in "isolation therefore reveals nothing about the treatment of export restraints under US countervailing duty law and could not be said to require any particular treatment of export restraints."[27]

The Statement of Administrative Action. The Panel then evaluated the Statement of Administrative Action. The Panel underscored the view articulated by Congress and reflected in the Statement itself that this is an authoritative expression of the Administration's views regarding the interpretation of the Uruguay Round Agreements and a source of primary interpretative guidance. The Panel did not see the Statement as having an operational life independent of the Uruguay Round Agreements Act (URAA). It did not see that it could, on its own, give rise to a violation of WTO rules.[28]

As to whether the Statement of Administrative Action requires the Department of Commerce to interpret the statutes such that export restraints are treated as financial contributions, the Panel noted that the statute is silent on the question of export restraints as such. On the question of its interpretive guidance on this question, the Statement offers conflicting commentary. It references certain past Department of Commerce cases where the Department treated export restraints as countervailable subsidies when they confer a benefit and are specific. Some portions of the Statement state that this practice will continue. Other portions suggest that this will be followed only under the new definition of a subsidy, referring to the requirement that there be a "financial contribution." It states that where the Department of Commerce is satisfied that the standard under section 771(5)(B)(iii) and Article 1.1(a)(1)(iv) of the SCM Agreement is satisfied, it will continue to countervail.[29]

Specifically, these different strands are evident in the section of the Statement of Administrative Action that discusses where a government entrusts or directs a private entity to make a financial contribution, which states:

---

[27] See para. 8.92.   [28] See para. 8.99.   [29] See para. 8.89.

The Administration intends that the "entrusts or directs" standard shall be interpreted broadly. The Administration plans to continue its policy of not permitting the indirect provision of a subsidy to become a loophole when unfairly traded imports enter the US and injure a US industry. In the past, the Department of Commerce has countervailed a variety of programs where the government has provided a benefit through private parties. (See, e.g., Certain Softwood Lumber Products from Canada, Leather from Argentina, Lamb from New Zealand, Oil Country Tubular Goods from Korea, Carbon Steel Wire Rod from Spain and certain Steel Products from Korea.) . . . . . In cases where the government acts through a private party, such as in Certain Softwood Lumber Products from Canada and Leather from Argentina . . . the Administration intends that the law continue to be administered on a case by case basis consistent with the preceeding paragraph. It is the Administration's view that Article 1.1(a)(1)(iv) of the Subsidies Agreement and Section 771(5)(B)(ii) encompass indirect subsidy practices like those which Commerce has countervailed in the past, and that these types of indirect subsidies will continue to be countervailable, provided that Commerce is satisfied that the standard under Section 771(5)(B)(iii) has been met.[30]

The Panel examined these conflicting passages and concluded that while the passages suggest a "a certain tension," the Department of Commerce's past practice will be followed in the future "only to the extent that there is no inconsistency with the definition of subsidy under the URAA." In this way, the Statement does not require the Department to interpret the statute in such a manner whereby export restraints are to be treated as a "financial contribution."[31]

The Preamble. A further legal question was whether the Preamble to the US countervailing duty regulations has an independent operational life that could give rise to the violations alleged by Canada. On this point the US and Canada had differed as well, with the US claiming that only the Regulations have the force of law and Canada claiming that the Preamble is an integral part of the Regulations. The Panel examined the preambular language and concluded that it has no operational life of its own separate from the regulations. Nevertheless, the Panel held that there was no reason to exclude the Preamble from consideration as a possible interpretative tool in the treatment of export restraints in US countervailing duty investigations.

---

[30] See para. 2.5.   [31] para. 8.103–8.106.

On this point, the Preamble references the Statement of Administrative Action as "directing" the Department of Commerce to proceed on a case-by-case basis with respect to the definitional elements of a "subsidy" and the Preamble incorporates by reference and defers to the Statement "in respect of the interpretation of the definitional element of a subsidy, in particular the meaning of *entrusts* or *directs.*"[32]

The Preamble does speak about export restraints specifically and states that they can "in certain circumstances lead those parties to provide the restrained good to domestic purchases for less than adequate remuneration. This was recognized by Commerce in *US – Softwood Lumber III* and *Argentina – Hides and Leather.* Further, as indicated by the Statement at 926 and as we confirm in these Final Regulations, if the Department were to investigate situations and facts similar to those examined in *US – Softwood Lumber* and *Argentina – Hides and Leather* in the future, the new statute would permit the Department of Commerce to reach the same result."[33]

The Panel held that this "would permit" language in the Preamble is consistent with the interpretation of the statute that the Department of Commerce is not required under US law to treat export restraints as financial contributions.[34]

US Practice. Canada also argued that the Department of Commerce "practice" was an institutional/administrative commitment to treat export restraints as financial contributions and that this is reflected in earlier cases that foreclose any discretionary consideration of the treatment of export restraints. As examples of US practice that reflected the institutional commitment to treat export restraints as financial contributions, Canada pointed to the pre-WTO practice of countervailing export restraints where they "directly led to a discernible benefit." Canada argued that this practice was explicitly referenced in the Statement of Administrative Action and the Preamble, adding further support to an interpretation that it would continue to be operative in the future. Moreover, Canada mentioned two post-WTO cases where it was alleged that the Department had indicated it would continue to take this approach in the future.[35]

The Panel disagreed and found the Canadian interpretation imprecise and not contained in any defined cases of export restraints in US countervailing duty investigations in the post-Uruguay Round context. In other words, there has been no case since the WTO came into existence in which the US has countervailed against an export restraint. The Panel

[32] See para. 8.115.   [33] See para. 8.116.   [34] See para. 8.111.   [35] See para. 8.120–8.122.

also noted that while practice must normally be followed, it can also be departed from, so long as a reasoned explanation is provided.[36] Hence, with respect to the US government measures, the Panel found that only the statute has an independent operational life of its own, although it must be read in light of the Statement, and that the Statement is the principal interpretive guide thereto.

The Panel further argued that, when read in light of the Statement, the statute does not require the treatment of export restraints as financial contributions in countervailing duty investigations. The Preamble contributes very little substance. The Panel therefore concluded that there was insufficient clarity as to the meaning of US practice to draw a conclusion that it requires any particular treatment of export restraints. Thus, there is no mandatory treatment of export restraints as financial contributions.[37]

3.6   Decision of the Panel

In sum, the Panel concluded that: (1) an export restraint as defined in this case cannot constitute government entrusted or directed provision of goods and hence does not constitute a financial contribution in the sense of Article 1.1(a) of the SCM; (2) the contested US measures are not inconsistent with Article 1.1 of the SCM Agreement by *requiring* the application of countervailing duties against practices that are not deemed subsidies. Thus, the statute requires both a benefit and a financial contribution. Here, an export restraint was seen as conferring a benefit but was not deemed to confer a financial contribution, and hence no countervailable subsidy.

3.7   Interpretative legal and policy issues

Section 4 below evaluates the treatment of export restraints as subsidies from an economic perspective. Here, we examine the legal reasoning of the Panel with respect to several questions of law and fact that raise systemic questions.

First, was the decision to apply the so-called "classical test" consistent within WTO caselaw? Second, despite its decision that only mandatory measures matter, the panel decided to undertake a substantive analysis first and then turn to the procedural question of whether the measures

---

[36] See para. 8.126.   [37] See para. 8.130.

were mandatory or discretionary. Was this the appropriate sequencing of claims?

On the first point, there is now a considerable body of GATT and WTO dispute settlement practice that has considered the so-called "mandatory-discretionary" question.[38] What is called the "classical test" refers to GATT precedent that only national legislation which is mandatory in its application and in a manner inconsistent with its GATT obligations can be a violation. Discretionary legislation, that is, national measures that provide the government, e.g. the executive branch, with the discretionary authority as to how to act or indeed whether to act, and therefore provide the scope for acting inconsistently with a GATT/WTO obligation are not viewed as a prima facie violation of the WTO. It is possible for discretionary legislation to be inconsistent with a covered agreement and thereby constitute a violation thereof, but that requires its WTO inconsistent *application*. In the GATT context, with this distinction came the view that only mandatory measures could alter the competitive opportunities of international trade.[39]

The majority of WTO case law has followed this basic precedent as in the case of *US – Export Restraints*. The Panel aligned itself with the dominant jurisprudential trend on this question. Indeed, the Panel barely took heed of the most important case that suggested that discretionary

---

[38] This includes at least a dozen cases: *Argentina – Measures Affecting Imports of Footwear, Textiles, Apparel and Other Items* (WT/DS56); *Canada – Measures Affecting the Export of Civilian Aircraft* (WT/DS70); *Turkey – Restrictions on Imports of Textile and Clothing Products* (WT/DS34); *US – Anti-dumping Act of 1916* (WT/DS136); *US – Anti-dumping Act of 1916* (WT/DS/162); *US – Anti-dumping Measures on Certain Hot-Rolled Steel Products from Japan* (WT/DS184); *US – Section 301–310 of the Trade Act of 1974* (WT/DS152); *Brazil – Export Financing Program for Aircraft* (WT/DS46W); *US – Section 211 Omnibus Appropriations Act of 1998* (WT/DS176); *Canada – Export Credits and Loan Guarantees for Regional Aircraft* (WT/DS222); *US – Anti-dumping and Countervailing Measures on Steel Plate from India* (WT/DS206/r); *US – Countervailing Duties on Certain Corrosion-Resistant Carbon Steel Flat Products from Germany* (WT/DS213); *US – Section 129 (c)(1) of the Uruguay Round Agreements Act* (WT/DS221); *US – Continued Dumping and Subsidy Offset Act of 2000* (WT/DS217, WT/DS 234); *US – Preliminary Determinations with Respect to Certain Softwood Lumber from Canada* (WT/DS236); *US – Countervailing Measures Concerning Certain Products from the EC* (WT/DS212).

[39] See, *US – Superfund* para. 5.2.9; *US – Malt Beverages*, para. 5.39, *US – Tobacco. US – Tobacco* has a particularly clear statement on this issue: "Panels had consistently ruled that legislation which mandated action inconsistent with the General Agreement could be challenged as such, whereas legislation which merely gave the discretion to the executive authority of a contracting party to act inconsistently with the General Agreement could not be challenged as such; only the actual application of legislation could be subject to challenge" *US – Tobacco*, Panel Report, adopted October 4, 1994, BISD 41S/131, para. 118).

legislation, namely the *US – Section 301 Trade Act* dispute, could constitute a *prima facie* violation of the WTO.[40] That case involved the timeline in section 301 of the 1974 Trade Act, as amended, which calls for retaliatory measures within eighteen months when foreign countries have been found to breach their international obligations while the DSU procedures usually take longer.

The EC alleged that the section allowed for retaliation without going through the WTO dispute settlement system, as mandated by Article 23 of the DSU. The US, for its part, argued that language in the SAA made plain that no WTO inconsistent action could be taken. The Panel held that discretionary legislation may support a violation. It stressed that its test did not overturn earlier GATT jurisprudence. The Panel argued that a rule that only legislation mandating inconsistency could violate the WTO does not mean that legislation with discretion can never be found a violation.[41] The WTO Appellate Body has considered the question of mandatory/discretionary legislation to a degree.[42] In our view, it has not entirely shut the door to the view expressed in section 301 that discretionary legislation can be a WTO violation.[43]

US – Export Restraints is a somewhat unusual case in that the complainant challenged the legislation on its face and not with respect to a particular application. We can only speculate why this case was brought in the first place. Given the track record here of past cases where the US held that export restraints *did* constitute an export subsidy, and given the existence of language in the Preamble and the SAA that suggested the ability to continue past precedent, Canada with no doubt wished to obtain a holding from a panel to pre-empt a US action. It obtained such a ruling, at least with respect to the potential application of countervailing duties on export restraints as defined by Canada.

---

[40] While the Panel's decision seems reasonable, the Panel's stated grounds for differentiation, namely the fact that this dispute centered on the subsidy agreement rather than the DSU and thus covered a different part of the WTO, seems perfunctory. Moreover, the Panel's argument that it was applying the classical test because the parties agreed that that should be the approach taken is also not persuasive legal argumentation.

[41] See para. 7.43.

[42] See, for example, *US – 1916 Act* where it held that the meaning of discretion had to do with the discretion vested in the executive branch of government (para. 91).

[43] In *US – Countervailing Measures on Certain EC Products*, for example, the Appellate Body emphasized that it was "not by implication precluding the possibility that a Member could violate its WTO obligations by enacting legislation granting discretion to its authorities to act in violation of its WTO obligations" (footnote 334).

Yet, at the end of the day, the Panel concluded after a careful review of the challenged US measures that they were discretionary. Hence, the Panel's decision on sequencing of analysis allowed it to opine on whether the US treatment of export restraints is consistent or inconsistent with the SCM Agreement when arguably it was not obliged to do so. Here we are left with the impression that the Panel really wanted to evaluate the case on the merits while not being fully obliged to do so.[44]

This issue therefore raises the broader question of judicial philosophy: should the Panel have undertaken the substantive analysis or should it have been expected to terminate its inquiry having determined that the applicable US measures were discretionary in the first instance and therefore did not oblige a violation of the SCM Agreement?

Clearly this is an issue of judicial philosophy or policy where opinion will differ. One could arguably find the Panel's decision to undertake a substantive analysis (i.e. of whether a certain category of measures can constitute a financial contribution) before it has undertaken a determination on the nature of the measures as being of a speculative and abstract nature. Does this decision by the Panel overstep the authority of WTO Panels? There may not be clear answers to these questions in the rules of the WTO or the DSU.

A restrained approach to judicial interpretation may be particularly relevant with respect to legislation that is being evaluated on its face and not with respect to a particular dispute. Such a claim could be premature or overreaching because no nullification or impairment has yet occurred. In this dispute the United States asserted that the Panel was being asked

---

[44] The *US – Export Restraint* Panel relied on three earlier cases for its decision to tackle the substantive features before examining the nature of the challenged measures. These cases are distinguishable from *US – Export Restraints* by virtue of the relatively non-controversial nature of the legal matters in question as compared with the deeply contested legal questions arising in *US Export Restraints*. We are grateful to Professor Hudec for many of this comments on an early draft of this essay, including his observations on this point. The Panel, in para. 8.11, specifically referenced *US – SuperFund*, where the scheme involved a discriminatory penalty tax that would be imposed if certain information was not submitted. The Panel found that a penalty tax, if imposed, would violate Article II.2, and then went on to find that the Superfund Act did not require imposition of the tax, See Report of the Panel BISD 34S/136 para. 5.29; *Thailand Cigarettes*: where the GATT Panel found that certain discriminatory tax rates would violate GATT provisions, but the Panel went on to find that the Thai authorities had room to implement the rates in a consistent fashion, See BISD 37S/200 para. 84; and *US – Tobacco*, where the GATT Panel concluded that the US had discretion to interpret its legislation consistently with the GATT, see BISD 41S/131, para. 123. See para. 8.11 footnote 114.

to render an advisory opinion, which by most accounts is not within the jurisdiction of panels or the Appellate Body to grant.[45] It has surfaced in a number of disputes.[46] As a matter of practice, the current Chairman of the Appellate Body has stated plainly that "we do not render advisory opinions in the Appellate Body."[47]

A more supportive view could argue that the Panel was justified in examining the challenged measures because these practices had been sources of intergovernmental dispute in the past. Further, there was no bright line between process and substance and the Panel had to undertake a legal analysis of the US measures in order to determine whether they alone or in combination amounted to mandatory or discretionary actions.

On balance, our view is that it was possible to evaluate the discretionary or mandatory nature of the measures as a threshold matter. As a result, the Panel's decision to evaluate the merits of the claim when it was not obliged to do so was inappropriate.[48] This view does not mean, however, that the Panel's rendering amounts to an error of law. The result may be a set of declaratory statements or dicta that perhaps serve as a warning to WTO members that may be inclined to interpret their own laws in a fashion that would deem export restraints to be countervailable subsidies. It is

---

[45] One can draw textual support in certain DSU provisions for the proposition that the dispute settlement system is not designed to render advisory opinions. For example, Article 3 states that the dispute settlement system is aimed at securing a "positive solution to a dispute," and Article 11 states that the function of panels is to make an "objective assessment of the matter before it, including the objective assessment of the facts of the case and the applicability and conformity with the relevant covered agreements. . . ." Advisory opinions also raise issues of compliance and retaliation.

[46] By way of examples, and without speaking to the accuracy of the allegations, the assertion has arisen in at least the *EC – Bananas* dispute; *US – Byrd Amendment*, and *Korea – Dairy* Panel (WT/DS98/R).

[47] The Chairman went on to state, "we render opinions only when there are specific trade disputes." See, Bacchus (2002). It is also true that the SCM Agreement itself establishes a mechanism for obtaining advisory opinions from a committee of external experts, reflected in Articles 24.3 and 24.4 of the Agreement, and there is nothing to suggest that this function is expected from panel or Appellate Body review.

[48] A counter-argument to this position might begin from the view that the possible – even if not mandatory – use of countervailing duties against export restraints could induce exporting governments to refrain from using export restraints as long as there was significant uncertainty about the legality of such an application of countervailing duty measures. From this viewpoint, it might then be argued that the Panel was justified in evaluating the merits of the claim in order to resolve the legal uncertainty. Such an argument, while certainly reasonable, would have to be weighed against the risk of judicial over-reaching. Our view is that in this particular case the risks of the latter probably outweigh the benefits of the former.

not clear that such "guidance" from the chambers of dispute settlement panels is appropriate (though see also note 49).

4 Specific economic analysis

We now consider and evaluate the particular legal and economic issues and methodologies raised by the dispute. More specifically we ask: In light of the underlying goals of the relevant WTO provisions, and taking them as given, was the resolution of the substantive economic issues around which the case revolved based on sound economic principles? The central substantive economic issue of this case concerns whether an export restraint could ever (under any circumstances) be interpreted as conferring a subsidy within the meaning of the SCM Agreement.

Before turning to our specific economic analysis, it may be helpful to begin with a basic observation, in order to frame the subsequent discussion. As described by the Panel (paragraph 1.1), the issue under consideration is ". . . US measures that treat a restraint on exports of a product *as* a subsidy to other products made using or incorporating the restricted product if the domestic price of the restricted product is affected by the restraint" (emphasis added). As this statement indicates, at one level the issue under consideration comes down to a simple question: what other policy measure is an export restraint *most like* when it comes to the implications of the export restraint for other products? As it happens, economic arguments can give a precise analytical answer to this question.

To develop this answer, we begin by observing that basic economic arguments can be used to show that an export tax on a single export good is conceptually equivalent to (i.e. "exactly like") an alternative program in which an export subsidy of the same magnitude is placed on every other export good and an import tariff of the same magnitude is placed on each imported good.[49] Intuitively, an export tax on a good lowers the price of that good in the domestic market relative to all other domestic prices, and this induces domestic consumers to shift their consumption toward that good and away from others at the same time that it releases for use in other sectors domestic resources that were used in the production of that export good. These effects mirror the impact of the alternative program described just above.

---

[49] This follows from an application of Lerner's Symmetry Theorem (Lerner, [1936], pp. 308–13).

Perhaps surprisingly, the conceptual equivalence between an export tax and the alternative program described just above continues to hold even when, for example, the export good under consideration is used as an input into the production of certain other (export- or import-competing) goods in the economy.[50] As a consequence, it would be valid to assert this equivalence in a circumstance such as that considered in the case of *Argentina – Hides and Leather*, where a government embargo on exports of cattle hides was found to be a countervailable subsidy to leather producers, and in the case of *US – Softwood Lumber*, where export restraints on logs were found to be countervailable subsidies to lumber producers. The equivalence result described above would indicate that the export restraints on cattle hides and logs would, in each case, be conceptually equivalent to an alternative program in which an export subsidy of the same magnitude is placed on every other export good and an import tariff of the same magnitude is placed on each imported good.

Recalling now the previous discussion contained in section 2.2 above, in which it was observed that an import tariff can be decomposed into its two component parts of consumption tax and production subsidy, and observing analogously that an export subsidy may be decomposed into its two component parts of a consumption tax on the export good and a production subsidy to export producers, it may be concluded that basic economic arguments can be used to show that an export tax on a single export good is conceptually equivalent to an alternative program in which a production subsidy of the same magnitude is placed on every other good in the economy and a consumption tax of the same magnitude is placed on every other good in the economy.[51]

The above statement provides a precise economic interpretation of the view that an export tax can confer a subsidy to production in other sectors of an economy. In fact, however, as the statement above reveals, if the subsidy conferred by an export tax is to be highlighted, then it is more accurate to say that the export tax confers a subsidy to production in *every* other sector of the economy. But this interpretation, while valid

---

[50] An extension of Lerner's Symmetry Theorem to allow for intermediate inputs can be found in McKinnon (1966). The particular result that underlies the statement made above is contained in Theorem 4 of that paper.

[51] This statement asserts that the implied production subsidy in every other sector of the economy will be at a common *ad valorem* rate, but we emphasize that from this it does not follow that production in every other sector of the economy will expand at a common rate.

from an economic perspective, carries with it a potentially important implication for the treatment of export restraints as subsidies within the SCM Agreement.

We now suggest that this interpretation provides the basis for an alternative line of reasoning by which the Panel might have rejected the US position that export restraints could ever (under any circumstances) constitute countervailable subsidies under the SCM Agreement. Under this alternative reasoning, the Panel might have argued that the US's own "effects" approach, if followed to its logical conclusion, would imply that export restraints could never constitute specific subsidies within the meaning of Article 2 of the SCM Agreement, and as a consequence would not be actionable under the SCM Agreement.

In particular, in its arguments the US suggested the validity of adopting an effects approach in determining whether a government action constitutes a financial contribution. Under this approach, the US argued that an export restraint that has the effect of inducing domestic producers to sell their product to domestic purchasers is "conceptually equivalent" to an explicit and affirmative order by the government to do so, and therefore constitutes a financial contribution in the form of a government-entrusted or government-directed provision of goods. The Panel rejected this approach, and ultimately relied on the ordinary meanings of the words "entrusts" and "directs" to conclude that an explicit and affirmative action of delegation or command is required to constitute a financial contribution under the SCM Agreement, a requirement which it concluded an export restraint cannot satisfy (para. 8.44).

In rejecting the effects approach taken by the US, the Panel observed that under this approach a tariff would constitute a subsidy within the meaning of Article 1 of the SCM Agreement, because the effects of a tariff would be conceptually equivalent to a subsidy to domestic producers of the tariff-protected product, and even though the nature of the government action associated with these two forms of government intervention would be quite different, under the US effects approach differences in the nature of government actions would be irrelevant given the equivalence of effect (para. 8.37).[52]

---

[52] Notice that the "tariff-as-production-subsidy" argument made by the Panel can be given a formal basis according to the tariff-as-production-subsidy-and-consumption-tax argument explained in section 2.2 above. Unlike an export tax, then, which as we have observed according to Lerner's Symmetry Theorem can be said to confer a production subsidy to every other sector of the economy, an import tariff can be said to confer a production subsidy to only the tariff-protected producers.

We suggest here that, rather than rejecting the US effects approach and relying on the ordinary meanings of the words "entrusts" and "directs" to reach its final conclusion, the Panel might have come to the same final conclusion by: (i) accepting for the sake of argument the US effects approach; (ii) arguing on the basis of the economic principles described just above that an export tax on a single export good is conceptually equivalent to an alternative program in which a production subsidy of the same magnitude is placed on every other good in the economy and a consumption tax of the same magnitude is placed on every other good in the economy; (iii) observing that the production subsidy conferred by this export restraint could not qualify as a specific subsidy within the meaning of Article 2 of the SCM Agreement; and (iv) concluding therefore that by the US's own effects-approach logic, an export restraint could never (under any circumstances) be interpreted as conferring an actionable subsidy within the meaning of the SCM Agreement.

The statement that the subsidy conferred by an export restraint applies to every other sector of the economy is admittedly counter-intuitive, especially when applied in a case such as US – Softwood Lumber. So it is important to be clear on what the underlying equivalence result that supports this statement says and what it does not say. Recall that the equivalence result says that an export tax on a single export good is conceptually equivalent to an alternative program in which a production subsidy of the same magnitude is placed on every other good in the economy and a consumption tax of the same magnitude is placed on every other good in the economy. Note that this result says nothing about the expected effects of these (equivalent) policies on trade volumes relative to an alternative of no intervention. So in particular, this result does *not* for example rule out the possibility that an export tax on logs would have a large expansionary impact on the volume of exports of lumber, and dispelling the belief that this result carries with it such an implication may go some way toward reducing the counter-intuitiveness of the result. Rather, the result says only that, whatever the economic effects of the export tax are, those effects will be replicated if the export tax is replaced by the dual policies described above.

5   Concluding observations on the legal tests and economic analysis

In general, we are of the view that the problematical aspects of this case do not stem from poorly drafted treaty text. There may be some areas where the rules could have been crafted more precisely or when they could have included some additional examples that might have answered directly some questions of interpretation. However, these drafting refinements tend not to go to the heart of the issues raised by the case. Instead, the conceptual problems discussed herein stem from the ambiguity or disjunction between the stated goals of the agreement and the instruments and approaches selected.

Turning now to the conceptual foundations of the case, we make the following broad economic observations.

First, while the SCM Agreement represents an attempt to ". . . impose multilateral disciplines on subsidies which distort international trade," we have explained in section 2 that only some of these disciplines admit a natural economic efficiency-enhancing interpretation. This finding derives from a basic observation. As we noted in that section, standard economic arguments can be utilized to succinctly characterize the fundamental inefficiency associated with unilateral policy choices in a global economy: insufficient trade volume.

This basic observation underlies the following three broad conclusions. First, to the extent that the provisions of the SCM Agreement operate to reduce export subsidies and, ultimately, export volumes, they therefore tend to work against efficiency. Second, to the extent that the provisions of the SCM Agreement create ambiguity about the market-access implications of tariff commitments and thereby interfere with the ability to negotiate greater market access, they again tend to work against efficiency. And third, to the extent that the provisions of the SCM Agreement provide disciplines on the use of (new) subsidies that help governments negotiate more effective market access agreements through tariff commitments and achieve greater trade volumes, then these provisions may be interpreted as contributing to efficiency from an economic perspective.

We have offered two interpretations of these conclusions. A first interpretation emphasizes the limits of existing formal economic reasoning in this instance, and casts doubt on the ability of existing formal economic models to adequately capture the role that international agreements to restrict subsidies can play. According to this interpretation, it is important to seek and develop further alternative modeling approaches that might better reflect some critical feature associated with the issue of subsidies that the standard models have failed to capture. A second interpretation would place more weight on the presumptions implied by the standard economic arguments reviewed above, and this second interpretation casts doubt on the general rationale for international agreements to limit subsidies.[53]

At the least, the conclusions we report in section 2 reflect the need for further articulation of the rationale for the treatment of subsidies within the GATT/WTO. At most, the GATT/WTO's approach to subsidies might benefit from a fundamental overhaul.

Second, our analysis indicates that as a general matter export restraints should not be viewed as specific subsidies within the meaning of the SCM Agreement. We offer an argument to support this view from an economic perspective. According to this argument, an export tax can be interpreted as providing a production subsidy to *every* other sector of the economy, because its effects are conceptually equivalent to imposing an export subsidy in every other export sector and an import tariff in every import-competing sector, and each of these policies can in turn be decomposed into a production subsidy and a consumption tax. Therefore, the subsidy implied by an export restraint would not appear to qualify as a "specific" subsidy as defined in Article 2 of the SCM Agreement, and on this basis Part II, III and V of the SCM Agreement would not apply.

If the specificity requirement is sufficient to exclude export restraints from consideration within the SCM Agreement, then no changes to legal text seem warranted (though this was not the legal basis for the finding in the US Export Restraints Case). If the specificity requirement by itself would not serve this purpose, then a change in the legal text to rule out the application of the SCM Agreement in cases of export restraints seems appropriate.

Turning now to the legal character of the case, we have considered issues such as the approach to treaty interpretation taken by the reviewing Panel, and if relevant, the Appellate Body. With respect to the sequencing of analysis, as noted above, we believe that the Panel could have looked to the nature of the US measures and reached a judgment with respect to the mandatory versus discretionary nature of the measures without necessarily going the next step and undertaking a full substantive review of the circumstances where export restraints could be deemed a subsidy within

---

[53] In this regard, the conclusions we report in section 2 may be difficult to accept for those who put emphasis on other, less analyzed or proven factors such as transaction costs, the stage of economic development of the importing country, the perception that export subsidies are particularly aimed at transferring the costs of adjustment abroad, etc. The lawyer co-author here is not fully convinced, although appreciative, of the force of overall economic observation on the effects of subsidies.

the meaning of the SCM Agreement. That exercise of judicial restraint would have been warranted and appropriate.

It is also instructive to compare the *US – Export Restraints* case to the *Canada – Dairy* case (see our companion review of that case) because both of these recent cases implicate the SCM Agreement. Consistency of interpretation is not the hallmark of these cases when taken together. *Canada – Dairy*, which concluded after *US – Export Restraints*, was a particularly noteworthy case from a legal perspective in that it represented the first interpretation of the Agriculture Agreement. However, the *Canada – Dairy* case also considered the SCM Agreement. These two cases viewed together do not present a coherent or comprehensive set of interpretations on the relationship between the SCM Agreement and the Agriculture Agreement.

References

Bagwell, Kyle and Robert W. Staiger. 2002. *The Economics of the World Trading System*. Boston, MA: MIT Press.

Bagwell, Kyle and Robert W. Staiger. In process. Subsidy agreements.

Lerner, A. P. 1939. The symmetry between import and export taxes. *Economica* 3 (August): 308–13.

McKinnon, Ronald I. 1966. Intermediate products and differential tariffs: a generalization of Lerner's symmetry theorem. Quarterly Journal of Economics 80 (November): 584–615.

10

Canada – Dairy
Canada – Measures Affecting the Importation of Dairy Products and the Exportation of Milk*

MERIT E. JANOW AND ROBERT W. STAIGER

1 Introduction

This paper summarizes and critically reviews the dispute brought before the World Trade Organization (WTO) concerning *Canada – Measures Affecting the Importation of Dairy Products and the Exportation of Milk*, euphemistically referred to herein as *Canada – Dairy*. This dispute is centered on the WTO Agricultural Agreement, though it also involves the WTO Subsidies and Countervailing Measures (SCM) Agreement and GATT – 1994.

Many analysts have argued that a significant accomplishment of the Uruguay Round of negotiations was the development of a set of rules on agricultural supports, that covered the three main policy instruments of such support: border measures, domestic supports, and export subsidies. The national commitments made as part of the Agreement on Agriculture clearly represented just the beginning of agricultural reform, reflected by the fact that agriculture was earmarked as part of the built-in agenda going forward. It is widely recognized that the agricultural sector is one of the most highly subsidized sectors in the world. Liberalization of trade in agriculture was deemed the "linchpin" of the Uruguay Round for the United States and a number of other jurisdictions. It remains controversial today. Hence, this political and economic backdrop adds a special importance to this dispute.

* This study has benefited from the suggestions of seminar participants at the Conference on the Principles of Trade Law: The World Trade Organization, held on February 6–7, 2003 in Philadelphia, and especially from the comments of Steve Charnovitz, William Davey, Wilfred Ethier, Henrik Horn, Robert Howse, Petros C. Mavroidis, David Palmeter, and John Ragosta. We are particularly indebted to Robert Hudec for extensive comments on earlier drafts of this study.

Contextually the dispute is also significant because it brings to light the systemic question of whether the Agriculture Agreement and the SCM Agreement are structured and drafted to strike the proper balance among the support measures, especially when there are spillover consequences of domestic support measures on export markets. Although the domestic price-setting mechanism is a distinct instrument from the export-pricing instrument, these instruments cannot be evaluated in isolation. Hence, in an environment of regulated prices and other domestic support measures, distortions introduced in one area (e.g. domestic supports) may have an impact on prices in another area, even if somewhat less regulated (e.g. export prices).

From a legal perspective, an important systemic feature of the case has to do with the relationship between the SCM Agreement and the Agriculture Agreement. The question of how the SCM Agreement should inform the Agriculture Agreement was raised but not answered in this dispute.

The discussion that follows undertakes a three-step analysis. In each step, we begin with the most general and turn in sequence to the more specific legal and economic issues raised by the *Canada – Dairy* dispute.

First, we consider the economic basis for the WTO provisions that are at the heart of this dispute. We ask: What are the underlying goals of the various WTO provisions touched upon in the *Canada – Dairy* case, and are the goals themselves sensible from an economic perspective?

Second, we present and evaluate the key factual and legal elements of the case, focusing primarily on the legal issues raised by the case in its final disposition (e.g. whether at the Panel or the Appellate Body level) that seem particularly important to understanding the stated legal and economic logic of the case. More specifically we ask: Have the reviewing panels and the AB applied the law consistently, mindful of WTO precedent? Are the panelists and the AB doing what they state they are doing? Are the judgments well grounded in legal argument? Is there ambiguity in the applicable law, as drafted? If so, how is it resolved – e.g. with deference to national measures, or through judicial license?

And third, we consider and evaluate the particular legal and economic issues and methodologies raised by the dispute. More specifically we ask: In light of the underlying goals of the relevant WTO provisions, was the resolution of the substantive economic issues around which the case revolved based on sound economic principles?

2 General economic analysis

The *Canada – Dairy* case raises several levels of questions from an economic perspective. A first-level question is: What are the goals of the various WTO provisions touched upon in this case, and are the goals themselves sensible from an economic perspective? This is the question that we review in this section. A second-level question is: In light of these goals, and taking them as given, was the resolution of the substantive economic issues around which the case revolved based on sound economic principles? This second-level question will be taken up in section 4, after the legal aspects of the case have been presented and evaluated in section 3.

What, then, are the goals of the various WTO provisions touched upon in this case? This case centers on the question of whether Canada's milk support schemes violated its export-subsidy-reduction commitments under Articles 3.3, 9, and 10 of Agriculture Agreement. Hence, we evaluate in this section the general economic basis for international commitments to reduce export subsidies on agricultural products such as those embodied in these Articles.

As a general matter, it is instructive to begin by considering the stated rationale for limiting export subsidies generally as contained in paragraph 2, section B of Article XVI GATT: "The contracting parties recognize that the granting by a contracting party of a subsidy on the export of any product may have harmful effects for other contracting parties, both importing and exporting, may cause undue disturbance to their normal commercial interests, and may hinder the achievement of the objectives of this Agreement." From an economic perspective, what is interesting about this statement is its assertion that export subsidies may have harmful effects for *both importing and exporting* governments.

By contrast, the Preamble of the Agreement on Agriculture and the Articles themselves suggest a more nuanced view of the impacts of agricultural export subsidies on importing and exporting governments. For instance, the Preamble lists as one of the four areas for achieving binding commitments the area of "export competition," and indeed Article 8 of the Agreement is entitled "Export Competition Commitments." This suggests that the commitments to reduce agricultural export subsidies are seen by WTO members as primarily serving the interests of competing exporters of agricultural products, but not necessarily the interests of importing governments. This suggestion is made more explicit in the last paragraph of the Preamble, which states: ". . . and taking into account the possible negative effects of the implementation of the reform programme on least-developed and net food-importing developing countries."

In fact, it might be said that the Preamble of the Agriculture Agreement reflects an underlying tension of interests between exporting and importing governments on the issue of export subsidies that is absent in the stance against export subsidies taken in the name of exporters and importers in section B of Article XVI GATT. As we explain below, tension between exporting and importing governments over the issue of export subsidies is more readily understood with standard economic arguments than is a unanimous stance against export subsidies. However, as we also explain below, standard economic analysis does not help us explain the way in which the tension between exporting and importing governments was resolved in the Agriculture Agreement. Thus, though for somewhat different reasons, the goals of the export subsidy provisions in both the Agricultural Agreement and section B of Article XVI GATT (and by implication, Article 3.1(a) of the SCM Agreement) are puzzling from an economic perspective.

2.1   The economic puzzle of international agreements to limit export subsidies

To appreciate the economic puzzle posed by international agreements to limit export subsidies, let us begin by trying to explain with standard economic arguments the interests of exporting and importing governments as expressed in Part B of Article XVI GATT. To this end, consider a hypothetical world in which export subsidies were not prohibited and where no government had yet bound a tariff in a GATT negotiation. We might think of this hypothetical world as approximating in very broad terms the world as it might have existed during the early years of GATT, had Part B of Article XVI GATT not been introduced.[1]

In this hypothetical world, with governments then free to respond to an export subsidy with tariffs and/or export subsidies of their own, it can be generally shown that one country's export subsidy must be seen as harmful to the governments of competing exporting countries, but *beneficial* to the governments of importing countries (we explain this benefit below).[2]

---

[1] Part B of Article XVI GATT was introduced during the 1955 Review Session. We do not mean to suggest that there were in fact no tariff bindings in 1955, but only that at the time Part B of Article XVI GATT was introduced the tariff choices of most GATT Contracting Parties remained largely unrestrained by existing GATT tariff bindings.

[2] See Bagwell and Staiger (2002), chapter 10.

Hence, the position evidently taken by importing governments in the drafting of Article XVI GATT section B is not easily interpreted with standard economic arguments.

Perhaps surprisingly, the difficulty in making sense of the position taken by importing governments in Article XVI GATT section B cannot be overcome by allowing that real-world governments seem often to be driven more by special-interest politics than economics. Intuitively, the reason that an export subsidy could not be harmful to an importing government even in this setting is that, regardless of its underlying objectives, the importing government could always respond to an export subsidy by raising its import tariff so as to prevent the extra export volume from crossing its borders – thereby preventing any "disturbance" in the domestic economy – and simply collect more tariff revenue. If the importing government chooses not to "countervail" the export subsidy in this way, it is presumably because it has found a response that it likes even better. Either way, the importing government is guaranteed to gain.

Figure 10.1 illustrates. Let us consider a country that imports good y. In the right-hand quadrant of figure 10.1, the price of good y is measured on the vertical axis while the quantity of good y is measured on the horizontal axis. The downward sloping curve labeled $M(p)$ depicts the domestic country's import demand for good y as a function of the price, p, paid by importers of good y and prevailing for sales of good y in the domestic economy. The horizontal line labeled $E_0^*(p^*)$ depicts the export supply of good y from the foreign country as a function of the price, p^*, received by foreign exporters and in the absence of a foreign export subsidy.[3] Imposing an import tariff t, the domestic country imports the quantity m_0, foreign exporters receive the price p_0^*, and the price of good y prevailing in the domestic economy behind the tariff wall is p_0. These magnitudes are each depicted in the right-hand quadrant of figure 10.1.

In the left-hand quadrant of figure 10.1, the price of good y is again measured on the vertical axis while the quantity of good y is measured on the horizontal axis, but the left-hand quadrant of figure 10.1 depicts the underlying demand and supply curves for good y in the domestic economy. The domestic demand curve is labeled $D(p)$, and as reflected

---

[3] The horizontal foreign export supply curve reflects the simplifying assumption that the domestic country is "small" on world markets. This assumption simplifies the exposition, but is inessential to the point being made.

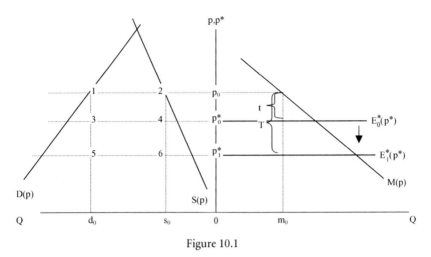

Figure 10.1

in the left-hand quadrant of figure 10.1, the quantity of good y demanded in the domestic economy is decreasing in the domestic price of good y. The domestic supply curve is labeled $S(p)$ and, as reflected in the left-hand quadrant of figure 10.1, the quantity of good y supplied by domestic producers is increasing in the domestic price of good y. At the price p_0 prevailing in the domestic economy, the quantity demanded in the domestic country is depicted as d_0, while the quantity supplied by domestic producers is depicted as s_0. The difference between d_0 and s_0 is the import quantity m_0, and the box labeled 1342 depicts the tariff revenue collected under the tariff t.

Now suppose that the foreign government applies an export subsidy to good y. In the right-hand quadrant of figure 10.1, this will shift the foreign export supply curve down, lowering the price at which foreign exports of good y are available to the domestic country. In the right-hand quadrant of figure 10.1, this lower price is labeled p_1^*, and the foreign export supply curve in the presence of the foreign export subsidy is labeled $E_1^*(p^*)$. If the domestic government responds to the foreign export subsidy with an increase in the tariff above t, it can maintain at the level p_0 the price of good y that prevails in the domestic economy behind the tariff wall. In the right-hand quadrant of figure 10.1, the tariff that achieves this domestic price preservation is labeled T.

The left-hand quadrant of figure 10.1 then depicts the impact on the domestic economy of the foreign-export-subsidy-cum-domestic-tariff-response just described. By design, the tariff T preserves the domestic price level p_0, and so neither the quantity demanded d_0 nor the quantity supplied s_0 in the domestic economy is altered. The only change experienced in the domestic economy is an increase in tariff revenue collected from the (unchanged) import volume m_0. The tariff revenue collected by the domestic government grows from the original box 1342 to the new larger box 1562 depicted in the left-hand quadrant, with the increased tariff revenue then corresponding to the box 3564.

Hence, as figure 10.1 makes clear, whatever the underlying objectives that might motivate a government to intervene with an import tariff, it can only benefit from the introduction of a foreign export subsidy, *provided it is free to make adjustments to its tariff.* This is because, as figure 10.1 depicts, the importing government can always continue to maintain the same domestic price level and import volume behind an extended tariff wall, and simply collect more tariff revenue.

For export subsidies to actually harm an importing government, standard economic arguments indicate that this importing government would have to (a) be concerned about the injury to domestic producers caused by the increased foreign exports resulting from the foreign export subsidy, *and* (b) lack the ability to use tariffs (or other policy instruments) to respond to this injury. Common-sense explanations of why export subsidies are harmful to importing governments often emphasize (a) without acknowledging that (b) is also required. But if (b) were emphasized as well, the position that importing governments are hurt by export subsidies might be taken less as an article of faith. Instead, whether or not an importing government considers export subsidies harmful to it would depend on the particular circumstances of the importing economy, and specifically on the degree of freedom that the importing government had to respond to the export subsidy with its tariff policy.

Of course, with the creation of GATT, governments surely anticipated that they would bind the majority of their tariffs through subsequent negotiation, and so perhaps this anticipation explains the position that export subsidies are expected to be harmful to importing governments. But within the GATT/WTO, the freedom arguably still exists to respond to an export subsidy with an increased tariff even after tariffs are bound. For example, an importing government has the freedom to respond to an export subsidy by imposing a countervailing duty under GATT Article VI (which would require no compensation and would be a discriminatory tariff action) or by renegotiating its tariff level under GATT Article XXVIII (which would involve compensation and would be a non-discriminatory tariff action). To the extent that these avenues of response are viable, standard economic arguments imply that agreements that attempt to place limits on export subsidies are not serving the interests of importing governments.

It is true that in practice, due to a variety of possible "transaction costs," these escapes may indeed be quite costly to use, and the resulting inflexibility of tariff commitments might then serve as the basis for understanding why export subsidies could be viewed as harmful by the governments of importing countries who had bound their tariffs. At a general level, this observation would seem to suggest a promising direction for further consideration of the degree to which the conclusions of the standard economic arguments reviewed above are robust. But the economics literature has yet to develop a formal treatment of the transaction-cost position in this context.

Hence, we may articulate a first piece of the economic puzzle posed by international agreements to limit export subsidies: standard economic arguments predict a tension between the interests of exporter governments and importer governments in this context, and so these arguments cannot account for the mutuality of interests expressed by exporting and importing governments in Part B of Article XVI GATT.

As we observed above, while the tension between the interests of exporter governments and importer governments that is predicted by standard economic arguments is absent from Part B of Article XVI GATT, this tension can be seen in the Preamble of the Agriculture Agreement. Nevertheless, it would be wrong to conclude from this observation that the export subsidy provisions of the Agriculture Agreement can find support from standard economic arguments. This is because, if followed to their logical conclusion, the standard economic arguments carry with them an even more provocative implication about the way in which this tension should be resolved. This is the second piece of the economic puzzle posed by international agreements to limit export subsidies: from a worldwide perspective, governments that choose to subsidize their exporters in the absence of international agreements should be encouraged to subsidize *more* under international agreements, not less.

The essential reason for this provocative implication of standard economic arguments is that, when the impacts on both competing exporter and importing governments are taken into account, an export subsidy can always be shown to confer a net benefit on the rest of the world. Through an international agreement, this net benefit can be "internalized" by the grantor of the export subsidy, resulting in an expansion of its export-subsidy program.

Why is it that an export subsidy can always be shown to confer a net benefit on the rest of the world? We may gain an intuitive understanding of this fact by returning to figure 10.1 above. Let us suppose that the foreign export supply of good y actually comes from two foreign countries, foreign country 1 and foreign country 2, whose exporters of good y are competing for sales in the domestic-country market. In the right-hand quadrant of figure 10.1, the horizontal line labeled $E_0^*(p^*)$ then depicts the total export supply of good y from the foreign countries 1 and 2 as a function of the price, p^*, received by foreign exporters and in the absence of a foreign export subsidy.

Now suppose that foreign country 1 applies an export subsidy to good y. Suppose further that, in response to the export subsidy of foreign country 1, foreign country 2 introduces an export subsidy of its own that permits its exporters to continue to export the original volume of good y to the domestic country and receive (inclusive of its export subsidy payment to them) the original price for their export sales. Notice that, under this response, the entire impact on foreign country 2 of foreign country 1's decision to offer an export subsidy is reduced to the *budgetary cost* of foreign country 2's export subsidy program, since under this export-subsidy program foreign country 2's exporters are completely insulated from any effects of foreign country 1's export subsidy. Suppose, then, that the upshot of foreign country 1's export subsidy and foreign country 2's described response is reflected in the right-hand quadrant of figure 10.1 by the downward shift of the foreign export supply curve to that labeled $E_1^*(p^*)$.

Figure 10.1 may now be used to develop an intuitive understanding of why an export subsidy can always be shown to confer a net benefit on the rest of the world. In the case under consideration, we may ask: How is it that we can be sure that foreign country 1's export subsidy confers a net benefit on the domestic importing country and the competing exporter foreign country 2? We can be sure of this fact for a simple reason: the extra tariff revenue collected by the domestic country under the tariff T in the presence of the foreign export subsidies, labeled as the box 3564 in the left-hand quadrant of figure 10.1, is more than sufficient to pay for the budgetary cost of foreign country 2's described export subsidy program.[4]

---

[4] This can be seen with the aid of figure 10.1 by observing that foreign country 2's described export subsidy must be at a (per-sales-unit) level which equals the difference between the original price received by foreign exporters, p_0^*, and the new price received by foreign exporters (excluding their subsidy receipts), p_1^*. This difference is the height of the box 3564 in the left-hand quadrant of figure 10.1. For foreign country 2, the budgetary cost

Hence, it follows that the domestic importing government could fully compensate foreign country 2 for the harm done to it by foreign country 1's export subsidy (i.e. the domestic importing government could pay for the budgetary cost of foreign country 2's described export-subsidy program) and still enjoy some remainder of the box 3564 for itself.[5]

For the reasons described above, it is difficult to utilize standard economic reasoning to offer broad support for worldwide benefits from export subsidy provisions which seek to place limits on export subsidies such as those touched upon in the *Canada – Dairy* case. Instead, standard economic reasoning leads to the conclusion that negotiated commitments to reduce the level of export subsidies from their unilateral levels represent an inefficient victory of exporter interests over importing – and world – welfare. The bottom line, then, is that the standard economic perspective does not provide broad support for the position that facilitating agreements to restrain export subsidies is an activity that the WTO should be involved in.[6]

2.2   What is wrong with the standard argument against export subsidies?

At this point it would be reasonable to ask: What is wrong with the standard argument against export subsidies? After all, standard economic arguments imply that free trade is the efficient outcome for the world, and that international agreements that reduce the level of intervention toward free trade – such as those that reduce export subsidies – are therefore efficiency-enhancing. Why do these standard arguments not provide formal support for the position that international agreements to limit export subsidies make economic sense?

---

of its described export-subsidy program is then this per-sales-unit export subsidy level multiplied by the total export volume of its good-y-exporting firms. But the total export volume of foreign country 2's good-y-exporting firms must be less than $m_0 = d_0 - s_0$ in figure 10.1, because foreign country 1's exporters are also supplying a portion of the trade volume m_0. As $d_0 - s_0$ is the length of the box 3564, it then follows that the box 3564 is larger than the budgetary cost of foreign country 2's described export subsidy program.

[5] As before, if in the present case under discussion the importing government or the competing exporter government chooses not to respond to the export subsidy of foreign country 1 in the described fashion, then it is presumably because an even better response has been found. Either way, the two governments can always be assured of a net benefit from foreign country 1's export subsidy.

[6] See Bagwell and Staiger (2002), chapter 10. This conclusion follows provided that the goal of the WTO is to serve the interests of its member governments, and that those interests are represented at the WTO bargaining table.

The difficulty with this position is that the formal conditions that are necessary to make free trade efficient when the interests of all governments are accounted for rule out the possibility that these governments would also choose to subsidize exports in a unilateral policy setting. In fact, such formal models predict that governments would *tax* exports in the absence of an international agreement, and hence a negotiated movement to free trade, while efficiency-enhancing in these models implies an international agreement that eliminates export taxes and thereby expands trade volumes.

Once these formal models are augmented with ingredients – such as political economy considerations or imperfect competition – that are capable of converting the predicted government policy choices from export taxes to export subsidies, the augmented models themselves no longer imply that free trade is efficient when the interests of all governments are accounted for (see also note 6). Efficiency continues to require international agreements that expand trade volumes from the levels implied by unilateral policy choices in these augmented models, but this is now accomplished in these augmented models by international agreements to increase export subsidies.

As a consequence, the contention that agreements to reduce export subsidies serve the interests of WTO Member governments because they represent a movement away from policy intervention and toward free trade does not stand up to formal scrutiny.[7] We are thus left with the bottom line that formed the concluding observation of the previous sub-section: the standard economic perspective does not provide broad support for the position that facilitating agreements to restrain export subsidies is an activity that the WTO should be involved in.

2.3   Interpretation 1: rethink economic explanations of export subsidy agreements

This observation invites at least two possible interpretations. A first interpretation emphasizes the limits of existing formal economic reasoning in this instance, and casts doubts on the ability of existing formal economic

---

[7] It is also interesting to observe that current efforts in the developed world to further restrict export subsidies in agriculture so as to help developing countries are driven by the interests of developing countries who are themselves competing exporters of agricultural products. The economic perspective outlined above would nevertheless predict that food-importing developing countries, food-importing countries more generally, and the world as a whole stand to lose if these efforts are successful.

models to adequately capture the role that international agreements to limit export subsidies can play. According to this interpretation, it is important to seek and develop further alternative modeling approaches that might better reflect some critical feature associated with the issue of export subsidies that the standard models have failed to capture. We have already mentioned the possibly important role of transaction costs in this regard. It is also possible that modeling approaches which see international agreements as helping governments make commitments to their own private sectors – rather than to other governments – may point the way to a more complete understanding of the role that international agreements to limit export subsidies can play.[8]

In the case of agricultural markets, the notion that governments might seek international agreements as a way to make commitments to their own private sectors – that is, to "tie their own hands" against intervention in the face of otherwise irresistible pressure from strong special interests – has a special appeal. Intuition would suggest that, given the extreme domestic political forces at work in agricultural markets, national governments might well seek ways to stand up to these pressures, and international agreements are a likely tool in this regard. Indeed, at a general level there is some empirical evidence that GATT/WTO commitments do play this role.[9]

Nevertheless, it is important to point out that, as yet, there is little formal understanding of the way in which international commitments might actually work toward this purpose. And there is even less formal understanding of the way that such international commitments might be structured to serve this purpose more effectively. A greater formal understanding of these issues could yield important dividends.

As one illustrative example, if governments seek to "tie their own hands" when it comes to resisting political pressures over domestic agricultural policies, then the ability to make commitments that afford very little discretion or ex-post flexibility can be very valuable in serving this purpose.[10] But when it comes to international commitments, the realities of international enforcement may call for a fairly high degree of flexibility in these commitments.[11] From this perspective, provisions of the Agriculture Agreement that give a government ex-post flexibility to "untie its hands," such as the special safeguard provisions contained in Article 5, would work

---

[8] For a recent review of the commitment approach to the study of trade agreements, see Bagwell and Staiger (2002), chapter 2.
[9] See Staiger and Tabellini (1999).   [10] See Staiger and Tabellini (1987).
[11] See Bagwell and Staiger (1990).

against the purpose of "hand tying," but may reflect a pragmatic position on the limits of international enforcement. This perspective might then in turn suggest that the flexibility afforded to governments under Article 5 could be further restricted – and the "hand-tying" purpose of the Agreement thereby better served – if the WTO dispute settlement procedures as they apply to the Agriculture Agreement were further enhanced.

In any event, under this first interpretation, while the way in which international agreements over export subsidies should be understood from an economic perspective is still an open question, and while the most effective design of these agreements may therefore still be an open question as well, the wisdom of GATT/WTO efforts to restrain the use of export subsidies is not really in doubt.

2.4   Interpretation 2: rethink WTO efforts to limit export subsidies

A second interpretation would place more weight on the presumptions implied by the standard economic arguments reviewed above, and this second interpretation casts doubts on the rationale for international agreements to limit export subsidies.

While this second interpretation may seem far-fetched and thus easily dismissed by those familiar with the GATT/WTO's long history of attempts to restrain export subsidies, it actually reflects a logic that is familiar in other settings. An intuitive appreciation of this logic can be gained by considering a simple analogy from the study of domestic antitrust policy.

Let us consider a single market, and suppose there are a small number of "big" sellers and "big" buyers in this market.[12] Due to the small numbers, each seller realizes that its sales will have an impact on the market-clearing price, and so each seller will tend to restrain its supply somewhat so as to raise the market-clearing price. That is, on the sellers' side, we have an oligopoly situation, in which the quantity supplied by the industry will tend to be lower than the efficient competitive level. Likewise, due to the small numbers, each buyer realizes that its purchases will have an impact on the market-clearing price, and so each buyer will tend to restrain its demand somewhat so as to lower the market-clearing price. That is, on the buyers' side, we have an oligopsony situation, in which

---

[12] Implicitly, the description that follows assumes that demand in this market is characterized by a small number of big buyers that coexist with a "competitive fringe" of additional small buyers. Since the existence of this competitive fringe is important only for technical reasons, we highlight in the text only the role of the big buyers.

the quantity demanded by the industry will tend to be lower than the efficient competitive level. The upshot is that, at the resulting market-clearing price, this market will have fewer sales – that is, less trade volume between buyers and sellers – than is efficient from the perspective of both the buyers and the sellers in total.

Consider now two possibilities for negotiation among the players in this market. A first possibility is that both buyers and sellers sit down at the negotiating table. A second possibility is that only the sellers meet to negotiate.

Under the first possibility for negotiation, both buyers and sellers can gain relative to their initial positions if each buyer agrees to increase its demand and each seller agrees to increase its supply in a "reciprocal" fashion, so that the original market-clearing price is preserved. To see how such an agreement can be beneficial to both buyers and sellers, recall that their initial positions reflect an inefficient situation in which there is too little trade between them at the market-clearing price. But the reciprocal agreement just described would induce a greater volume of trade without changing the market-clearing price. Hence, by agreeing to expand trade in this reciprocal fashion, buyers and sellers can together reduce the inefficiency and thereby each share in the resulting gains. In fact, it can be shown that achieving greater trade volume will be a necessary condition for all parties to gain from the negotiation in this situation. And as negotiations are voluntary, it may be expected that each party to the negotiation does indeed gain.

We may conclude that trade-volume-expanding agreements are needed to solve the inefficiency in this situation, and that negotiations that involve both buyers and sellers are therefore likely to result in efficiency-enhancing volume-expanding agreements.

Under the second possibility for negotiation, only the sellers are present at the negotiating table. Now it is no longer possible to negotiate an expansion of trade volume that preserves the original market-clearing price, because to do so would require reciprocal commitments on both sides of the market (i.e. by both sellers and buyers). The sellers can still gain from their negotiations, though, but to do so they must agree to *restrict* trade, not expand it, and thereby jointly raise the market-clearing price. In effect, as every student of anti-trust policy is taught, if oligopoly suppliers are allowed to cooperate through mutual agreements, they will combine to restrict trade. Such an agreement is beneficial to the suppliers, as it moves their joint supply decisions closer to the monopoly outcome, but it is bad for buyers and for overall efficiency when the interests of both sellers and buyers are counted, because it moves joint supply farther from the competitive outcome.

We may conclude that, while trade-volume-expanding agreements are still needed to solve the inefficiency in this situation, negotiations that involve only sellers are likely to result in restrictions in trade and further worldwide inefficiency.

What does this have to do with the WTO and its export-subsidy provisions? We may think of typical market-access negotiations within the GATT/WTO as corresponding to the situation in which both the buyers and the sellers are themselves each small players in a competitive market, but are represented at the international bargaining table by their respective governments, who in turn have the ability to affect (world) market-clearing prices with their trade policy choices.[13]

In a typical situation, sellers of good 1 in country 1 seek access to buyers of good 1 in country 2, while sellers of good 2 in country 2 seek access to buyers of good 2 in country 1, and the governments of countries 1 and 2 then come together to negotiate an exchange of market access commitments. Importantly, in these negotiations the interests of both the sellers of goods 1 and 2 (represented by the governments of countries 1 and 2, respectively) and the buyers of goods 1 and 2 (represented by the governments of countries 2 and 1, respectively) are represented. As a consequence of this representation, the negotiated market-access agreements are naturally trade-expanding in their effect, taking the form of various commitments to policy changes that increase trade volumes from the levels implied by unilateral policy choices.[14]

In the same way, we may think of negotiations over export subsidies within the GATT/WTO as corresponding to the situation in which only sellers are represented.[15] As a consequence of this representation, the negotiated commitments are naturally trade-restricting in their effect, taking the form of various commitments to policy changes that reduce trade (export) volumes. From this vantage point, agreements by exporting

[13] In fact, while we develop this argument in the context of trading economies with perfectly competitive export sectors, an identical logic applies if instead the export industry is characterized as an oligopoly (see Bagwell and Staiger, 2002, chapter 10).

[14] Here the GATT/WTO negotiating norm of "reciprocity" can serve the role of fixing (world) market-clearing prices in the presence of negotiated increases in trade volumes (see Bagwell and Staiger, 2002, chapter 4), completing the analogy with the oligopoly/oligopsony negotiations discussed above.

[15] More accurately, those represented at the negotiating table are net sellers (i.e. exporters), and what is important is that the interests of the other side of the market, namely the net buyers (i.e. importers) are not being served by such negotiations.

governments to limit export subsidies can be interpreted as a "sellers' combination in restraint of trade," with the consequent implications for overall efficiency (i.e. good for the sellers, but not for the buyers, and not for the sellers and buyers on the whole).[16]

The simple point is that the standard economic rationale for the purpose of negotiations over trade policy is that trade volumes are inefficiently low when governments set their trade policies unilaterally. As a consequence, from this perspective, the central task of trade negotiations is to expand trade volumes beyond their unilateral levels to more efficient levels. Since agreements to restrict export subsidies are agreements to restrict trade volumes below unilateral levels, such agreements appear to run counter to efficiency. Any economic argument in support of international agreements to restrict export subsidies must overcome this basic dilemma.

3 Factual and legal claims

3.1 Introduction and overview

In this dispute the United States and New Zealand challenged certain Canadian government domestic milk-production and export supports that were provided through Canada's Special Milk Classes Scheme as well as the Canadian government's application of its tariff rate quota for imports of fluid milk. The Canadian government has a comprehensive system of supply management for industrial milk that includes production quotas, administered price supports and border measures.

This dispute centered on allegations of excessive use of export subsidies and the Canadian government's misuse of its tariff rate quota. However, more broadly this case arises out of the tensions between the instruments of supply management. Indeed, it may not be possible to understand the

---

[16] We observe that the same logic is at work on the import-policy side. If, for example, importers of a product come together to negotiate a customs union, then as they harmonize their external tariffs on the products they jointly import from outside the customs union, they will have an incentive to agree to external tariffs that more effectively exert their combined oligopsony power, which is to say they will have incentive to negotiate higher external tariffs that restrict external trade volume. This incentive is inefficient from the point of view of world (buyer and seller) welfare, and if the exporters of these products from outside the customs union were also represented in these negotiations, trade volumes would presumably not be restricted in this way. In some ways, the provisions of Article XXIV GATT that specifically prohibit raising external tariffs in this circumstance may serve to give exporters outside of the customs union some representation in these negotiations, and thereby contribute toward ensuring that inefficiencies do not arise from this incentive.

nature of this dispute – export subsidies – without examining the governmental interventions that have affected the relationship between export and domestic prices. Substantively, the case is important in part because of the balance that was struck when evaluating the relationship between domestic and export subsidies. In terms of the WTO-covered agreements, the dispute is important in its interpretation of the Agricultural Agreement.

From a legal point of view, the most significant interpretative judgments are contained in the rulings of the AB in its evaluation of the 21.5 panel findings on implementation of a revised Milk Classes Scheme. However, the discussion that follows takes us through all of the phases of this dispute.

The regulatory features and entities responsible for implementation and management of the Canadian dairy regime are complex, and will not be fully recounted here.[17] Suffice it to say that regulatory control over trade in dairy products is divided between federal and provincial governments, and there are three main entities that have decision-making roles with respect to the production and sale of milk in Canada:

- the Canadian Dairy Commission (CDC), which can establish national target prices and sell and buy dairy products and pool products;
- the provincial milk marketing boards, which regulate production and marketing in intraprovincial trade of dairy products, comprised "mostly or exclusively" of dairy producers; and
- the Canadian Milk Supply Management Committee (CMSMC), which is a federal–provincial agreement that regulates the marketing of milk and cream products in Canada.

The CMSMC, which is composed of representatives from the provincial market boards and provincial governments, oversees implementation of a comprehensive pooling scheme, which is the basis for the Special Milk Classes Scheme. The Boards develop an annual plan through the National Milk Marketing Plan, which develops an annual production target for industrial milk, which is called the Market Sharing Quota, allocated among the provinces, which in turn allocate targets to individual farmers.

The Special Milk Classes Scheme established five different classes, four of which are designed for the domestic market and the fifth which is comprised of a cluster of five sub-classes for "Special Milk." A purpose of the Scheme was to fund the CDC's losses in exporting surplus milk.

---

[17] See the Panel Report para. 2.1 to 2.66 for full details.

Class 5(d) is for milk used in products exported, notably for the US and UK markets under a negotiated quota system, and 5(e) is for removal of surplus milk from the domestic market, which can be in- or over-quota. Prices in the first four classes are developed by provincial marketing boards. Special Class 5, which is the class at issue in this dispute, requires processors and exporters to apply for a permit from the CDC. The permit is then used as the basis for gaining provincial access to the milk. Classes 5(a) through (c) provide permits on an annual basis while classes (d) and (e) require exporters/processors to negotiate prices with the CDC on a transaction-by-transaction basis.

Pricing differs by class.[18] Returns to producers are calculated on the basis of a system of pooling, separated between those that are in-quota and over-quota. In-quota sales are pooled regionally, while over-quota sales are more limited.

The complainants, the United States and New Zealand, challenged Special Classes 5(d) and 5(e) of the Special Milk Classes Scheme under Articles 9.1(a), 9.1(c) and 3.3 of the Agricultural Agreement, and in the alternative under Article 10.1 of this same agreement. They argued that Canada's scheme provided export subsidies within the meaning of Article 9 of the Agricultural Agreement which exceeded Canada's reduction commitments and therefore constituted a violation of Article 3 of the Agriculture Agreement. The US also challenged the Scheme under Article 3 of the SCM Agreement. And both the United States and New Zealand challenged Canada's application of its tariff rate quota for fluid milk.

To summarize the overall conclusion of the case: the Panel found that the Canadian Scheme represented a violation of Articles 9.1(a), 9.1(c), 3.3 and 10.1 of the Agriculture Agreement. Further, it held that some of the restrictions imposed by Canada under its tariff rate quota violated GATT Article II.1(b). These findings were appealed by Canada. The AB reversed on a number of elements. A "reasonable period of time" after the DSB ruling when implementation was expected to be complete, the complainants again challenged Canada for failure to bring its system into conformity with the DSB ruling. A reviewing panel on implementation was formed, hereinafter called the first 21.5 panel, which held that the revised scheme continued to provide export subsidies to the Canadian

---

[18] For example, (a) and (b) are by formula; (c) reflects a negotiation between the CMSMC and manufacturers; (d) and (e) are case-by-case negotiations between the CDC and exporters/processors.

industry. Canada appealed and the AB reversed in part. A second 21.5
Panel completed its evaluation pursuant to the AB ruling on the first 21.5
Panel report in July 2002. Again Canada appealed certain issues in the
second 21.5 Panel report and the AB issued its report in December 2002.

The discussion that follows breaks this history into two parts: the first
phase, including the Panel and AB ruling, and the second phase, which
includes the rulings of the 21.5 Panels and the AB.

3.2   Phase I: the Panel and the AB report

Article 9.1(a) of the Agreement on Agriculture: The complainants argued
that Classes 5(d) and (e) under the Scheme amount to export subsidies
under Articles 9.1(a) of the Agricultural Agreement, which obliges governments to reduce their direct export subsidies. This provision requires
reductions of

> [t]he provision by governments or their agencies of direct subsidies, in-
> cluding payments in kind, to a firm, to an industry, to producers of an
> agricultural product, to a cooperative or other association of such produc-
> ers, or to a marketing board, contingent on export performance.

The Panel noted that under 9.1(a) an export subsidy comprised four
different elements: (1) direct subsidies, including payments in kind (2)
provided by governments or their agencies (3) to a firm, an industry,
to producers of an agricultural cooperation or other association of producers, or to a marketing board and (4) which are contingent on export
performance.[19]

The Panel examined the applicability of each of these elements in turn
and concluded that the milk made available under Special Classes 5(d)
and (e) constituted export subsidy subject to reduction commitments.
Summarizing this discussion in brief, the Panel noted that since processors
and exporters obtain the milk and the milk is made available for exports,
the facts support elements three and four above.[20]

The question of whether these facts support a finding of direct subsidies,
including payments in kind, stand at the heart of the legal controversy. The
Panel noted that this connotes a "gratuitous act," and that a payment connotes in turn the granting of a benefit. Payments in kind include the provision of a good free of charge or at less than the normal price.[21] Under the
Scheme, the exporters and processors obtain the milk at less than the price

---

[19] See para. 7.38.   [20] See para. 7.39.   [21] See para. 7.43.

for use on the domestic market. Indeed, the milk prices available under Classes 5(d) and (e) were significantly lower than domestic prices or other prices and, given high tariffs on imports, they were also lower than the price of imported milk.[22] Hence, these facts and others led the Panel to conclude that the elements of "payment in kind/direct subsidy" as well as the "benefit" elements were met.

The remaining element was whether the payments were provided "by governments or their agencies."[23] The Panel examined the character and operation of the Scheme and the role of the regulatory bodies. It emphasized the decision-making roles played by the CDC, which is a Crown corporation under the Federal Government of Canada, the role of provincial marketing boards and the CMSMC. Considering the role of government involvement in the Scheme, the Panel identified the CDC as the ultimate decision maker on the question of whether or not domestic requirements were met and whether milk constituted surplus for export, among other variables. Since all elements of 9.1(a) were present, the Panel held that Special Classes 5(d) and (e) milk amounted to an export subsidy that was subject to reduction commitments.

On appeal, the AB reversed on several of these elements. Specifically, it reversed on the availability of "direct subsidies" and "payments in kind" and therefore disagreed with the Panel's conclusion that the measures constitute an inconsistency under the Agricultural Agreement Article 9.1(a).[24]

While arguing that the Panel properly looked to the SCM Agreement for guidance on the general definition of a subsidy contained in its Article 1.1, the AB argued that the Panel applied this definition improperly. The AB did not agree with the concept of "benefit" being equated with the term "payment in kind" given that the latter was simply a form of payment. It was theoretically possible to receive full consideration for a payment in kind thereby failing to meet the requirement of "benefit" or a gratuitous act.[25] Further, the AB argued that the Panel had also "failed entirely to make any mention of the other integral aspect of a subsidy under Article 1.1 of the SCM Agreement, namely the need for a financial contribution." Having reached a different finding on the meaning of the terms "direct subsidies" and "payment in kind," the AB therefore reversed the Panel's conclusion that the Canadian measures involved export subsidies under Article 9.1(a).

---

[22] See para. 7.58.   [23] See para. 7.63.

[24] The AB did, however, concur with the Panel that the provincial milk marketing boards constituted "agencies of Canada's Government" for purposes of Article 9.1(a).

[25] See paras. 87–91.

Article 9.1 (c): The complainants also alleged that certain classes of milk under the Scheme were a violation of Article 9.1(c) of the Agriculture Agreement. This provision covers "payments on the export of an agricultural product that are financed by virtue of governmental action."[26] The Panel interpreted the first part of this provision that requires that the payment is "conditional or contingent on exports" to be analogous to the finding of export conditionality under Article 9.1(a). The Panel also considered and answered in the affirmative that the term "payments in kind" is covered by the terminology of "payment" in 9.1(c).[27] Given the role of the provincial boards in paying milk producers a monthly income and the intermediary role of the boards, the financial function of governmental action was also deemed present. The Panel found that lower-priced milk provided to processors for export under the Scheme constituted a subsidy under Article 9.1(c) of the Agricultural Agreement. This issue was also appealed and the AB upheld the Panel findings.

Article 3.3 of the Agricultural Agreement: Article 3.3 is designed to prohibit export subsidies, as defined in Article 9.1, that exceed a Member's commitment levels.[28] The Panel held that the actions were inconsistent with Article 3.3 given that the total quantity of exports generated through subsidies provided to classes 5(d) and (e) under the Scheme were clearly in excess of Canada's quantity-reduction commitment levels identified in its Schedule.[29]

Articles 10.1 and 8 of the Agriculture Agreement: The Panel also concluded that the treatment of Classes 5(d) and (e) under the Scheme constituted a violation of Articles 10.1 and 8 of the Agriculture Agreement. Article 10.1 is an alternative basis for determining whether an export subsidy exists. It provides that "export subsidies not listed in paragraph 1 of Article 9 shall not be applied in a manner which results in, or which threatens or leads to, circumvention of export subsidy commitments; nor shall non-commercial transactions be used to circumvent such commitments."[30] Focusing on the question of whether "other" export subsidies exist that are not listed in Article 9.1, the Panel looked particularly to 10.1(e) which "covers a wider range of export subsidies than the

---

[26] See para. 7.88.   [27] See para. 7.92.

[28] Specifically it states: "Subject to the provisions of paragraphs 2(b) and 4 of Article 9, a Member shall not provide export subsidies listed in paragraph 1 of Article 9 in respect of the agricultural products or groups of products specified in Section II of Part IV of its Schedule in excess of the budgetary outlay and quantity commitment levels specified therein and shall not provide such subsidies in respect of any agricultural product not specified in that Section of its Schedule."

[29] See para. 7.115.   [30] See para. 7.117.

specified practices listed in Article 9.1." The Panel also looked to Article 1 of the SCM Agreement.[31]

Noting the arguments under 9.1(a) and (c), the Panel held that assuming in the alternative that the treatment of Classes 5(d) and (e) did not constitute an export subsidy as listed in 9.1(a) or (c), it would come under the "other" category of export subsidy for purposes of Article 10.1.[32] Since Article 8 requires Members "not to provide export subsidies otherwise in conformity with this Agreement," the Panel held that Canada's measures were inconsistent with Article 8.

The United States also claimed that Article 3 of the SCM Agreement was violated by virtue of the provision of milk in Classes 5(d) and (e), but the Panel decided to apply the principle of judicial economy and did not examine US claims under Article 3.

The AB reversed the Panel's findings that Canada acted inconsistently with its obligations under Articles 3.3 and 8 of the Agriculture Agreement by providing export subsidies within the meaning of Article 9.1(a). However, it concurred that its scheme of Special Milk Classes 5(d) and 5(e) was inconsistent with 3.3 and 8 by providing export subsidies within the meaning of 9.1(c). It elected not to speak to coverage under Article 10.1.

Tariff Rate Quota: The final aspect of this case at the Panel level related to Canada's tariff rate quota for imports of fluid milk, which provided for a quota of 64,500 tons, with differential duties for in-quota imports of 17.5% and over-quota imports of 283.8%. Access to the lower in-quota rate was restricted to "cross-border imports by Canadians of consumer packaged milk for personal use, valued at less than C\$20 per entry." The United States argued that Canada's restrictions on access to its tariff rate quota for fluid milk amounted to treatment less favorable to imports of fluid milk than it had provided in its WTO schedule, which thereby constituted a violation of GATT Article II.1(b).[33]

---

[31] With respect to the SCM Agreement, the Panel argued that item (d) of the Illustrative List (Annex 1) requires the presence of three elements: the provision of "imported or domestic products . . . for use in the production of exported goods, on terms or conditions more favourable than for provision of like or directly competitive products . . . for use in the production of goods for domestic consumption"; the provision of products by "governments or their agencies either directly or indirectly through government-mandated schemes"; and the "more favorable terms or conditions for such products for use in the production of exported goods . . ." (para 7.128).

[32] See para. 7.129.

[33] Article 11.1(b) provides that "the Products described in Part I of the Schedule relating to any contracting party, which are the products of territories of other contracting parties, shall, on their importation into the territory to which the Schedule relates, and subject to the terms, conditions or qualifications set forth in that Schedule, be exempt from ordinary customs duties in excess of those set forth and provided herein."

By comparing the conditions applied by Canada on access to the tariff rate quota and the conditions set forth in its Schedule, the Panel found various differences in treatment and concluded that "by restricting the access to the tariff rate quota for fluid milk to (i) consumer packaged milk for personal use and (ii) entries valued at less than C$20, [Canada] acts inconsistently with its obligations under Article II:1(b) of GATT 1994."[34]

On appeal, the AB reversed certain features of the Panel's determination on the question of the legal effect of the "conditions" as stated in Canada's Schedule and it also reversed the Panel's findings that restrictions of tariff rate quota to consumer packaged milk for personal use was a violation of GATT Article II.1(b).

The AB argued that the Panel failed to give appropriate legal effect to the "terms and conditions" of Canada's schedule.[35] Finding the terms ambiguous, the AB turned to negotiating history and found that Canada's commitment was understood to be a commitment to continue current access. However, given that there was a value limitation imposed by Canada, this feature of the tariff rate quota was inconsistent with GATT Article II:1(b).

3.3   Phase two: the 21.5 Panel determinations and AB reviews thereof

Resolution of this dispute has proven elusive. On October 27, 1999, the DSB adopted the Panel and AB reports. It was agreed that the reasonable period of time for implementation would expire on January 31, 2001. After that date, the United States and New Zealand again challenged Canada for failing to comply with the recommendations of the DSB. The matter was referred to a Panel under Article 21.5, which found that the new measures were inconsistent with the WTO rules. This ruling was in turn appealed and the AB reversed on several important points of law. As discussed in greater detail below, it is this second AB ruling that has advanced the most significant interpretations of the Agriculture Agreement and its relationship to the SCM Agreement. This 21.5 proceeding also raised a number of procedural issues but the factual record is not discussed in any detail herein.[36]

---

[34] See para. 7.156.   [35] See para. 134.

[36] For example, the Panel denied Canada's request to adopt procedures governing business confidential information; third parties were granted access to rebuttal submissions; the burden of proof requirements under the Agriculture Agreement 10.3 and 21.5 where the Panel held that Canada has the burden of proof with respect to 3.3, 9 and 10.

Subsequently, the United States and New Zealand requested a second Article 21.5 Panel to examine the revised Canadian measures and the second 21.5 Panel Report was released in July, 2002. As noted, Canada contested certain features of that second 21.5 Panel Report and the AB has issued a report on that second report.

First 21.5 Panel Ruling: As a result of the adverse ruling by the WTO DSB, Canada eliminated the Special Milk Class 5(e) and restricted Class 5(d) exports to Canada's export-subsidy-commitment levels. Canada did maintain its basic milk-supply management scheme, including an annual quota for industrial milk and allocation to producers and regulation of supplies and prices of different classes of milk through Classes 1 to 4. It also created a new class of domestic milk, Class 4(m), under which any over-quota milk could be sold only as animal feed. And the regime also included a new class of export-oriented milk labelled as "commercial export milk."

Under this commercial export milk (CEM), domestic producers can sell any quantity of commercial export milk to processors for export on terms that are freely negotiated between them. Such CEM sales do not require a quota or permission from the government and the revenues are collected without government involvement. If, however, a processed dairy product using CEM is sold on the domestic market, there are penalties applied to the processor for diverting such product to the domestic market.[37] The United States and New Zealand challenged that the CEM market system and the continued operation of Special Milk Class 5(d) was inconsistent with Articles 3.3, 8, 9.1c, and 10.1 of the Agriculture Agreement. The US argued that this revised scheme was inconsistent with Articles 1.1 and 3.3 of the SCM Agreement.

As discussed below, the 21.5 Panel held that the supply of CEM by domestic milk producers involves payments that are financed by virtue of government action, thereby making such payments inconsistent with Article 9.1(c) of the Agriculture Agreement.[38] This was also the main issue on appeal.

9.1(c) The Question of Payments: The first substantive issue that was addressed by the Panel was whether the measures amount to export subsidy "payments" under Article 9.1(c). The Panel argued that a determination that CEM is sold at discounted or reduced prices meets the standard

---

[37] See para. 4 of the AB Report.   [38] See para. 62–63.

of a transfer of economic resources as suggested by the AB in its statement outlining the meaning of 9.1(c). A judgment on what constitutes "below market rates," as expressed by the AB in its review of the first Panel findings, requires in turn a judgment on the appropriate benchmark for prices. To the 21.5 Panel, the appropriate benchmark was the price of milk sold by producers domestically. The Panel also noted that an alternative benchmark was world market prices.

Canada argued on appeal that this determination by the Panel failed to fully appreciate that CEM is "no longer subject to government regulation."[39] Further, it argued that CEM prices are freely negotiated in the market place and hence there is no "payment" when the producer sells CEM to a processor.

In the original proceedings, in order to determine whether there were payments under Special Milk Classes 5(d) and (e), the Panel had identified two benchmarks for comparing prices: domestic prices and the price of milk available to processors through imports under the Imports for Re-export Program. The Panel had found that the export prices were less than the prices under these two benchmarks. In its 21.5 appeal, Canada challenged the Panel's pricing benchmarks that were used as a basis for determining whether or not there were "payments" within the meaning of the Agriculture Agreement.

The AB reviewed the history and concluded that when determining whether there are "payments" under article 9.1(c), the question turns to whether the price charged by the producer is less than the milk's "proper value."[40] This requires a comparison of prices actually charged for CEM and some objective standard or benchmark which reflects the proper value of the goods or services.

Before turning to the question of how to determine "proper value," the AB examined the adjustments that Canada had made in its regulatory setting. It noted that CEM is now substantially deregulated and does not require governmental permits. However, it also took note of the fact that CEM cannot be directed to the domestic market and that the domestic price is an administered price that is favorable to the domestic producers. The AB argued that given this character of the overall environment, it was inappropriate to use as a benchmark and compare domestic prices (which are set by the government) with the CEM price that is freely negotiated. Hence, the AB reversed the Panel's finding that the right benchmark is the domestic market prices.[41]

---

[39] See AB Report para. 69.   [40] See AB Report para. 73.   [41] See AB Report para. 81.

World market prices, another comparator identified by the 21.5 Panel, may provide one possible measure of the value of the milk to the producer. Looking at that price, however, still does not answer the fundamental question as to whether CEM can be sold competitively on world markets because it involves subsidies that make it competitive.[42] If the basis were world prices, the AB noted that "it would be possible for WTO members to subsidize domestic inputs for export processing while taking care to maintain the price of these inputs to the processors at a level which equaled or marginally exceeded world market prices. There would then be no 'payments' under Article 9.1(c) of the Agreement on Agriculture and WTO members could easily defeat the export subsidy commitments that they have undertaken in Article 3 on the Agreement on Agriculture."[43]

Instead of looking to world market prices, the AB argued that the total cost of production, which reflected the fixed and variable costs which the producer must spend in order to produce the milk and the total amount that it must recoup, in the long term, to avoid losses, were the important variables for determining whether payments were made within the meaning of Article 9.1(c).[44] This formulation, in the view of the AB, struck the proper "harmony" with the disciplines under the Agriculture Agreement.

The AB noted that there could be some "spillover" effects between WTO-consistent domestic supports to exports. The distinction between domestic support and export-subsidy disciplines would be ended, however, if two consistent supports were automatically characterized as export subsidies because they produced spillover economic benefits for export production. At the same time, the AB noted that this notion could also not operate in an unbounded fashion. The best way to strike a balance between domestic and export supports, in the view of the AB, is to rely on the "total cost of production" to determine whether there are payments.

The "total cost of production" involves all fixed and variable costs. In circumstances such as this, where independent operators are making payments and where domestic prices are administered, the AB held that the average total cost of production is the appropriate standard for determining whether sales of CEM involve payments under 9.1(c). The AB then considered the factual findings made by the 21.5 Panel to see if it was possible to complete the analysis under what it had identified as the proper legal standard. It concluded that the record was not clear and the data was not sufficient.

---

[42] See AB Report, para. 84.   [43] Ibid.   [44] See ibid., para. 88.

The Question of Financing by Government Action: As to the question of whether the payments are being "financed by virtue of government action," the Panel formulated the issue as whether "milk processors for export have access to lower priced commercial export milk *but for* governmental action".[45] The Panel considered that this standard would be met if it could demonstrate that de jure or de facto governmental action (i) prevents the Canadian milk producers from selling more milk on the regulated domestic market at a higher price than to the extent of the quota allocation to them; and (ii) obliges Canadian milk processors to export all milk contracted as lower-priced CEM and therefore penalizes the diversion of milk from the export market to the domestic market.[46]

The Panel argued that "the choice left to the Canadian producer is not a real choice."[47] Since the government had taken away the first-best option, which was domestic sales, producers would rationally opt for the second-best possibility, export sales. The Panel found that CEM "would not be available to Canadian producers but for . . . the federal and provincial actions . . . obliging producers, at least de facto, to sell outside quota milk for export."[48]

The AB disagreed that producers are obliged or driven to produce additional milk for export sale. However, the AB acknowledged the logic of the Panel's reasoning as a means of establishing a *demonstrable* link between governmental action and the financing of payments. Given its judgment to reverse on the issue of payments, the AB did not feel it necessary to consider the Panel's findings on the phrase "financed by virtue of governmental action" with any further detail.

On the issue of Article 10.1 of the Agriculture Agreement, given that the AB was unable to speak of the legal character of the measure under Article 9.1, it was unwilling or unable to discuss the legal character of the measure under Article 10.[49]

4 The second 21.5 Panel and AB rulings

New Zealand and the United States requested the establishment of a second 21.5 panel to evaluate the consistency of the Canadian measures with

---

[45] See ibid., para. 107.   [46] See Panel Report, paras. 6.41–6.42

[47] See ibid., para. 6.45.   [48] Ibid., para. 6.42.

[49] With respect to the claim under Article 3.1 of the SCM Agreement, the AB held that a WTO-consistent subsidy for exports must be reviewed under the Agriculture Agreement and since there is not final determination under Article 9 thereof, it cannot opine on Article 3 of the SCM Agreement.

the DSB rulings and Canada appealed. Given the rulings of the AB in response to the first 21.5 panel report, it is hardly surprising to see the complainants seeking additional consideration of the meaning of what the AB had stated to be the proper methodology for evaluating the existence of a subsidy – namely, the average total cost of production. The brief summary that follows focuses primarily on the evolving clarification of this concept.

4.1   The question of payments redux

The second 21.5 panel proceedings brought to the surface two alternative formulations of what constituted "average total cost of production." The complainants argued that the cost of production should be interpreted to mean industry-wide average costs with industry-wide average CEM prices along with imputed costs. The objective would be to determine whether prices are below the average total cost of production. Canada, in contrast, argued that individual producer costs were the appropriate comparison, excluding imputed and certain other costs. The Panel appeared not to have confidence in the data presented by Canada as being complete and instead represented an "extrapolation" regarding individual producer prices.[50] It expressed doubts that the individual producer's costs should be the basis for the determination. The Panel also argued that the evidence did not support Canada's position that payments were not made and it ultimately elected not to opine on which methodology was definitive.[51] It also disagreed with Canada on the exclusion of other costs.

The AB ruling on this second 21.5 panel upheld the basic finding.[52] On the methodology, however, the AB went further and suggested that the nature of the obligations imposed under the Agriculture Agreement speak to export subsidies provided through private party action. And the AB suggested that the question "is not whether one or more individual milk producers, efficient or not, are selling CEM at a price above or below their individual costs of production. The issue is whether Canada, on a national basis, has respected its WTO obligations."[53] As a result of this perception of the Agreement implicating a national obligation, the AB suggests that the benchmark should be a "single, industry wide cost of production figure rather than an indefinite number of cost of production

---

[50] See Panel Report, para. 5.63.   [51] See, ibid., paras. 5.65, 5.87.
[52] The AB disagreed with the Panel's treatment of burden of proof, but nevertheless did not disagree with the overall conclusion.
[53] See, AB Report *Canada – Dairy*, para. 96.

figures for each individual producer."[54] The AB further held that all costs should be included.

On the question of whether these payments were "financed by virtue of governmental action," the Panel focused on a number of attributes of the scheme and its incentives, and concluded that Canada had failed to establish that governmental action is not demonstrably linked to these payments.[55] The AB upheld this finding and articulated for the first time a detailed interpretation of this provision. It reiterated the view that "payments" can be made by private parties and need not be made by the government, and the standard requires careful scrutiny of the factual and regulatory setting.[56] Indeed, the AB argued that governmental action can be an act or an omission, and the scope of government action includes circumstances where no compulsion is involved in the making of payments.[57]

With respect to the terminology "by virtue of," the AB argued that simply enabling payments was insufficient, a "tighter nexus" between the mechanism or process by which the payments are financed being necessary.[58] With respect to the question of financing, the AB accepted that it could encompass situations where significant aspects of financing might not involve the government, but the government "must play a sufficiently important part in the process by which a private party funds payments, such that the requisite nexus exists between 'governmental action' and 'financing.'"

On the facts of this case, the AB focused on the issue that milk was produced "using a single line of production, but sold in two different markets," and the fixed costs of production are shared. Moreover, the AB stressed that the price of milk is fixed by a governmental agency that has a statutory mandate to ensure a "fair return" for "efficient producers."[59] It also emphasized that "governmental action" controls virtually every aspect of domestic milk supply management, a fact which ensures a highly remunerative system for domestic milk producers which covers their fixed costs and permits them "to sell export milk at prices that are below the costs of production."[60]

4.1.1   Comments and questions on legal and policy matters

As noted at the beginning of this study, the Agricultural Agreement has been seen as an accomplishment in no small measure because it set up a

---

[54] Ibid.   [55] See, Panel Report, paras. 5.133–5.135.
[56] See AB Report, para. 87.   [57] Ibid., paras. 127–28.
[58] Ibid., paras. 129–31.   [59] Ibid., paras. 132–41.   [60] Ibid., para. 145.

framework of rules for evaluating agricultural supports and because countries committed to phased reductions or improvements in the three core areas of domestic supports, export subsidies, and market access commitments. Of these, legal experts are often inclined to see the rules on export subsidies as representing the clearest improvement made by the Agricultural Agreement as compared with the GATT rules, particularly when reflected in numerical commitments in country schedules.[61]

Yet neither the Agriculture Agreement nor the SCM Agreement provides a complete methodology for interpreting core concepts – e.g. what constitutes a "subsidy," whether there is a "payment," and what is deemed an empirically sound and consistent basis for a judgment on that point. And it remains to be seen whether the definitions will prove workable. With respect to the second example, on payments, the 21.5 panel elected to focus on domestic and world market prices as a means of arriving at a judgment on this question, in an environment of a price floor and production ceilings. That Panel's approach seems to be founded, in part, on the AB's response to the first Panel methodology, and in the first review by the AB it stressed that "below market rates" was decisive. Given that guidance by the AB, the 21.5 Panel's decision to focus on internal (domestic) and external (world) prices is understandable. But then the AB went a step further and identified another standard, "total cost of production," because it argued that an "objective benchmark" was necessary, which implied the price methodology was not.

The AB's formulation in response to the 21.5 Panel Report appears to be an altogether new methodology for determining the existence of a "payment." Putting aside for the moment whether it represents an improved economic rationale, as a matter of legal methodology this approach does not seem grounded in a strict legal interpretation of the applicable agreements. In other words, neither the Agricultural Agreement nor the SCM Agreement explicated the use of this methodology. Moreover, since this methodology was not delineated in the covered agreements, not surprisingly the parties had generated a factual report that permitted neither the Panel nor the Appellate Body to complete the analysis. Having called certain pertinent facts and the applicable methodology into question, the AB was unable to reach a judgment on the law, and the case was sent back to be re-reviewed by a second 21.5 Panel. In a word, it appears that the

---

[61] See, Hudec, (1998 draft), "Does the Agricultural Agreement Work?" available at http://www.harvard.cid.edu. GATT/WTO Constraints on National Regulation: Requiem for an Aims and Effect Test, 32 *International Lawyer*, 619–649.

AB developed its own methodology because it was dissatisfied with that employed by the Panel.

The second Panel was in turn understandably hesitant to be conclusory with respect to the methodology that might be used as a reliable basis for determining total average production cost. At a minimum, the AB had not spoken on this point in sufficient detail to guide the Panel. As between industry averages and firm specific information, the Panel leaned in the direction of industry averages, partly owing to the nature of the data that was presented to it in this instance. The AB took this a step further and affirmatively supported the notion of industry averages under the stated logic that WTO obligations flowed to the nation as a whole and hence this aggregate data was more appropriate.

We shall turn presently to an overall economic assessment of this case. The legal reasoning and stated logic on this single methodological point, however, also warrants further consideration. The AB introduced whole cloth the concept of "average total cost of production" because it was thought to offer a more precise basis for determining whether a payment is present. In the following section, we question the reliability of that measurement. Nevertheless, using the logic articulated, would it not make more sense to lean toward the methodology that delivers the most rigorous and precise assessment possible of actual costs? If so, that would lead one toward developing detailed firm-specific data and then aggregating and averaging that data. If such detailed micro-economic data is not available then other methodologies might need to be utilized so it may not be the only choice available.

Hence, the AB could have attempted to delineate or articulate some hierarchy of possible approaches, leaning to the most rigorous method available in the first place. Instead, it chose to reject the microeconomic methodology because it considered this analysis as firm-oriented while WTO obligations occur at the level of the nation-state. Given that this provision is attempting to assess the impact of government action on private costs, it is curious not to see the aggregation of such firm-level data as a more precise starting point than some general averages.

From a legal and policy perspective, this case is also noteworthy for its treatment of State responsibility and attribution. The issue of public versus private conduct and the scope of government measures that can come under the GATT/WTO system has surfaced periodically for many years.[62] There have been several GATT/WTO cases that considered the

---

[62] See, for example, a 1960 GATT study that looked at the question of whether subsidies financed by a governmental levy were notifiable under Article XVI. That study stated that

extent of government responsibility over the actions of private parties and the outer limits of what constitutes a government measure. *Canada – Dairy* reviewed that issue in the context of a particular covered agreement. In *Japan – Semiconductor*, the GATT panel held that even non-binding administrative guidance by the Government of Japan could constitute a "government measure" if certain criteria were met.[63]

Later, in *Japan – Film*, the WTO held against the US complainant on the facts of the case but on the general question of actionable government measures, the panel built upon the semiconductor case to support an expansive view of government-covered measures.[64] That Panel noted that "past GATT cases demonstrate that the fact that action is taken by private parties does not rule out the possibility that it may be deemed to be governmental if there is sufficient government involvement with it . . ."[65]

Within the context of Article 9.1(c) of the Agricultural Agreement, we see in *Canada – Dairy* even more detailed consideration of the extent of government responsibility over private practices, which the respondent had asserted were fully deregulated private sector decisions. As discussed above, the 21.5 Panel's interpretation of the extent of government

the "question depends on the source of funds and the extent of government action, if any, in their collection" (Report on Review Pursuant to Article XVI:5, adopted on May 24, 1960 BISD 9S/188 192).

[63] *See* Report of the GATT Panel (adopted), *Japan – Trade in Semiconductors*, BISD 35th Supp. 116, at 155 (1988). In that case, which involved restraints on exports of semiconductors by the Government of Japan, the specific criteria identified by the panel included (1) that reasonable grounds exist for believing that the government measures created sufficient incentives to persuade private parties to conform their conduct to the non-mandatory measures, and (2) that the effectiveness of the private conduct was "essentially dependent" on the non-mandatory actions taken by the government.

[64] See WTO/DS44/R (*Japan – films*). The Panel found that "government policy or action need not necessarily have a substantially binding or compulsory nature for it to entail a likelihood of compliance by private actors in a way so as to nullify or impair legitimately expected benefits within the purview of Article XXIII.1(b). Indeed, it is clear that non-binding actions, which include sufficient incentives or disincentives for private parties to act in a particular manner can potentially have adverse effects on competitive conditions of market access." Another case that involved private activities was *Restrictions on Imports of Dessert Apples*, which involved market withdrawal of fruits by consumer organizations. That Panel found that the formal system for apples was a hybrid one, and the buy in and withdrawal systems could be considered a government measure. See, *Restrictions on Imports of Dessert Apples* adopted on June 22, 1989, 36th Supp BISD 93, 1990 BISD 93, 1990.

[65] See *Japan – films* (WT/DS44/R), para. 10.56. That panel also looked to the semiconductor panel report for the proposition that "where administrative guidance creates incentives or disincentives largely dependent upon government action for private parties to act in a particular manner, it may be considered a government measure." See paras. 10.43–10.46.

responsibility hinged on a "but for" standard. The AB held that there had to be a "demonstrable link" between the government action and the financing of payments. The final articulation of that link by the AB goes quite some distance into the deconstruction of what constitutes "payments financed by virtue of governmental action." In making its evaluation, the AB has indicated a willingness to consider the entire regulatory scheme and its consequences for private entities. In this case, private activities were seen as having lost (or never having had) their private character, operating as they were under the comprehensive supply management scheme.

5   Specific economic analysis

We now consider and evaluate the particular legal and economic issues and methodologies raised by the dispute. More specifically we ask: in light of the underlying goals of the relevant WTO provisions, and taking them as given, was the resolution of the substantive economic issues around which the case revolved based on sound economic principles? The central substantive economic issue of this case concerns the identification of export subsidies, and more specifically the methodology for detecting the presence of "payments" to exporters within the meaning of Article 9.1(c) of the Agriculture Agreement.

The AB report in response to the first 21.5 Panel determination (especially paragraphs 89–92) provides the rationale for the measure of "payments" to exporters of processed dairy products that was proposed by the AB, namely, the difference between the average total cost of domestic milk production and the milk price paid by exporters of processed dairy products. In essence, the AB suggests that the milk's "proper value" is its average total cost of production; and further the AB suggests that, measuring proper value in this way, its methodology for measuring payments strikes a balance between, on the one hand, permitting domestic supports for milk producers even when these supports may have some "spillover" economic benefits for exporters of processed dairy products, and on the other, not going so far as to permit the provision of unlimited support for exporters of processed dairy products so long as this support is generated by the domestic support provisions for milk producers.

This raises a key question: Does the suggested comparison of the average total cost of milk production with the milk price paid by exporters of processed dairy products provide a reliable measure of how much support exporters of processed dairy products are receiving? By way of the following hypothetical scenarios, we suggest that the reliability of the measure suggested by the AB is problematic. We then reconsider an alternative measure of proper value which the AB considered and rejected, namely world market prices.

5.1   What is wrong with average total cost as a measure of proper value?

Consider the following hypothetical scenario. Suppose that a government wishes to redistribute income from its general population toward its dairy farmers, who are currently earning a below-normal economic rate of return on their sunk investments (e.g. dairy cattle, land improvements tailored toward dairy farming, physical and human capital specific to the dairy industry) but, due to the "sunk" nature of these investments, do not find it in their economic interest to exit from dairy farming.[66] Suppose further for the sake of argument that this country is initially a textbook laissez-faire perfectly competitive market economy, and that it is an exporter of processed dairy products ("cheese") on world markets (and for simplicity, let us assume for now that unprocessed milk is not directly tradable internationally, due perhaps to high costs of transport).

To accomplish the desired redistribution, suppose that the government imposes a tax on all milk that is consumed by domestic households – whether consumed directly, or rather indirectly in the form of cheese – and uses the revenue generated by this tax to pay for direct "lump-sum" transfers to its dairy farmers. Should this program be viewed as providing an export subsidy to cheese exporters?

The immediate reaction to this question would probably be a puzzled look and the answer "Of course not." However, a little reflection reveals that the country's exports of cheese on world markets would likely rise as a result of this program, and so the answer may not be quite as obvious as it first appears. Still, upon further reflection, most observers would probably agree that the answer to this question is "No." It is true that, under typical economic conditions, the impact of this program would be to increase the country's cheese exports. But the increased exports would not come about as a result of "payments" made to domestic producers of cheese as a reward for exporting. Instead exports, which we now recall are simply the difference between a country's domestic production and its domestic

---

[66] Introducing other fixed costs of production that are not also sunk would leave unaltered the basic argument.

consumption, would increase with the introduction of this program only because domestic consumption of cheese would be reduced.

In fact, total domestic production of cheese at given world prices would not be altered at all with the introduction of this program: each domestic cheese producer can always export all of its production to world markets and receive the given world price for its foreign sales, and so the domestic production of cheese continues to occur at the point where this (unchanged) world price equals the (unchanged) domestic marginal cost of cheese production. Moreover, these producers would be willing to sell cheese to domestic consumers only if the producers receive this same (i.e. world) price for domestic sales. This means that the full incidence of the milk tax will be passed on to domestic consumers of cheese, who will see the prices they pay for cheese rise by the full cost implications of the milk tax.

As a consequence, the total quantity of cheese produced in the domestic country at a given world price is unchanged with the introduction of this program. And the increased exports at a given world price associated with the introduction of this program would come about as a result of the diminished domestic consumption of cheese, which in turn results from the tax-induced price increase for cheese faced by domestic consumers. For these reasons, any export effects of the program will be dependent upon features of domestic demand for cheese (such as how "price elastic" this demand is).

Figure 10.2 illustrates the main ideas. In the left-hand quadrant of figure 10.2, the price of cheese charged by domestic cheese producers is measured on the vertical axis while the quantity of cheese is measured on the horizontal axis. As there are assumed to be no impediments to the export of cheese, the price of cheese charged by domestic producers for domestic sales, which we denote by p, must be the same as the price these producers could charge for sales on the world market, which we denote by p^* (that is, we must have $p = p^*$). The quantity of cheese supplied by domestic producers (for domestic or foreign sales) at any given producer price p is then depicted as the upward-sloping curve in the left-hand quadrant of figure 10.2, which we label S(p). In the absence of a tax on the domestic consumption of milk and the milk content of cheese, domestic demand for cheese is depicted by the downward-sloping curve in the left-hand quadrant, which we label $D_0(p)$.

At any given world-market price p^*, we may use the fact that $p = p^*$ to determine the export supply of cheese from the domestic country as

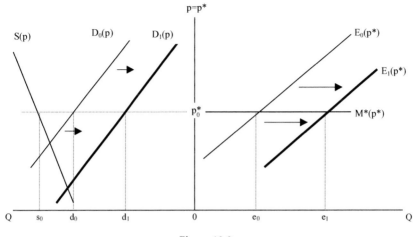

Figure 10.2

the difference between domestic supply and demand in the left-hand quadrant. This difference is plotted in the right-hand quadrant of figure 10.2, which measures p^* on the vertical axis and the quantity of cheese on the horizontal axis, and the associated domestic export supply curve for cheese is labeled $E_0(p^*)$. The foreign import demand for cheese can be plotted in the right-hand quadrant of figure 10.2 as well, and it is depicted as the horizontal line labeled $M^*(p^*)$.[67] As shown in the two quadrants of figure 10.2, in the absence of a tax on the domestic consumption of milk and the milk content of cheese, domestic cheese producers make domestic and foreign sales at a common price level equal to p_0^* and supply a quantity of cheese equal to s_0, while domestic cheese consumers pay the price $p = p_0^*$ and demand a quantity of cheese equal to d_0, with the difference between s_0 and d_0 corresponding to the volume of cheese exported to world markets by the domestic country, e_0.

Now consider the impact in the cheese market of a tax on the domestic consumption of milk and the milk content of cheese. Since domestic cheese producers can continue to sell all the cheese they want on world markets and receive the world price p^* (this is reflected in the horizontal foreign import demand curve M^*, p^*, in the right-hand quadrant of figure 10.2), these domestic cheese producers will only sell cheese to

[67] The horizontal foreign import demand curve reflects the simplifying assumption that the domestic country is "small" on world markets. This assumption simplifies the exposition, but is inessential to the point being made.

domestic consumers if they continue to receive $p = p_0^*$ for each unit of cheese sold on the domestic market. This implies that domestic cheese consumers must bear the entire incidence of the tax, and therefore must pay a higher price for each unit of cheese consumed in order to cover the tax payment collected by the government and still provide domestic cheese producers with a price $p = p_0^*$. In terms of the left-hand quadrant of figure 10.2, this implies that the domestic demand curve shifts back to the bold curve labeled $D_1(p)$.

The right-hand quadrant of figure 10.2 depicts the implication of this shift in domestic cheese demand for the domestic export supply curve, which shifts out correspondingly to the bold curve labeled $E_1(p^*)$. As depicted, the impact of the milk-tax-and-redistribution program described above is then to reduce domestic cheese demand to the quantity d_1 and raise domestic exports of cheese to the quantity e_1, without altering the quantity of cheese produced in the domestic country from its initial level of s_0.

In light of the above discussion, it seems reasonable to conclude that this program offers no support whatsoever to domestic cheese producers, whether this cheese is produced for the domestic market or for export: the domestic production of cheese is simply unaffected by the milk-tax-and-redistribution program. By this logic, the program could not be interpreted as an export subsidy to domestic cheese producers, even though it will typically result in some "spillover" increase in domestic exports of cheese. And indeed, if we apply the methodology suggested by the AB for calculating "payments" to cheese exporters, we would find that the payments are zero, provided that proper account were taken of the below-normal economic profit rate earned by domestic dairy farmers that we assumed at the start.

The simple point is, under this program, domestic milk producers will receive the same price for their milk from every buyer, whether that buyer is a final domestic consumer of milk or an industrial milk processor (i.e. "cheese" producer): there is no "cross-subsidization" implied by the pattern of domestic-milk sale prices. Hence, the milk price received by a domestic milk producer will bear the same relation to its average total cost, regardless of whether this milk is sold for domestic consumption or to be processed for export. And the relation between price and average total cost will be an equivalence relationship, and measured payments will therefore be zero, provided that the costs of the sunk factors are calculated appropriately (i.e. they are imputed as a residual return on each dairy farmer's milk production).

Consider now an alternative redistribution program, in which the government (i) announces a regulated price (above the initial price) at which all domestically produced milk consumed by domestic households – whether consumed directly, or indirectly in the form of cheese – is to be sold; (ii) imposes a prohibitive tariff on cheese imports; (iii) institutes a quota system to allocate domestic milk sales among domestic dairy farmers; and (iv) allows domestic dairy farmers to continue to make unregulated milk sales at unregulated "market" prices for milk that is used in the production of cheese for export. Should this program be viewed as providing an export subsidy to cheese exporters?

On its face, this program looks like a complicated scheme for increasing the incomes of dairy farmers through a system of domestic supports that keep domestic milk prices high while permitting the "excess" milk production to become available at low ("cross-subsidized") prices to the exporters of processed dairy products. And this sounds suspiciously like an export subsidy to exporters of processed dairy products.

However, it can be shown that, for any tax level chosen under the first program described above, there is an associated regulated price level under (i) and system of quotas under (iii) that together with (ii) and (iv) make the second program *identical* to the first program in every relevant economic dimension. Essentially, both programs orchestrate a redistribution from the domestic consumers of milk and cheese to the domestic milk producers, and both programs accomplish this by facing domestic consumers with higher prices for their (direct and indirect) milk consumption. The only difference between the two programs is the method by which domestic dairy farmers receive the "transfer": under the first program, they receive this transfer as a lump sum distribution of tax revenue from the government, while under the second program they receive the transfer "directly" in the form of higher regulated milk prices. This difference, though, is immaterial to each and every production and consumption decision in the domestic economy.

In essence, figure 10.2 applies (with some appropriate programmatic re-labeling) as a description of the impact of the milk program on the cheese market, whether the milk program takes the first (tax-based) form or the second (regulation-based) form. In analogy with the tax-based program, it can be argued using figure 10.2 that with the introduction of the regulation-based program, the higher regulated price of milk paid by domestic households for their direct and indirect milk consumption shifts the domestic demand for cheese back, but leaves the domestic supply curve for cheese unaffected, with the consequent outward shift of the domestic export supply curve for cheese.

Hence, if it is agreed that the first program described above does not qualify as an export-subsidy program, then the second program logically cannot either. And yet, under the methodology suggested by the AB for calculating "payments" to cheese exporters, we would find that the payments are positive, provided that proper account were taken of the impact of the regulatory program on the profit rate for milk producers.[68]

The simple point is, under this second program, domestic milk producers will receive the high domestic regulated price for milk sales that ultimately find their way to domestic consumers, while these producers will receive a lower unregulated price for milk sales that are used to produce exports: there is now a degree of "cross-subsidization" implied by the pattern of domestic-milk sale prices. As a consequence, the milk price received by a domestic milk producer will be higher in relation to its average total cost when this milk is sold for domestic consumption than when it is sold to a processor for eventual export. And since the average price across all milk sales must equal the average total cost (again, provided that the costs of the sunk factors are calculated appropriately, i.e. they are imputed as a residual return on each dairy farmer's milk production), a finding that the average total cost of domestic milk production is above the price of milk paid by export processors – that is, a finding of positive payments to exporters of processed dairy products – is assured.[69]

Hence, the pattern of domestic-milk sale prices under this second program will appear as "cross-subsidization" of cheese exporters, even though the program itself has identical economic implications to the first program described above, and therefore has no impact whatsoever on the domestic production of cheese whether destined for the domestic or export

---

[68] At a more specific level, this discussion also raises a question as to whether the Canadian Dairy Program should in fact be seen as operating as an export subsidy program. If the second program described above captures the essence of the Canadian Dairy Program, then as we have observed above the domestic production of processed dairy products would be unaffected by this program, and it can then be argued that this program should not be seen as an export subsidy program within the meaning of the Agriculture Agreement. As this is not our main point here, we simply raise the possibility and leave a more careful assessment of this possibility for future work.

[69] In effect, we are arguing that in the presence of sunk investments, a comparison of average total cost of milk production to milk price is guaranteed to imply positive "payments" to any processor that pays less than the average milk price. Hence, if exporters do not have to pay the high regulated price of milk that processors for domestic consumption must pay, then the methodology proposed by the AB will indicate that these exporters are receiving payments.

markets. Moreover, in this case the second step of the AB's methodology for determining the presence of export subsidies will be met as well: the payments so defined will be "financed by virtue of government action," since it is true that without the government's regulatory program this "cross subsidization" would not occur.

This suggests a basic and fundamental problem with the methodology for identifying the presence of export subsidies as suggested by the AB. In effect, whenever sunk investments earning a below-market rate of return are present – a condition that is likely to be met in "declining" industries that are also the most likely to be receiving domestic support – the measurement of average total cost for use in the AB's suggested methodology becomes problematic. If the rental costs of the sunk investments are imputed as their residual returns in the industry, then the measured average total cost must equal the industry average price. This "endogeneity" between the prices charged in the industry and the measured average total costs implies in turn that the AB's methodology will find that payments are being received by any purchaser of the products of that industry that pays a price below the industry average price. As the hypothetical scenario considered above illustrates, this does not provide a reliable guide for identifying the presence of export subsidies.

An alternative measurement procedure would be to exclude fixed costs that are also sunk from the calculation of average total cost for the purposes of the AB's methodology. This alternative procedure would solve the "endogeneity" problem described above, but it would lead to other problems. For example, this alternative procedure would overlook a government subsidy program that induced suppliers to offer low prices to some buyers when they would not have done so absent the government program, but where the low prices are not so low as to fall below the measured average total cost. A related, though perhaps less relevant, flaw in the AB methodology is that, by basing its proposed calculation of average total cost on the assumption of an "ordinary" profit rate (paragraph 95), the methodology could overlook subsidy payments in an industry where profits were extraordinarily high.

Finally, it is interesting to observe that in the second 21.5 Panel Report, a central part of the dispute revolved around whether imputed costs should be included in the average total cost calculation or not. The US and New Zealand (complainants) argued for including these imputed costs, much as we have done in our hypothetical scenario above, while Canada argued for excluding them. The Panel chose not to rule on which procedure for measuring the average total cost was correct, stating that ". . . we have made findings of the existence of 'payments' based on both the Complainants' and Canada's interpretation of how to apply the Appellate Body's benchmark, thus making it unnecessary to decide *in this* case which of these two interpretations is the correct one" (paragraph 5.90). In its second report on the 21.5 Panel, the AB offered further guidance on its proposed methodology, stating (paragraph 110) that imputed costs should indeed be included in the calculation of average total cost.

We have illustrated here by way of our hypothetical scenarios a difficulty with including imputed costs in this calculation, but as we have observed above there are also obvious difficulties with excluding such costs from the calculation. As a consequence, we would suggest that neither of these approaches is likely to be entirely satisfactory, and further analysis of this question seems appropriate and important.

5.2   What is wrong with world market prices as a measure of proper value?

In light of the difficulties in the AB's suggested methodology as pointed out in section 5.1 above, we suggest briefly here that the AB might usefully reconsider an approach to the measurement of "proper value" that it had previously considered and rejected, namely, world market prices. In rejecting this measure of proper value, the AB argued in its response to the first 21.5 Panel determination (paragraph 84) that, since it would be possible that CEM could be sold at terms competitive with world market prices precisely because CEM involves subsidies that make it competitive, ". . . a comparison between commercial export milk prices and world market prices gives no indication on the crucial question, namely, whether Canadian export production has been given an advantage." The implication of this statement appears to be that Canadian export production will have been given an advantage if and only if CEM prices do not reflect the milk's "proper value," which is to say that CEM prices do not cover the average total cost of milk production.

Why, though, should it be concluded that Canadian export production has been given an advantage in this circumstance, if the CEM price simply provides cheese exporters with an alternative and *equivalent-cost* source of milk supply to the supply that can be attained from world markets? Put differently, what advantage can cheese exporters be receiving if they are essentially indifferent between buying milk inputs on the world market at world market prices and buying milk inputs instead on the domestic market from (possibly subsidized) domestic milk producers? From this perspective, a comparison between CEM prices and world market prices would seem to provide a reasonable measure of the precise amount of the advantage which could be deemed a "payment" to exporters under Article 9.1(c) of the Agriculture Agreement.

We therefore suggest, to the extent that purchases of milk on world markets is an option that is readily commercially available to processors of milk products, that world market prices of milk are a reasonable comparator to the CEM price, and that under this comparison the existence of "payments" within the meaning of Article 9.1(c) of the Agriculture Agreement could be reasonably determined. In light of the limitations of the AB's suggested methodology in this regard, reconsidering the use of world market prices in this fashion may be appropriate.

6   Concluding observations on the legal tests and economic analysis

This final section summarizes the relationship between the legal rules and economic assessments of the analyzed dispute. In general, we are of the view that the problematical aspects of this case do not stem from problems in legal drafting. Instead, this case points out complexities associated with the underlying conceptual foundations of the Agriculture Agreement. It provides some questions as to whether the treaty rules and the AB-developed methodologies are fully workable. Turning first to the conceptual foundations of the case, we make the following broad economic observations.

First, the overall approach to export subsidies within the GATT/WTO lacks a sound economic underpinning. As the discussion of exporter versus importer interests in section 2.1 above sought to reveal, even in a world of bound tariffs importing nations have some tools under the WTO to respond to the perceived adverse effects of export subsidies – e.g. through the imposition of countervailing duties or renegotiation of tariffs. Thus, additional prohibitions on export subsidies do not factor in the full economic interests of all importing nations. From this perspective, such prohibitions do not serve the interests of importing governments' – or world – welfare. This conclusion runs counter to the long history of efforts in the GATT/WTO to eliminate export subsidies, but it is derived from formal economic thinking under standard arguments.

We have offered two interpretations of this conclusion. A first interpretation emphasizes the limits of existing formal economic reasoning in this instance, and casts doubt on the ability of existing formal economic models to adequately capture the role that international agreements to limit export subsidies can play. According to this interpretation, it is important to seek and develop further alternative modeling approaches that might better reflect some critical feature associated with the issue of export subsidies that the standard models have failed to capture. A second interpretation would place more weight on the presumptions implied by the standard economic arguments reviewed above, and this second interpretation casts doubt on the rationale for international agreements to limit export subsidies.[70]

At the least, the conclusion we report in section 2.1 reflects the need for further articulation of the rationale for the treatment of export subsidies within the GATT/WTO. At most, the GATT/WTO's approach to export subsidies might benefit from a fundamental overhaul.

Second, our analysis points to a basic and fundamental problem with the methodology for identifying the presence of export subsidies as suggested by the AB in the *Canada – Dairy* case. We appreciate the systemic tension faced by the AB and the Panels, in that the Agriculture Agreement permits domestic supports and prohibits export subsidies in excess of reduction commitments, and the adjudicators are then faced with a dilemma as to how to give both effect when the domestic subsidy fosters the export subsidy. However, the particular methodology developed by the AB, as we argued, does not isolate the presence of export subsidies.

In effect, whenever sunk investments earning a below-market rate of return are present – a condition that is likely to be met in industries receiving domestic support – the measurement of average total cost for use in the AB's suggested methodology becomes problematic. If the rental costs of the sunk investments are imputed as their residual returns in the industry, then as an accounting matter the measured average total cost must equal the industry average price. This implies in turn that the AB's methodology will find that payments are being received by any purchaser of the products of that industry that pays a price below the industry average price. As the hypothetical scenario considered in our analysis above illustrates, this does not provide a reliable guide for identifying

---

[70] In this regard, the conclusion we report in section 2.1 may be difficult to accept for those who put emphasis on other, less analyzed or proven factors such as transaction costs, the stage of economic development of the importing country, the perception that export subsidies are particularly aimed at transferring the costs of adjustment abroad, etc. The lawyer co-author here is not fully convinced, although appreciative, of the force of overall economic observation on the effects of export subsidies.

the presence of export subsidies. This suggests the possible advisability of additional legal text within the GATT/WTO Agreements that would offer guidance to member governments in their identification and calculation of export subsidies, along the lines offered in the WTO Agreement on Implementation of Article VI.

In light of the problems with the AB's suggested methodology in this regard, we also suggest an alternative: to the extent that purchases of milk on world markets is an option that is readily commercially available to processors of milk products, world market prices of milk are a reasonable comparator to the CEM price, and under this comparison the existence of "payments" within the meaning of Article 9.1(c) of the Agriculture Agreement could be reasonably determined. While the AB considered and rejected the use of world market prices as a measure of milk's "proper value," we suggest that reconsidering the use of world market prices in this fashion may be appropriate.

Turning now to the legal character of the case, we have considered issues such as the approach to treaty interpretation taken by the reviewing Panel and the AB. How broadly or narrowly did the reviewing body define its mission? Within the body of relevant WTO case law, was the case reviewed in a manner consistent with past WTO practice? How might we evaluate the legal methodology employed?

Canada – Dairy has already produced a long record. Despite the absence of formal remand authority under the rules of the DSU, this case has already produced two 21.5 panels and three AB rulings. It has been a particularly noteworthy case from a legal perspective in that it represented the first interpretation of the Agriculture Agreement. The findings of the AB with respect to the methodology appropriate for evaluating whether an export subsidy was present was particularly novel. As the economic discussion showed, the methodology may not introduce meaningful or reliable economic distinctions.

This case also considered the SCM Agreement to a limited degree. In this regard, it is interesting to compare *Canada – Dairy* to the *US – Export Restraints* case (see our companion review of that case). The *US – Export Restraints* case was centrally focused on the SCM Agreement. These two cases viewed together do not present a coherent or comprehensive set of interpretations on the relationship between the SCM Agreement and the Agriculture Agreement. More specifically, how the definition of export subsidies in the SCM Agreement should inform interpretations of the Agriculture Agreement has not been well clarified by these two cases. The Canadian government invoked the SCM Agreement (notably

Article 1.1(a)(iv) and *US – Export Restraints*) as important contextual guidance for interpreting Article 9.1 (c) of the Agreement on Agriculture. If that case and its ruling regarding Article 1 of the SCM Agreement were applied in the context of *Canada – Dairy*, it would suggest a somewhat narrow range of governmental action that would be sufficiently targeted and purposeful to meet the terms of the Agriculture Agreement.[71] As of this time, the exact relationship between the SCM Agreement and the Agriculture Agreement remains to be clarified and will doubtless take place over a period of some years.

References

Bagwell, Kyle and Robert W. Staiger. 1990. A theory of managed trade. *American Economic Review* September.
    2002. *The Economics of the World Trading System.* Boston, MA: MIT Press.
Staiger, Robert W. and Guido Tabellini. 1999. Do GATT rules help governments make domestic commitments? *Economics and Politics* July.

---

[71] The second 21.5 Panel tried to speak more generally to the question of the extent to which the SCM Agreement informs or provides guidance to the Agriculture Agreement, notably with regard to the definition of prohibited export subsidies in Article 3 of the SCM and the Illustrative List in Annex I thereto as it provides guidance for export subsidies as used in Article 10.1 of the Agreement on Agriculture. See para. 5.154.

11

US – Section 110(5) Copyright Act
United States – Section 110(5) of the US Copyright Act, Recourse to Arbitration under Article 25 of the DSU: Would've or Should've? Impaired Benefits due to Copyright Infringement*

GENE M. GROSSMAN AND PETROS C. MAVROIDIS

1 Facts of the case

This dispute between the European Communities and the United States originated when the United States amended its copyright law in a way that nullified and impaired certain benefits promised to the European Communities under the Agreement on Trade Related Aspects of Intellectual Property (TRIPs). Article 9.1 of TRIPs requires all WTO members to comply with Articles 1 through 21 of the Berne Convention of 1971. Among the provisions of the Berne Convention thus incorporated into the TRIPs Agreement is one that grants to authors of literary and artistic works the exclusive right to authorize "the public communication by loudspeaker or any analogous instrument transmitting, by signs, sounds or images, the broadcast of the work," and another that grants to authors of dramatic and musical works the exclusive right to authorize "any communication to the public of the performance of these works."[1]

In 1998, the United States amended its Copyright Act of 1976 to expand substantially the exemption enjoyed by certain establishments from the obligation to pay royalties on some copyrighted music.[2] Subparagraph (A) of amended Section 110(5) of the US Copyright Act exempts

---

* This study was prepared for the American Law Institute project on "The Principles of World Trade Law." We are grateful to Yves Renouf and Hannu Wager for helpful discussions and to Jane Ginsburg, Alice Haemmerli, and participants at the ALI conference held in Philadelphia, PA on February 6–7, 2003, for their comments on earlier drafts of this paper.
[1] See Article 11bis(1)(iii) and Article 11(1)(ii) of the Berne Convention (1971).
[2] See the Fairness in Music Licensing Act of October 27, 1998.

eating, drinking, and retail establishments that transmit music on a single receiving apparatus of the kind commonly used in private homes (this part of Section 110(5) remains essentially unchanged from its previous version). Sub-paragraph (B) excludes, on the one hand, bars and restaurants of less than 3,750 square feet that transmit radio and television music as well as larger bars and restaurants that communicate audio performances by means of six or fewer loudspeakers, or audiovisual performances by means of four or fewer audiovisual devices ((B)(ii) – (B)(iv)) and on the other hand establishments other than bars and restaurants ((B)(i), referred to as retail establishments).[3]

The European Communities challenged the legality of the US policy before a WTO Panel, using the dispute settlement procedures outlined in the Understanding on Rules and Procedures Governing the Settlement of Disputes (hereafter, the DSU). The European Communities claimed that the US amendment to Section 110(5) had denied holders of EC rights benefits that were promised to them by TRIPs. The European Communities objected to both the exemptions under sub-paragraph (A) for small establishments using one receiver and to the exemption under sub-paragraph (B). It should be noted that (B)(i) applies to all retail establishments, whereas (B)(ii)–(B)(iv) apply to all eating and drinking establishments. The European Communities in their complaint presented claims and arguments on all categories of sub-paragraph (B). The Panel upheld the EC claim with respect to sub-paragraph (B) of Section 110(5), while ruling that sub-paragraph (A) does not violate any WTO statutes. Neither side appealed the ruling.

The DSU (Article 22.1) allows a Member in violation of a WTO obligation to pay compensation to an injured Member to settle any dispute when both sides agree on the amount.[4] In case the parties cannot agree on a level of compensation, and if the offending Member continues policies that have been found to be in violation of the WTO Agreement, the WTO may authorize an equivalent withdrawal of concessions by the injured Member. In the case at hand, the United States and the European Communities met following the issuance of the Panel Report to discuss potential compensation. When they could not come to an agreement, they

---

[3] Non-eating and drinking establishments are also permitted under new sub-paragraph (B) to use up to six loudspeakers for audio, and up to four audiovisual devices for audiovisual performances. Although the amendment includes some limitations on the number of devices that can be placed in one room, it represents a radical enlargement in Section 110(5)'s scope. The 3,750 square feet statutory delimitation does not apply to retail establishments.

[4] The offending Member is still, however, obligated to bring its policies into conformity with WTO rules within a reasonable period of time.

turned to the WTO for binding arbitration to resolve the issue. The possibility of such arbitration was established in Article 25.2 of the DSU, which states in part that "except as otherwise provided in this Understanding, resort to arbitration shall be subject to mutual agreement of the parties which shall agree on the procedures to be followed." Article 25.3 further stipulates that "the parties to the proceedings shall agree to abide by the arbitration award."

The European Communities argued before the Arbitrators that the United States ought to pay compensation equal to the full amount of the royalties that would have been paid by US eating and drinking establishments of less than 3,750 square feet had all of them been duly licensed to transmit the copyright-protected music. It estimated this amount to be $25,486,974.

The United States countered that the actual level of benefits that had been nullified or impaired was dramatically smaller than this, amounting to somewhere between $446,000 and $733,000. It justified this smaller figure in two steps. First, it noted, not all of the eating and drinking establishments that might potentially be licensed actually pay royalties. Royalties are collected in the United States on behalf of copyright holders by collective management organizations. These organizations do not find it profitable to license all of the potential users of their works in view of the transactions costs that are involved. Indeed, in the years that immediately preceded the passage of the amendment to Section 110(5)(B), less than 20 percent of restaurants in the United States were licensed to transmit music, whereas almost three quarters of restaurants actually did play music.

Second, the United States argued, the impaired benefits of the European Communities should include not the gross amount of royalties that copyright holders would have collected but only the net payments copyright holders would have received from the collective management organizations had the licensing of small restaurants and bars taken place. The difference of course is the fees that would have been retained by the collective management organizations, which are two American corporations.[5] In effect, the European Communities requested compensation for the totality of royalties that *should have* been collected, whereas the United States asked that compensation be limited to the amount that *would have* been paid.

---

[5] These are the American Society of Authors, Composers and Publishers (ASCAP) and Broadcast Music Inc. (BMI). A third CMO, the Society of European Stage Authors and Composers is also active in the industry, but the parties and the Arbitrators did not include this organization in its calculations because they considered the royalties it pays to EC rights holders affected by this dispute to be insignificant.

2   The WTO Arbitration process

Before turning to the legal and economic issues involved in this case, it will be useful for us to discuss briefly the legal mandate of the WTO Arbitrators and the role that they are meant to play in the dispute settlement process.

As we noted in section 1, the possibility of arbitration as an alternative means of dispute resolution was introduced in Article 25 of the DSU. The appeal of the arbitration alternative presumably lies in its streamlined proceedings and in the prospect it offers to avert any mutually damaging retaliatory measures. Article 25 leaves the procedures to be followed by the Arbitrators as a matter to be agreed by the disputing parties. It places few restrictions on either the nature of the issues that can be considered or the reasoning that must be applied.[6] Moreover, the matter under consideration was the first time that WTO Members had resorted to the arbitration process after the adoption of the DSU. Precedents and prior jurisprudence are thus non-existent in this case.

The parties to the copyright dispute asked the Arbitrators to rule only on the size of the payment that the United States would make to the European Communities to compensate for its violation of TRIPs. In principle, the parties might have gone to the Arbitrators in lieu of pursuing their initial dispute before the WTO Panel. They might also have asked the Arbitrators to rule on whether the US enforcement procedures for copyright infringement are consistent with its obligations under TRIPs, an issue that we will touch upon later. But they did not elect to do either; instead, they limited the Arbitrators' mandate to one of quantifying the level of compensation. The Arbitrators, for their part, were not legally obliged to accept this mandate, inasmuch as the text of Article 25 of DSU does not address the issue of how the Arbitrators' mandate shall be determined. But neither does the DSU prohibit the parties from restricting the scope of the arbitration hearing. In the event, the Arbitrators accepted their limited mandate.

Given this mandate, the Arbitrators had few guidelines to follow in reaching a decision. Unlike in cases involving the suspension of concessions – which arise when the WTO adjudicating body finds in favor of a complainant and the offending party fails to change its practices so as to comply with the WTO rules – the DSU places no restriction on the size of any compensation payment, and in particular does not limit

---

[6] Article 25.4 of the DSU does require that "Articles 21 and 22 of the *DSU* shall apply *mutatis mutandis* to the arbitration awards."

compensation to the amount of the benefits that have been nullified or impaired. Article 25 of the DSU is also silent on the issue of punitive compensation and on the question of whether compensation should be paid retroactively (from the time that the offending party began to violate the WTO Agreement) or prospectively (from the time that the injured party filed its complaint). Article 25.3 of the DSU does require, however, that the parties abide by the Arbitrators' decision without recourse to appeal.

3   The Arbitrators' decision

3.1   The parties' arguments

As mentioned previously, the European Communities requested that compensation be set equal to the economic value of the exclusive rights that the United States denied to EC holders when it granted an exemption from royalties to small bars and restaurants. The value of these rights, it submitted, is the full amount of royalties that the establishments would have paid for the use of radio and television music copyrighted by EC rights holders had the TRIPs Agreement been perfectly enforced by the United States. To do less, the European Communities claimed, would be tantamount to sanctioning piracy.

The European Communities arrived at its estimate of the foregone licensing revenue using a "bottom–up" approach. It took as its starting point an estimate of the number of establishments in the United States that qualify for the exemption under Section 110(5)(B) of the Copyright Act but not Section 110(5)(A). It reduced this number to account for the estimated fraction of establishments that do not play music. For the remaining establishments, it applied the licensing fees found in the fee schedules of the two collective management organizations at the time.

The United States countered that lost benefits ought not to be based on potential revenues, but rather on legitimate expectations. The EC rights holders could not legitimately have expected to receive payments equal to the full *potential* value of the rights, because there are substantial costs associated with collecting the fees. In actuality, the rights in question are administered by the actions of the collective management organizations. These organizations decide which establishments to license based on a comparison of potential revenues and prospective costs. With respect to larger eating and drinking establishments, the collective management organizations (CMOs) do not in fact choose to collect royalties from every bar or restaurant with over 3,750 square feet of surface area that offers music. And prior to the introduction of the exemption for smaller establishments, the CMOs evidently considered it worthwhile to license only a modest fraction of those establishments that were potentially liable for royalty payments.

The United States further argued that the Arbitrators would be granting the European Communities a windfall profit if they disregarded the actual cost of collecting and distributing the royalties. The legitimate expectations of the EC rights holders could include only the net payment they would receive absent the exemption for small eating and drinking establishments, not the gross payments that include a part to cover the cost of doing business for the CMOs.

The United States used a "top–down" approach to estimate the benefits lost by the European Communities. It took as its starting point the total royalties paid to EC rights holders in the years preceding the amendment to Section 110(5) and proceeded to adjust this number by successive reductions to reflect the amount attributable to entities that do not meet the statutory definition of an "establishment," the amount due to music from sources other than radio and television, and the amount due to eating and drinking establishments that do not meet the size and equipment limitations of Section 110(5)(B) that would qualify them for an exemption.

3.2   The Arbitrators' reasoning

The Arbitrators basically concurred with the conceptual arguments put forth by the United States, although they did not accept all aspects of the US calculation of impaired benefits.

The Arbitrators noted that the benefits nullified or impaired by the US policy are not limited to the royalties lost by EC copyright holders. In principle, other EC citizens besides the rights holders might have suffered as a result of the US failure to abide by TRIPs. However, the European Communities had not made any arguments to the effect that there were other losers from the copyright exemption besides the rights holders, so the Arbitrators decided to treat the lost benefits of the EC rights holders and the lost benefits of the European Communities as equivalent.

Next, the Arbitrators ruled that the rights protected by Article 11.1 of the Berne Convention (but violated in part by the United States by dint of its exemptions) should not be considered to be self-enforcing. Enforcement imposes a cost, as is evident from the fact that EC rights holders choose to rely on collective management organizations to assist them in collecting their royalty fees. The Arbitrators found force in the US argument that enforcement activities ought to be planned on a cost–benefit basis. The collective management organizations license only those establishments for which the expected revenues exceed the transaction costs.

The Arbitrators were persuaded that revenues and costs of licensing will vary with characteristics of the user base, such as "the number, size and location of the users that play broadcast music as well as the extent to which users play such music" (Award of the Arbitrators, para. 3.29; hereafter, *Award*). Therefore, the Arbitrators ruled, the transaction costs can legitimately affect the level of licensing. Moreover, the actual size of these costs should not be neglected in calculating the benefits that the rights holders can expect to realize from the TRIPs Agreement.

However, it is not true that TRIPs leaves WTO Members free to choose any enforcement procedures they wish, perhaps thereby rendering the costs of enforcement to be prohibitively large. For intellectual property, the legal environment and the specific transactions costs associated with collecting the fees jointly determine the magnitude of the enforcement costs. Concerning the former, Article 41 of TRIPs obliges a Member to

> ensure that enforcement procedures . . . are available under their law so as to permit effective action against any act of infringement of intellectual property rights covered by this Agreement.

The European Communities could have challenged the enforcement procedures used by the United States in its complaint to the WTO Panel. However, as the Arbitrators note in footnote 44 of the Award of the Arbitrators, they did not elect to do so. Nor did the parties agree to make the question of whether the US enforcement provisions meet the requirements imposed by TRIPs part of the Arbitrators' mandate in this case. The Arbitrators ruled that it is beyond the scope of their investigation to assess the legality of the enforcement provisions that are included in US copyright law. Instead, they chose to "assume that the United States is acting consistently with the enforcement obligations contained in the TRIPs Agreement" and based their evaluation of the EC claim on the economic implications of the costs present in administering the rights according to the prevailing legal environment.

In short, the Arbitrators concluded that the level of EC benefits that are being nullified or impaired as a result of Section 110(5)(B) of the US Copyright Act is equal to the amount of royalty payments that would have been distributed by US collective management organizations to EC rights holders had the offending amendment not taken effect. They then turned to the task of estimating these payments in the hypothetical, "but-for" world.

3.3 The Arbitrators' calculations

The Arbitrators essentially adopted the "top–down" methodology proposed by the United States, but did not consider all of its adjustment and deductions to be appropriate. After confirming with the parties that they did not consider the Arbitrators to be bound to choose either one or the other of the party's proposed estimates, the Arbitrators set about to construct their own estimate of the EC benefits nullified or impaired by Section 110(5)(B).

The Arbitrators considered it appropriate to begin with an estimate of the actual licensing revenues paid to EC rights holders by US collective management organizations in the three-year period prior to 1998, when the Amendment of Section 110(5)(B) illegally extended the scope of exemptions from royalty payments. The first step in their calculation generated an estimate of the average annual amount for 1996 through 1998 of total royalties distributed for the benefit of EC right holders both "directly" (direct distribution by ASCAP and BMI to the EC collecting societies that represent EC musicians and music publishers) and "indirectly" (distribution to US publisher affiliates of EC publishers for the performance of EC works).[7]

Second, they deducted an estimate of the royalties paid on behalf of users other than eating, drinking, and retail establishments.[8] Third, from the resulting estimate of the total amount paid by the relevant establishments, the Arbitrators deducted an estimate of the amount due to music sources other than radio and television music, since these other sources were not exempted from payment under the amendment to Section 110(5). Fourth, the Arbitrators estimated the share of the revenues attributable to eating, drinking and retail establishments for the broadcast

---

[7] For ASCAP, the Arbitrators had access to these two categories of payments for the three years in question. For BMI, they had only the direct payments for 1996. They estimated the average annual amount for direct plus indirect payments for BMI by assuming that the ratio of direct to indirect payments and the growth rate of total payments was the same for BMI and for ASCAP.

[8] This would include both licensing from radio and television broadcasting and concerts, which are not part of "general licensing," and royalties paid in the general licensing category by users such as airlines, sports stadiums, motion-picture theatres, amusement parks, conventions, telephone-music services, colleges and universities, health clubs, and background-music services.

of radio and television music that was due to establishments newly exempted from royalties in 1998 by Section 110(5)(B) of the US Copyright Act. This required an estimate of the fraction of establishments that meet the size limit of 3,750 square feet of surface area and the fraction that are exempted based on the type of broadcast equipment they use.

The resulting figure after all of these deductions represents an estimate of the average annual royalties that were paid by the newly exempted establishments for their rights to broadcast radio and television music during the years 1996 through 1998. The Arbitrators adjusted this figure to allow for growth between that period and July 23, 2001, the date at which the matter was referred for arbitration. Their resulting estimate of the benefits nullified or impaired by dint of Section 110(5)(B) is $1,100,000 per year.

3.4 No punitive compensation and no retroactive payments

As we noted previously, the DSU is silent on the question of whether compensation should include any amount for punitive purposes and whether the injured party should be compensated retroactively for illegal actions that took place prior to the initiation of its complaint. The Arbitrators ruled that punitive compensation would be inappropriate in this case, because they would lead to a situation in which "the level of E.C. benefits nullified or impaired by the operation of Section 110(5)(B) would have been overestimated" (*Award*, para. 4.27). They did, however, recognize in footnote 84 of the *Award* that an overestimation of benefits is less consequential for matters of compensation than for matters involving the withdrawal of concessions, because Article 22.7 of DSU does not specify that compensation paid under Article 22.2 of DSU must be equivalent to the level of nullification or impairment.

The Arbitrators' decision on whether compensation should be prospective or retroactive was less explicit, but can be gleaned from their method of calculation. Nowhere did they rule on whether it would be appropriate for the United States to compensate the European Communities for nullified or impaired benefits incurred between the amendment of Section 110(5)(B) and the date at which the matter was referred to arbitration. But in calculating the size of the lost benefits, the Arbitrators allowed for growth in the but-for royalties between the historical period prior to the enactment of Section 110(5)(B) and July 23, 2001, the date at which the matter was referred for arbitration. They did not compute any estimate of what benefits had been nullified or impaired in the intervening period. Evidently, they meant their remedy to be prospective from the date of referral and not to include any compensation for the prior period.

4 Analysis and critique of the Arbitrators' decision

In this section, we shall analyze and critique the Arbitrators' decision. We begin by examining the objectives of TRIPs and discuss the strength of the protection of intellectual property rights that it is meant to provide. We briefly touch on the issue of optimal enforcement policy, but conclude as the Arbitrators did that the legality of the US enforcement provisions is beyond the scope of our task. We then turn to the principles the Arbitrators should have used in deciding an amount of compensation, once they had assumed that the US enforcement provisions were consistent with the objectives of TRIPs. We conclude that the Arbitrators were correct to evaluate the legitimate expectations of the EC rights holders and to use this as a basis for their compensation award. Finally, we discuss the calculations performed by the Arbitrators and their treatment of the issues of punitive and retroactive compensation.

4.1 Potential revenues or legitimate expectations?

TRIPs was designed to prevent Members from imposing negative externalities on their trading partners when they established their national systems for protecting intellectual property.[9] In a non-cooperative world regime of intellectual property protection, externalities might come in two main forms. First, governments may have a national incentive to discriminate against the intellectual property rights of foreign citizens (see, for example, Scotchmer, 2002). This explains the requirements for national treatment that are included in TRIPs, and in the Berne Convention and Paris Treaty before it. Second, even with national treatment, national governments may choose to provide insufficient protection for intellectual property relative to the strength of protection that would be globally efficient.

What determines the efficient level of protection of intellectual property? In choosing their patent and copyright policies, governments must balance the static costs of protection against dynamic benefits. Once intellectual property exists, it typically can be consumed by many different

---

[9] For an excellent overview of TRIPs and a detailed analysis of its objectives and provisions, see Maskus (2000).

users at little or no additional cost beyond the initial cost of creating it. For example, the creation of a new music album requires substantial investment of time and resources by songwriters, performing artists, and musical publishers. The cost of producing an extra compact disc of an existing piece of music is very much smaller. Once a musical work exists, it would be efficient to allow widespread use (without copyright protection) up to the point where the marginal benefit of the last listener matches the marginal cost of stamping out an extra disc. By granting copyright protection to the rights holders, the government induces a monopoly price of the disc in excess of the marginal production cost, thereby generating under-consumption. This is the static cost that derives from government protection of intellectual property.

Against this cost is the dynamic benefit. The presumption is that without any form of protection, the creators of intellectual property would reap little or no personal benefits from their investments in knowledge or art; they might then invest very little. By granting monopoly rights, the government provides private rewards to the creators of intellectual property that serve as an inducement for their efforts. The nationally optimal intellectual property regime is one that balances the marginal cost to national citizens of the distortions that derive from monopoly pricing against the marginal benefit that comes from having a greater stock of knowledge and artwork available.

As Grossman and Lai (2002) show, there are two reasons why intellectual property protection will be too weak when policies are set noncooperatively by national governments.[10] First, national governments do not take into account in their cost–benefit calculus the benefits that accrue to foreign citizens when protection induces additional investments in intellectual property. Second, national governments do not consider as an offset to the static cost of granting patent and copyright protection the monopoly profits that accrue to foreign rights holders. For both these reasons, a global regime of independently chosen patent and copyright policies will provide too little incentive for investment in intellectual property relative to the aggregate reward that would maximize world welfare. In effect, countries have an incentive to free ride on the intellectual property rights protection provided by their trading partners.

---

[10] On the related point of whether developing countries have an incentive to grant patent and copyright protection considering that relatively little intellectual property is created by their nationals, see Chin and Grossman (1990), Diwan and Rodrik (1991), Deardorff (1992), and Helpman (1993).

By forging an international treaty such as TRIPs, the WTO Members can ensure that each takes into account the interests of the others when setting its national policies. Overall, an efficient agreement should serve to strengthen global protection of intellectual property. Various combinations of policies in different countries can achieve the globally efficient level of protection for any particular type of intellectual property. Moreover, in each country, the strength of protection for a particular type of intellectual property reflects a number of different dimensions of the national policy. For musical and dramatic works such as those at issue in this dispute, copyright protection might vary in the number of years for which protection is provided, the breadth of protection against similar but not identical works, the range of uses that are regulated by copyright protection, and the enforcement provisions that are included in case of infringement, among others. For these reasons and others, TRIPs does not stipulate the exact package of policies that must be adopted in each member country.

Instead, TRIPs specifies some minimum standards that all Members must meet in all functional areas of intellectual property protection. On copyrights, as already indicated, TRIPs requires Members to obey many of the rules of the Berne Convention. This means, for example, that governments must grant copyrights that extend for the life of an author plus fifty years. The Agreement also stipulates that Members must protect computer software and data compilations by copyright under the terms of the Berne Convention, just as they would literary works.

At issue in this dispute is the extent and nature of US enforcement of copyright protection. The optimal enforcement policy for the United States – that is, the policy that would maximize world welfare – is not one that ensures licensing to 100 percent of the users of proprietary music. Even if such an objective were feasible, which it probably is not, the costs of ensuring such a high level of compliance would far outweigh the benefits. Rather, the optimal enforcement policy is one that balances the marginal cost of achieving slightly greater compliance with the marginal benefits that derive from doing so. Note that the optimal enforcement policy will vary with the other policy dimensions that are enacted. For example, a change in the duration of copyright protection alters the marginal benefit of greater compliance with the copyright laws and thus the resources that should be devoted to avoiding infringements.

Is the US policy with regard to the playing of music by eating and drinking establishments consistent with TRIPs? The WTO Panel determined that it is not, insofar as the US exempts establishments smaller than a certain size from the obligation to license certain music. But even if there were no such exemption, there remains the question of whether an enforcement system that requires the participation of private agents (the collective management organizations) and achieves a relatively modest level of compliance fulfils the US obligation to protect the exclusive rights of authors of artistic and musical works. As we have noted before, Article 41 of TRIPs requires Members to maintain a legal and regulatory environment that permits effective action against acts of infringement. The US policy, which relies on the collective management organizations to issue licenses and does not involve a high level of policing of bars and restaurants by government agents, might or might not be consistent with this provision of TRIPs. But as the Arbitrators correctly point out, this question is not one that has been posed by the European Communities in any complaint under the DSU, nor is it one that an adjudicating body of the WTO has ruled upon.

Like the Arbitrators, we consider the legality of US enforcement procedures for copyright-protected music played in eating, drinking, and retail establishments to be beyond the scope of this paper. To answer the economic question of whether the US procedures are (close to) efficient in the light of the enforcement costs and the potential benefits from greater compliance would require evidence and data that are not readily available to us. Instead, we will proceed with our analysis – as the Arbitrators did – by assuming that US enforcement procedures other than the one concerning the exemption of small eating, drinking, and retail establishment are legal, since they have not been shown to be otherwise.

By taking the objective of TRIPs to be the achievement of global efficiency in the creation of intellectual property, and by assuming that US enforcement procedures are legal and thus consistent with this objective, we are forced to conclude that the optimal level of investment in new musical works by EC songwriters and performing artists is one that equates the expected costs of creating music with the expected rewards. Thus, under the assumed legality of the enforcement procedures, EC artists would have faced the appropriate incentives to create new works had their prospective rewards been those they could legitimately have expected to obtain but for the (illegal) amendment to Section 110(5) of the US Copyright Act.

Accordingly, we concur with the Arbitrators when they write in paragraph 3.24 of the *Award* that they "consider the benefits which they should take into account in this case as those which the European Communities could reasonably expect to accrue to it under Articles 11*bis*(1)(iii) and 11(1)(ii)" of the Berne Convention. These benefits match the injury that EC rights holders have suffered as a result of the demonstrated US violation of TRIPs. Assuming that US practices and procedures in its copyright laws are legal except for those that the WTO Panel found to be otherwise, a compensatory payment equal to the benefits lost by reason of the illegal actions would enable the European Communities to restore the appropriate incentives for the creation of intellectual property.[11]

4.2   The calculations

It is difficult to find fault with the detailed calculations performed by the Arbitrators to estimate the revenues that would have been paid to EC rights holders but for the enactment of Section 110(5)(B). The Arbitrators identified the conceptually correct magnitude of impaired benefits as being the royalty fees that would have been distributed to the EC rights holders or their designated representatives as a result of payments made by eating, drinking, and retail establishments that had been exempted from royalties on radio and television music based on their small size or the nature of their broadcasting equipment. Constrained by the limited availability of data, the Arbitrators made a reasonable effort to find an empirical analogue to this unobserved magnitude.

We feel, however, that the Arbitrators toiled under unreasonable and unfortunate constraints with respect to their access to data and evidence. The Arbitrators recognized this problem themselves. They wrote in paragraph 4.15 of the *Award* that

> In this case, the Arbitrators have encountered particular difficulties due to the lack of precise information available. This problem originated either in the actual absence of specific data for the type of transactions concerned (payment of royalties to E.C. rights holders) or in the lack of co-operation on the part of some of the private entities which may have had the information. The absence of sufficiently specific information played a major role in the choices made by the Arbitrators with respect to methodology and calculations.

---

[11] One qualification here is that appropriate incentives for the creation and performance of musical works will only be restored if the European Communities distribute the moneys collected from the United States in compensation to those whose rights have been abrogated. But there is nothing in the DSU that requires the European Communities to use the funds received in compensation in this way.

And they reiterated in paragraph 4.35 that

> ... [the Arbitrators'] ability to make an accurate calculation has been limited by the fact that the data provided to them by the two parties were incomplete and included many estimations and assumptions. In their submissions, both parties have recognized this problem, noting that some of the relevant data are in the possession of private parties. As explained above, we sent letters to the two main US CMOs, ASCAP and BMI, requesting actual data on their collections and distributions that would have enabled us to base our calculations on specific information. In response to those letters, we obtained some information from BMI, but due to the conditions attached to its use, we decided not to include it in the record of the case.

We note that Article 13 of the DSU grants the WTO adjudicating bodies the authority to gather information from any source they deem appropriate. The Arbitrators made use of this provision in the case at hand, but only to a limited extent. Because the parties had instructed the Arbitrators to resolve the matter expeditiously, the Arbitrators felt constrained in their ability to exercise powers under Article 13 of the DSU.

Here we confront one of the most frequently debated aspects of the DSU: can a WTO adjudicating body disregard a mutually agreed request by the disputing parties in the interest of delivering a more reasoned verdict? Or must the adjudicating body accept that 'the dispute belongs to the parties'? Arguments can be made on both sides.

Inasmuch as the reports by the adjudicating bodies provide guidance in subsequent disputes, the WTO has an abiding interest in the accuracy and intellectual coherence of its reports. But a broad interpretation of the maxim of *non ultra petita* might suggest that the adjudicating bodies have little discretion to deviate from the requests of the disputants. Proponents of such an approach can find good support for their argument in the letter of Article 25.1 of the DSU: "Expeditious arbitration . . . can facilitate the solution of certain disputes that concern issues that are *clearly defined by both parties*" (emphasis added).

We prefer to interpret this maxim as applying only to the issues that the adjudicating body has been asked to resolve, and not to extend unduly so as to prejudge the powers of the WTO adjudicating bodies under the DSU. That is, in our view the maxim *non ultra petita* should be understood to provide a limit as to *what* (i.e. which claims and arguments) can be discussed by the WTO adjudicating bodies but not a limit as to how claims and arguments will be entertained. Article 13 of the DSU gives the Arbitrators a clear and unambiguous right to gather the information they need to assess impaired benefits. The Appendix to the DSU contains more hortatory language (which therefore is of lesser legal standing) that an adjudicating body's work should be finished within a pre-specified time period. Accordingly, we feel that the Arbitrators should have asserted their rights under Article 13 to delay their decision until the necessary data had become available.[12]

4.3   Punitive compensation

We believe that the Arbitrators were correct not to award punitive compensation in this case. From a legal perspective, the Arbitrators could have relied on the maxim of *non ultra petita* to exclude punitive payments, inasmuch as the European Communities had not suggested that compensation include any amount for punitive purposes and thus the Arbitrators were constrained by an established principle of international law not to recommend compensation in excess of what had been requested. Instead, the Arbitrators declined to award punitive compensation based on their understanding that the award should not exceed their estimate of the EC benefits nullified or impaired. We find this justification to be faulty, because the DSU allows for any "mutually agreeable compensation" and does not thereby exclude payments for punitive purposes. Since the parties themselves can agree to compensation that includes a portion for punitive reasons, there is no legal basis for excluding such an award by the Arbitrators when the injured Member requests it.

However, from an economic perspective, we do not believe that punitive compensation would be warranted in this case. In general, punitive damages have a role to play in contract enforcement when the parties understand reasonably well whether their potential actions are legal or not but the actions taken are difficult to verify by their partners and by third parties. Then punitive levies can be used as a tool to discourage opportunistic behavior. In this case, the consistency of Sections 110(5)(A) and 110(5)(B) with TRIPs was not well understood before the dispute

---

[12] We are mindful of the fact that the WTO contract is an agreement between governments, and that the WTO adjudicating bodies lack the legal means to ensure that private institutions in the United States or elsewhere will act in a cooperative manner as concerns the timely provision of data. However, this does not mean that a WTO body should always succumb to a request by the disputants to produce a report expeditiously and, as a result of this request, forfeit its rights under Article 13 of the DSU. Indeed, if the parties to the dispute truly are interested in a speedy resolution of a dispute, they have the ability to facilitate the process by obliging their nationals (private parties) to cooperate.

was brought to the WTO Panel. Indeed, the Panel found that one of these provisions was not in violation of US obligations under TRIPs. Since the Agreement was new and its interpretation still open to question, it cannot be said that the United States was attempting to act in a clearly illegal way when it amended its Copyright Act in 1998.[13] Nor can it be argued that the US action, once taken, was difficult to verify. The US legislation was publicly announced and readily observable to the European Communities and to the WTO adjudicating bodies.

4.4   Retroactive compensation

Insofar as the Arbitrators meant to compensate the European Communities only for the lost benefits that occurred after the dispute was referred for arbitration, we believe that they erred in assessing the appropriate time dimension for their award. Our argument has both legal and economic dimensions. On the legal side, it is a reasonably settled issue in public international law that remedies can be retroactive to the time when the violation(s) began.[14] In the particulars of this case, there is nothing that excludes retroactive compensation, because the DSU allows for any mutually agreeable compensation and the parties did not specify in their proposals to the Arbitrators the time period over which their estimates of annual losses ought to apply.[15]

From an economic perspective, we have argued that the objectives of the Arbitrators ought to be to estimate the losses suffered by EC rights holders by reason of the offending US legislation. In doing so, they would

---

[13] Moreover, it should be emphasized that the exclusions applied not only to royalties that otherwise would be paid to EC rights holders, but also to royalties that otherwise would be paid to US rights holders. Indeed, although we have no evidence on this, we strongly suspect that US music publishers and artists lost far more by reason of the amendment than their EC counterparts. Thus, it is likely the case that the US legislation was not motivated by an intentional desire to abrogate US obligations under TRIPs, but rather by purely domestic considerations.

[14] However, with only one exception – the case of *Australia – Subsidies Provided to Producers and Exporters of Automotive Leather*, Recourse to Article 21.5 of the DSU (WTO Doc. WT/DS126 of February 20, 2000) – the WTO adjudicating bodies have preferred prospective remedies to retroactive remedies in all cases that have been brought before them since the signing of the DSU. It should be noted that the WTO contract does not make retroactive compensation illegal. Rather, the contract provides no specific normative guidance on this issue.

[15] Had the European Communities specified that it was seeking compensation only for the period after the referral of the matter to arbitration, the Arbitrators would have been constrained by the maxim of *non ultra petita* not to include any compensation for benefits lost in earlier periods.

make good the legitimate expectations of these rights holders at the time the Agreement was signed, and thereby would ensure that the rewards to creativity provide the appropriate incentives for the generation of new musical works. Surely, it was legitimate for EC songwriters, musicians, and musical publishers to expect royalties from their copyrighted works not only in the period from July 23, 2001 onward, but also from the period between January 26, 1999 (when the amendment to the US copyright law went into effect) and July 23, 2001. Only by providing retroactive compensation can the rewards in the event of a violation of the Agreement match the hypothetical rewards in the but-for world.

5 Conclusions

To conclude, we summarize our main findings. We believe that the WTO Arbitrators were legally justified and economically correct in using a but-for standard in calculating the compensation that would be paid to the European Communities in recognition of the US violation of TRIPs. The Arbitrators sought to estimate the royalties that EC rights holders would have received from American collective management organizations had the United States not illegally exempted certain eating and drinking establishments from the obligation to license certain forms of music. The European Communities had argued instead for an amount that equals the total royalties that these establishments should have paid in a hypothetical world with 100 percent enforcement. The Arbitrators noted that intellectual property rights are not self-enforcing, and that enforcement entails real costs. By replacing the reward that EC songwriters, musical performers, and musical publishers could legitimately have expected to receive, the Arbitrators were restoring the optimal incentives for creative activity under the working hypothesis that US enforcement procedures are consistent with the objectives of TRIPs.

We emphasize, however, that the legality of the US enforcement procedures has not been resolved in this case. The United States tolerates a system in which only about one quarter of the bars and restaurants that ought to be liable for royalty payments actually acquire licenses for the copyrighted music they play. Such a system may or may not be consistent with the US obligation under Article 41 of TRIPs to "ensure that enforcement procedures . . . are available under [each country's] law so as to permit effective action against any act of infringement of intellectual property rights covered by this Agreement." Surely, 100 percent enforcement should not be expected in the light of the transaction costs that are involved. The Arbitrators argued that they did not have any mandate to judge the legality of the US enforcement procedures. We too lack sufficient information to judge what level of compliance would be sufficient to meet the requirements of TRIPs. We consider this issue to be unresolved.

Finally, we have considered whether the Arbitrators were correct to exclude any levy for punitive purposes in the award to the European Communities and whether they should have taken a retroactive perspective for purposes of calculating the size of the compensation payment. We argued that a punitive levy would not be appropriate in this case, because the illegal actions of the United States were not hidden and not clearly intended to violate an international agreement. As for the time dimension, the legitimate expectations of EC rights holders would have included royalty payments throughout the period following the signing of TRIPs. Therefore, the Arbitrators' award should have included an amount for retroactive compensation.

References

Chin, Judith and Grossman, Gene M. 1990. Intellectual Property Rights and North South Trade. Pp. 90–107 in R.W. Jones and A.O. Krueger, eds. *The Political Economy of International Trade*. Cambridge MA: Basil Blackwell Publishers.

Deardorff, Alan V. 1992. Welfare Effects of Global Patent Protection. *Economica* 59: 35–51.

Diwan, Ishac and Rodrik, Dani. 1991. Patents, Appropriate Technology, and North-South Trade. *Journal of International Economics* 30: 27–48.

Grossman, Gene M. and Lai, Edwin L.-C. 2002. International Protection of Intellectual Property. *NBER Working Paper No. 8704.*

Helpman, Elhanan. 1993. Innovation, Imitation, and Intellectual Property Rights. *Econometrica* 61: 1247–1280.

Maskus, Keith E. 2000. *Intellectual Property Rights in the Global Economy.* Washington DC: The Institute for International Economics.

Scotchmer, Suzanne. 2002. The Political Economy of Intellectual Property Treaties. *NBER Working Paper No. 9114.*

INDEX

Agriculture Agreements: *see also*
    Canada – Dairy; export
    subsidies, economic rationale
    for limiting; SCM (Agreement
    on Subsidies and
    Countervailing Measures)
conformity with agreement and
    commitments thereunder (AA
    8) 256–257
direct subsidies
    (AA 9.1(a)) 257
    "contingent on export
      performance" 254
    financial contribution, need for
      (SCM 1.1(a)(1)) 255–256
    payment in kind, as
      benefit/gratuitous act
      255–255
    provided by government or
      agency 255; demonstrable link,
      need for 261–262
    to a firm, industry, producer,
      association or marketing board
      254
as major achievement of Uruguay
    Round 236, 264–265
absence of methodology for core
    concepts 265–266
payment on export financed by
    government action (AA 9.1(c))
    257, 259–262
    "contingent on export
      performance" (AA 9.1(a)) and
      256
    financed by government 256; act
      of agency 264; act or omission
      as 264; "by virtue of" 264

as national obligation 263–264;
    payment by private parties and
    264
payment in kind and 256
price benchmark: *see* price
    benchmark *below*
price benchmark 259–261
    total cost of production 261,
      263–264, 265–266, 268–276;
      cross-subsidization and
      272–275; declining industry,
      problems related to 275;
      high-profit industry and 275;
      milk-tax-and-redistribution-
      programme 269–272; sunk
      costs, exclusion 275, 278–279
    world market prices 276–277, 279
SCM as aid to interpretation 255
subsidy in excess of commitments
    (AA 3.3) 256, 257
subsidy not listed in AA 9.1 (AA
    10.1) 256–257, 262
anti-dumping and countervailing
    duties, Anti-dumping
    Agreement
"constructed value" (AD 2.2.2) 123
developing countries, need to seek
    constructive remedies (AD 15)
    123–124
disclosure of essential facts (AD 6.9)
    167–168
economic rationale 115, 133–137,
    168–169: *see also* anti-dumping
    and countervailing duties,
    GATT VI, economic rationale;
    export subsidies, economic
    rationale for limiting